VOICE
from the
STARS

◇◇◇

by
TOM
SCOTLAND

Tom Scotland.

ISBN 1 875317 09 0

Design & Production by WordsWork *Express*
156 Mills Street, Welshpool WA
Ph: 350 5311 Fax: 350 5572

Illustrations by Edgar Riley (Newcastle on Tyne)

VOICE FROM THE STARS

CONTENTS

VOICE FROM THE STARS

PREFACE

By Air Commodore Peter Cribb
CBE,DSO,DFC, RAF (Retired)

I have known this West Australian author for some years as a fellow member of the Pathfinder Association of Western Australia. Like Tom, I too flew in the Path Finder Force based in England, both before and during Tom's tour of duty with 614 Squadron in Italy.

Coming from opposite sides of the world, and operating from opposite sides of Germany, we both attacked many targets deep inside Germany and Italy, flying a four engined Halifax in the Pathfinder role. We both experienced the hazards and trauma of mechanical disorders, the hostility of European weather towards war-time fliers, the flak and the fighters, and the team-work and trust of a good crew.

From this stand point I can assuredly testify to the truthfulness of Tom's account, told simply and faithfully, without exaggeration or embellishment. I am particularly impressed with the wealth of detail Tom is able to recall of his surroundings and companions, their conversations and their activities. This is a gift I do not share, but greatly admire in those who are blessed with it.

Tom completed sixty two raids without a break, except for short leave periods. I don't think this is a record, but in England, forty five was the usual Pathfinder tour, followed by six months or more away from the front line, before returning for another tour. The mathematical chances of surviving sixty raids of the kind Tom flew, are at least ten to one against.

It takes a very resolute character, and exceptional leader to hold a crew together for that length of tour. In the course of it one would see most of the aircrews you started with become casualties. There would be more than a few occasions when the same fate seemed only a whisker away from you. Who would not ask "Why them; why not me?" "Is there such a thing as a Guardian Angel?" "How did I get one?" "Why don't we all have them?"

There is more to this book than just the reminiscences of an old war-horse. The title itself hints at a mystical experience. There will be more than one. There are times of fear, and of pride in a job well done.

Those who fly high at night time are often privileged to find themselves in a grandstand seat for some of Nature's most awesome and beautiful displays; the brilliant canopy of stars, sunrise and sunset above the snowy cloudscape, the snow covered mountains by moonlight. Is this God's handiwork? What does it mean? Is there hope for humanity in a world racked by senseless destruction?

Through seeking answers, perhaps subconsciously, Tom's life underwent a dramatic change after his return to Perth. This is a story he must tell you himself.

P.H.C., Greenwood,
Western Australia,
July 1990.

✧✧✧

_____

FOREWORD

By Tony Wheeler DFC

In "A Voice from the stars", the author has captured with uncanny accuracy and graphic detail, his experiences during World War 11.

From enlistment as a rookie trainee airman, he takes you step by step through challenging and, on many occasions, hazardous training programmes of the remarkable Empire Air Training Scheme. Mounting aircrew losses on all sides made the success of the scheme a vital part of the Allied war effort. Its purpose was to provide pilots and crew to man aircraft used to attack and destroy the enemy war machine and installations.

On completion of training, the author and his crew were selected to join, in Italy, a squadron of the famous Path Finder Force. Only the most talented aircrews were invited to operate with this elite, distinguished group.

The role of Pathfinders was to lead the Bomber Squadrons through the night to heavily defended military installations and to clearly identify and mark these targets for the Bombers to accurately follow up, bomb and destroy. Being first over the target called for a high level of courage as casualties were heavy.

The skills employed, the hazards encountered and evasive counter actions taken during 60 such operations made by this crew, are truly and graphically described and make compelling reading as they fight for survival on every mission.

The toll on mind and body that pilot and crew were subjected to night after night by these hazards, is revealed with remarkable compassion and perception. A high percentage of Air Crews live with these experiences to this day, many at the expense of their health.

The story is always greater than the author, it is said. The truth of that statement is questioned in this case. The author is unique! After serving his country and its people with such distinction during World War 11, he returned to civilian life in Civil Engineering but a short time later his chosen career path took a dramatic change in direction.

Tom felt a deep need to again serve. This call truly came during the War when on more than one bombing raid, he received a clear message from "somewhere above" - hence the title of his book, "Voice from the Stars". These experiences plus a miracle escape from a burning aircraft, following a crash landing in England, left a vivid impact on his mind and lead him on a new course. He joined an Australian Missionary Society and with the loving help and support of his wife Laurel, became totally committed to assisting and counselling less privileged persons, only recently retiring due to war related injuries.

Thus Tom Scotland, distinguished airman and citizen, has served half a century in the interests of others — both in war and peace. This surely places him in a unique group. I commend this factual war-time account of a dedicated airman — one of thousands who were prepared to sacrifice all to defend the interests of free people.

This is a true story. I know. I was there. I can confirm all his writings and feelings through my personal experiences in a similar career path in the RAAF.

A.T.W.
Sydney,
June, 1990.

1

THE MAN FROM MUNICH

Professor Frew (Glasgow University) spoke to students at the University of Western Australia in 1948. Predicting the problems that lay ahead for post war society he said,"Man seems to have lost his way, he needs a star to guide him."

The idea of a voice from the stars was not new to me then, and I seemed to be hearing it again in 1964 during a surprising encounter. In hitchhiking around the world, a young German had been given our Australian address, and now sought accommodation with us in our community in Sydney. Fair, blue eyed, Nordic in appearance, he came from Munich.

He settled into a room, and wandered out to join me in coffee. "What did you do during the war?" he asked. "I flew as a pilot, with the RAF," I answered, wondering how he had survived the chaos of Germany after the second world war. "Did you fly over Germany?" he asked in accented English. "Yes," I responded feeling his questions prodding me. "Did you fly over Munich?" "Yes." How much deeper into my wartime past would this young German want to get?

My questioner, not yet ready to let go, continued, "Were you over Munich on thirteenth June 1944?" The date could have been significant, I could not be sure, for twenty years had passed since those tempestuous years of my life. My mind flicked over crowded incidents from my past. "Why do you ask?" I queried. "It was my birthday of eleven years and now I have come to my 31st," replied Helmut drawing attention to the present date, June 1964.

After work, late in the evening, my wife and I unearthed my old, worn pilot's log book from amongst our cases. I opened its pages and searched for a date. There written in red ink, I read the details of June 13th 1944, a night attack on Munich. Some seven days after Allied soldiers had made their memorable invasion of the coast of France, my Pathfinder Squadron had taken off from our base in southern Italy and led a night attack on Munich, the capital of Bavaria in southern Germany.

I had been a 21 year old pilot when my crew and I had flown our Halifax bomber into the defensive maze of guns and searchlights of southern Germany. My mind switched to a seemingly insignificant event that had occurred on that flight.

For a moment, in the midst of war over Munich, my Scottish flight engineer had accidentally switched on the powerful Aldis signalling lamp. Illuminating the interior of our Halifax, the light had made my windscreen a mirror. In that moment, I had viewed a perfect reflection of myself.

The light had flicked off and my reflection had disappeared. But in that critical interval of time, my eyes had met those in the reflection. The unusual thing about seeing my own reflection was the shock it gave me, the impression it made on me, the surprise of coming face to face with myself over Germany. For at that instant, despite the headgear and bulging ear phones, I looked at a face that belonged 12,000 miles away in Australia.

How could the reflection be myself, for the aircraft flew over my mother's home country. Somewhere down there, my mother's town, the ancient home of the Pustkuchens had long ago given honour to her family as they migrated to Australia.

As quick as the reflection had taken my attention, I had thrown off its impact. The night's work demanded concentration as the following RAF squadrons from Italy depended on my Pathfinder aircraft being one to get in and drop markers on the rail facilities of Munich. We had to mark them from the sky, in a way visible for the following bomber aircraft.

On this night, the RAF planes from Italy and the RAF planes from England, approximated one another over Germany. I recalled the experience of flying right through the boiling pot of searchlights and guns over Munich and in sheer amazement at our survival, set course for the return flight to our base in Italy.

Next day newspaper headlines in England read, "The Hammer from the south meets the Hammer from the North." The newspapers referred to RAF aircraft from Italy meeting over Germany with RAF aircraft from England. But the newspapers did not report the shock one Halifax pilot had, at eighteen thousand feet above Munich, in seeing his own image momentarily reflected in the windscreen of his plane.

ENMITIES

Many years had passed since then, and now in 1964, my wife and I hosted the young man from Munich. At various intervals over a period of several days, he sat in my office in Sydney, and talked about the events in 1944 that had brought our lives so mysteriously close to each other .

Now this present confrontation made me aware of something that I needed to accept about myself. The end of the war had not meant an end to the enmities I had felt against Germany and German people. I had painful areas that were as yet unhealed. Coming close to the young German felt like coming close to the enemy and my enmities surfaced.

A dichotomy of feelings came from two streams within me. I had German and British blood in my veins. I needed to face the animosity that made me look on him as enemy, and part of my own heritage as deserving hostility also. In spending time together, we both faced the truth of our feelings; I experiencing the air war over Europe; he as a young boy seeing the devastation of his city in Germany, and experiencing all the fear that engendered.

He went on his way hitchhiking around Australia. By that time he and I allowed the seeds of reconciliation from our past to germinate, and grow. But something of his visit remained, reminding me of a voice from long ago, a voice that had spoken from the stars.

VOICE FROM THE STARS

There and then I decided that I must write down in order how that voice came to me during my involvement in the air war. I had kept documents, letters, records and photographs of those years, and contacted the men who flew with me to check over the details of the story. I have entitled it "Voice from the stars." You may well ask, "Do the stars have a voice?" That same intriguing question faced me during those turbulent wartime events.

2

SCOTLANDS CORNER

The ten year old freckle faced boy first became aware that war clouds threatened his world in 1933. It was the year Bert Brindal came to live with us on our farm at Wellard, 30 miles south of Perth. At that time, my father had been away for several years. He and my Uncle Leo were opening up a gold mine at Ora Banda on the Kalgoorlie goldfields. Bert came to help us run the farm, milk the cows and generally help take the load off us kids who had been trying to keep the farm going.

I doubt that Bert ever received much payment for his work; my mother received too little for our farm produce to be able to pay him. Bert stayed because he secretly loved being near my three older sisters, belles of our farming area. Being on our farm, he was nearer than his competitors, the young bloods of the district who knew the bend in the road known as "Scotland's Corner", the corner where the Scotland girls lived.

I loved being with Bert, a man to whom I could talk, and I chose to help him at every opportunity. Work ended in the evening, when he drew water for the cows. Afterwards, he leaned against the railing of the well, and told stories about the sea. He backed up his stories with a rich tenor voice singing his favourite, "A life on the sea, singing happy and free ...." He helped me decide I must be a sailor, nothing else in life mattered.

One day he surprised me. I helped him cut firewood from one of the large jarrah trees felled by lightning. A piece of wood flew off from Bert's log, and hit him in the face. My immediate reaction imitated an exclamation I had heard Bert use so often, "Jesus bloody Christ". The expletive rolled off my tongue and I felt six foot tall, a man! Bert put down the axe, rubbed his face where the wood had hit him, then looked hard at me. His eyes pierced through me with anger. I felt the heat of his fury and then he cut me with the words, "Do not ever use those words like that again!" His anger was so unexpected, and I felt thoroughly deflated. I did not hear Bert use those words again, and for the next few years I quit using them myself.

Our livelihood rested on a continuing troublesome question. How could we keep our farm operating when the milk company collected our milk each day, and their transport charges were higher than the price paid for our milk? We tried all ways we knew. My mother took in local teachers as boarders and used the board money for payments on the farm. But even then, our payments fell further and further behind. Finally she faced the inevitable heartbreak; the farm no longer earned a living for us. She made arrangements to sign the title deeds back to the bank.

I sat with her as the bank agent, Mr Staker, came and completed the paperwork. "You've done all you can Mrs Scotland," he said, "there's nothing more you can do, nothing more."

Word went around our area that the Scotlands were having a sale of farm goods. From near and far they came, poor farmers hoping to purchase items they could never otherwise afford. When my dad's rifle was sold, I no longer had interest in staying on the farm. From the money we received at the sale we moved to the city.

NEW SIGHTS, SOUNDS AND SMELLS

Perth! For a long time I missed working with Bert and hearing that rich tenor voice. However, the sights, sounds and smells around the house intrigued me. I had never before experienced such things as gas, water supply and the electric power that came into our rented house, and I determined to find out all I could about them. With brash country rawness, I turned on the electric power and tried to understand how the lights worked. When no one was home, I placed a chair within easy reach of the light bulb, removed the bulb, and put my finger in the ceiling light socket. At last I would discover how this thing called electricity really felt. The jolt sent me sprawling, worse than the kick from Kingy our horse on the farm. It took me some months before I had enough courage to try it again. The second shock frightened me into total respect for electric power.

We were in the city alright and with exciting possibilities of discovering new things. But the battle to find a necessary twenty one shillings a week for rent went on relentlessly. My elder sisters, one by one, rose to the challenge. Norah became a secretary with Roland Smith and Company, a clothing warehouse. Melita had done well in dressmaking in our farming district and she began taking orders for dresses. Helen began minding children in the home of Mr and Mrs Digby Leach an engineer with the Main Roads Department. Then my mother took in boarders. There were already eight of us, but she still took in boarders!

FIRECRACKERS

A mother and her two adult sons Tim and Pat came. The mother with son Pat went out daily to school teaching, while Tim fascinated us as a radio announcer with 6PM. The mother rented our number three bedroom, and the men slept on our verandah. I took every opportunity to converse with the men, and was proud I had the job of erecting a curtained area for them because there were so many beds on the verandah already. One memorable morning, the lady jammed a drawer at the bottom of one of our prized wardrobes. She kicked and pulled, but the drawer resisted her attempts to open it. Then her rage blew up, and she wrecked the drawer. She yelled and screamed about being poor and having to limit herself to one room and a part of our verandah. The drawer seemed her release to an inner tidal wave of fury.

I was aghast at the lady's display, and believed her destruction needed redress. She and her sons used a separate table for meals, and one morning as she sat for breakfast, I let off a firecracker right under her part of the table. In the closed room it made our ears ring. After the firecracker, a greater explosion occurred, "You wicked, wicked boy .....
......"

Her angry response made me feel my effort well worth while, but my mother, whom I was trying to protect, showed her horror at my action. Grossly misunderstood, I smouldered.

WAR CLOUDS

Being an avid reader of the newspaper, I followed the reports of an increasing number of wars in the world. In 1932, Japan made war in Manchuria. In 1935, Italy invaded Ethiopia and the carnage went on for four years. In 1936, Spain plunged into years of bloody civil war.

Germany poured in help for one side and the Russians helped the other. In 1937 Japanese forces flooded into China and spewed destruction and terror. Then the newspaper featured accounts of the German army invading Czechoslovakia and Austria. War in Europe seemed a fearful possibility. I looked into our northern sky from where the angry heat of war could roll in upon my small world, and I felt very insecure.

With the end of high school, I needed a job to help with family expenses. I still dreamed of the wide world of Bert Brindal's songs and wanted to go to sea. Pestering mother about joining the navy, I inspired her with an idea. Why should she not write and get advice from my father's brother in England, a Captain in the British Navy.

My uncle helpfully sent the paper work for me to enter Dartmouth Naval College and train to be an officer. But Dartmouth needed the sons of the rich to pay for its courses. We faced the fact that we did not have the finance for me to go there and finally I acknowledged it as an impossible dream. Being then fourteen, my world, that had seemed to be enlarging, became small again. I looked for employment.

Men and boys lined up for the same jobs I wanted, and I was often on the end of a long queue. Unable to get a job I liked, and inhibited from continuing studies because of the cost, I became a garage attendant servicing cars. I hated the filthy work, but talking to car drivers from all over Western Australia, enlarged my world.

GAZING SKYWARDS

1938 came, and with it the heightening threat of approaching war in Europe. Part of Australia's rearmament programme included opening the Pearce air base north of Perth. Single engine Hawker Demon aircraft and twin engine Hudson bombers filled Perth skies with their noisy presence. Gazing skyward, a fresh spirit of adventure arose within me.

A new job saw me excitedly becoming a "pen pusher" in the office of the clothing warehouse of Goode Durrant and Murray. It also added an unexpected pleasure; I cycled to work with Jim Layton, my closest friend, who also had a job in a city office.

We rode to work and our main conversations surrounded the rumbling of war in Europe being reported in our daily papers. Jim Layton asked, "If there is war Tommy, what will you do?" I replied,

"I'm set for the navy Jim." "I'm going to fly," said Jim.

Despite my assurances about the navy, I became more and more drawn to the activities of planes flying from Pearce air base. We saw them daily and their noise activated my mind. Slowly but surely I began talking to Jim of my increasing interest in flying.

On September 3rd 1939, Mr Neville Chamberlain, Prime Minister of Great Britain, came on the radio. In dramatic sombre voice, he announced Britain had declared war on Germany! He had worked for peace, but the German invasion of Poland had triggered Britain's protection treaty with Poland.

Shortly after the declaration of war by Britain, Mr Menzies, Prime Minister of Australia, spoke to the nation. His doleful voice phrased the sombre words, "Fellow Australians, it is my melancholy duty to tell you, Australia is now at war with Germany!" Mr Menzies outlined the terrifying events in Europe that had led the Australian Government to join Britain in declaring war on Germany.

MOTHER

I stood by the piano in the drawing room of our house in Nedlands, and listened to the announcements. My mother sat in her comfortable chair by the hearth of a gently burning fire. The afternoon of this cold spring day drew to a close. Shades of evening made the room seem quite dark; a dull glow came from the fireplace. I pictured the nations of the world crowding beneath the shadow cast by the declaration of war in Europe.

Mother looked at me, "Tom do you think you'll have to be in it, do you think you will have to go?" It stunned me to have to confront my feelings about Australia and Britain being at war with Germany. Mother's question came into my whirling and turning multitude of thoughts.

I considered my reply carefully, "I'm sixteen, a bit young mother, but if the war goes on I suppose I will surely be in it." I recognised this moment of truth for myself, and goose pimples moved across my body in a tremendous sense of awe at the responsibility I felt.

My mother had lived through seeing my dad go overseas with the 10th Light Horse Cavalry to fight in World War 1. What memories filled her as we sat in our darkened room and tried to communicate our thoughts. Age tried to understand youth and youth tried to share with age. But the manhood thinking that seemed expected of me, evaded me.

COUNTRY BOYS AND SOLDIERS

Jim and I rode off to work each day and soon we began to notice that people with whom we worked disappeared and then reappeared dressed in the khaki uniform of Australian Army units. Soldiers from nearby army camps, came to our home. They were fine solid farming men; I loved their fun and enjoyment of being in our home.

While going out to post mail from work one day, I saw our streets filled with soldiers in a type of uniform I had not seen before. They were New Zealanders, pouring into our city from big ships anchored near Fremantle. I arrived at the Perth Post Office, where a group of them carried a small car up the steps. Inside the car, a lone lady driver looked most embarrassed. She had spoken provocatively to the Kiwis, and they had reacted by making her car a monument on the post office steps.

Despite their strange ideas of fun, the Kiwis were loved, lauded and welcomed to Perth. The City opened its heart to them in unforgettable warmth. Their good natured fun touched the heart strings of Perth people and offers of hospitality for them flooded in.

VAST ARMADA

When Saturday came, my friends and I decided to ride our cycles to Fremantle to see the convoy of ships. We topped the last rise and stopped to view the ocean. A vast armada of ships met our gaze. We had never before seen such huge liners anchored off our coast: the Queen Mary, the Aquitania, and many others. Not only were there big passenger ships, but like shepherds around their flock, warships of the Australian navy. The sight from our vantage point, was just awesome.

We learnt that the convoy was taking on board Western Australian regiments; adding them to the New Zealand and other Australian contingents already on board. My family had to say farewell to khaki clad Tim and his brother Pat, the men who had lived in our home so long.

From my first floor vantage point in the city, I saw Tim and Pat march with their regiments. There was no public announcement, but the crowds gathered to say goodbye. I watched as onwards they came, line after line, slouch hats, square jaws, rifles at the slope. There was something fearful about them, long ranks of khaki, strong men, going off to battle in distant places.

Later we saw the convoy sail from Fremantle. Big ships moved sedately off shore; Australian warships leading them out along our ocean front, their destination unknown, probably North Africa. War news from North Africa informed us that a huge German and Italian Army swept towards the Suez Canal and the Australians were needed to help keep the canal open for shipping to India and Australia.

However, several ships, with a division of Australian troops on board, cut through to Singapore and Malaya, where threats of Japanese invasion were rife. On one of those ships, Tim, our friend and ex boarder, sat down to write to us about his feelings on leaving Australia.

NEW WORKPLACE

The ships departed, and a vacuum seemed to be left in our home and even in Perth itself, where people missed seeing their fighting men. I experienced my own sort of vacuum as I began working in the office of the West Australian Government Railways. I really only wanted the job because it offered me an extra five shillings a week.

My work, amongst a huge hall of men, concentrated on accounts and audits at numerous tables. Ages ranged from near retirement in the front rows, to those of junior clerk years at the rear. It depressed me when I let my eye rove over the groups. I saw my future years of service locking me up in this place, and I wanted to scream out, "No, I won't stay here!" My whole upbringing in country life rose up in rebellion against being closed in, separated from the outside world. The world around me had now become very small. Then slowly I began to appreciate my fellow workers.

Day by day, the men began to befriend me. I chatted to different ones and several showed particular kindness. One man, a serious forty year old, had an incurable disease. He talked about it to me and I asked a lot of questions to help me understand how he coped. One morning we received news he had gassed himself in his oven.

The suicide stunned me, and all my fellow workers, for we were like a family. I had been aware of the man's feelings of hopelessness but I had not realised that such feelings could lead to self destruction. I understood a little about dying, but not suicide. My first introduction came when my grandmother had died; Grossie we called her and we loved her. The funeral exemplified flowers and beauty. I felt sad but I experienced the loving warmth of family around me as she went away from us.

A later event occurred while my friend Lin Berryman and I ate school lunch together. He went a terrible colour, vomited violently, and then went limp. I ran to get the headmaster, but Lin had a burst appendix, and he died on the way to hospital. I felt devastated.

At his funeral with others of our class, I gazed at the coffin and felt bereft of my friend, not knowing what to do with the ache inside me. It was a sun filled day, and the clear transparent sky overhead made me wonder if Lin was somewhere in the blue above, "I wonder if he is really there?"

Eight years later, the suicide of my fellow worker at the railways office, spoke to me of his painful loneliness, and it took me a long while to reconcile myself to his suffering.

EUROPE

1940 came. The war had been going some months. Newspapers seemed to indicate it would soon be over. Then everything changed. The French army collapsed, the British Army retreated, and German Forces advanced towards Paris. The British, in trying to save themselves from annihilation, moved at full speed towards the French port of Dunkirk, and hoped for evacuation back to Britain.

Australians were shocked. British defeat had not been considered a possibility. Australia's Prime Minister Menzies called for a day of prayer across the nation, asking for deliverance of the British Army at Dunkirk. Thousands of people packed Forrest Place in Perth to unite in prayer to God. Never before had Australians been so united, with one aim.

My avid reading kept me aware of events on the beaches of Dunkirk. Four hundred thousand British soldiers were waiting there to board ships and be transported back to Britain. A powerful German army and air force were poised, ready to pounce on the British units before any reasonable rescue could be mounted.

Then came a miracle. A rearguard of chosen British regiments held the German advance as evacuation from the beaches began. Amidst this heroism, heavy clouds settled over the Channel area, limiting the German Air Force to sporadic bombing. British naval ships hauled soldiers off the beaches. Then came merchant ships, sending in their long boats to rescue the troops. Lastly, an armada of small boats, often, seemingly too small, came floating out from England's shores: Thames launches, private motor boats, sail boats, fishing boats, trawlers. The greatest miracle seemed to lie with those small boats. They came right in to the shallow beaches alongside groups of soldiers waiting up to their necks in water. Smooth seas and cloud covered skies enabled 330,000 troops to be lifted out and returned to England. It was explained as intervention by the Almighty.

I thrilled to radio and newspaper accounts of this deliverance. Britain had saved her army, however, most of their guns and equipment stayed in France and Belgium. Germany was now poised to land her troops on English soil, and Britain prepared for invasion.

MEANWHILE

Meanwhile, Jim Layton and I continued to ride to work along Mounts Bay Road and discussed the war situation in Europe. Joined by another good friend, Jimmy Dodds, we enjoyed magnificent river views as a delightful backdrop to the momentous decisions now forming in our minds. We discoursed daily on the news of British Hurricane and Spitfire fighters climbing into British skies to defend their nation against German air fleets. Impending German invasion of Britain assured us that our involvement in a lengthening war was inevitable. We determined we must learn to fly and play our part in the defeat of Germany. Debating ways in which we could prepare ourselves, we heard the Australian Air Force had a preparatory programme of study for men like ourselves. We decided that was the way we would go. We applied for the course, and soon our minds were grappling with the intricacies of navigation and radio.

WE WILL NEVER SURRENDER

While the world expected Britain's early defeat, Britain became bestirred by a voice; newly appointed Prime Minister Winston Churchill. He broadcast Britain's intentions after the fall of France, *"The news from France is very bad, and I grieve for the gallant French people who*

---

have fallen into this terrible misfortune. .... We shall defend our island home, and with the British Empire, we shall fight on unconquerable until the curse of Hitler is lifted from the brows of mankind." My friends and I were aroused, challenged with our urgent need of flying training.

France fell. Some of her soldiers escaped to become the Army of the Free French in Britain. But French territory, like Syria, became an enemy stronghold. Australian Army units were sent to capture it, and in time, Syria fell. Australian newspapers were jubilant. Then, in January the next year, 1941, Aussie soldiers captured Tobruk in Libya. They had defeated a seemingly invincible German Army under the control of that desert fox, General Rommel. Australia was elated.

However, tragedy was waiting. Australian units, hastily called out of North Africa, went north to help safeguard the security of Greece and the Island of Crete. But it was hopeless. Overwhelming German air power combined with battle trained ground forces crushed the Allied regiments. Australian newspapers now featured increasing lists of Aussie boys slain in battle and Australia mourned her lost sons. Included in the lists of battle casualties was our friend and boarder, Pat. Notified of his death by telegram, his mother was devastated. Her favourite was no more. My family stood by her, but no one could comfort her in the torture she felt at his loss.

MOTHER'S SIGNATURE

Mother was tidying the dining room table one morning when I asked for her signature on my application to join the Air Force. The worried lines on her face showed the long nights she had spent in trying to prepare herself for this step. She hesitated, stopped her tidying motions, and asked me to talk with her about what I proposed to do. Moving slowly along the wide hallway ahead of me on her walking sticks, she entered her bedroom and said, "Sit down Tom."

Slowly and deliberately she asked, "If you send this form in, when would you expect to be called up?" I explained, "Mother, if I pass the medical and education tests, they'll call me up straight away. You see I am already partly enrolled by doing the one year training course." Mother continued, "Would you have an opportunity for a ground staff role if they don't accept you as a pilot?" I could see that my possible pilot role was of great concern to her, but I answered, "I am applying for aircrew and I do hope to become a pilot. If I fail in that, I would have to think about a ground staff role."

She asked, "Do you think that you will be sent to England?" The deep lines of concern on her face made me pause. This question seemed to trouble her most. I said, "Mother, the RAF in England has a big job to do. I think it is a possibility that I be sent there." I explained that the RAF had a great need for pilots and my friends, Jim Layton and Jimmy Dodds also saw this need.

My words seemed to add to the deep anguish within her. She gave a very deep sigh, then stoically signed her name to my form.

THAT TEST

The big day arrived for my Air Force medical test. I had practised for one particularly difficult test I expected to grapple with. I wanted to pass well in that one, as it would take me one step nearer to becoming a pilot. I had to blow into a tube of mercury until reaching my maximum, then hold the mercury at that height until I ran out of breath. It transpired I passed that test easily but nearly burst my insides in making sure that I did pass. The doctor smiled as he told me my results and said he recognised my zeal and determination. He looked at my papers, and noted that it was my eighteenth birthday, August 5th 1941. "Hmmm!" he said, looking at me seriously, "You aren't wasting any time are you. Good luck to you!"

3

THE FORTY CLUB

Surrounded by one hundred and twenty men, I marched through the main entrance gate to my new home at the Pearce air base on September 14th 1941. I had been an avid follower of events at Pearce, and now, in becoming a participant there, I was like one who dreamed. Then I met our drill corporal.

With all our men lined up, and standing to attention, the silence was suddenly broken, "That man, stop scratching!" I did not believe "that man" existed apart from the drill corporal's imagination. His barking voice aimed at gaining control over us, and I hated him for it. His discipline earned him the name, "Ming the Merciless".

So life began anew for us in number twenty course of the Empire Air Training Scheme, a scheme co-ordinating the air training facilities of Australia, South Africa, New Zealand, Rhodesia and Canada. The Air Forces of these countries and Britain, needed pilots, navigators, bomb aimers, wireless operators and air gunners to operate the planes now being planned and produced in British and American factories. But time would prove that flying was not the only activity the Air Force had in mind for us!

DISTINCTIVE AROMA

Arriving at the supply store to receive my uniform, I delighted in the distinctive aroma of the dark blue cloth, and held it to my face. There was a chuckle behind me. A husky voice asked, "What are you sniffing there?" A tall, long faced trainee with black hair combed tightly back, smiled as I said, "I'm enjoying the smell of this uniform. What did you think I was doing?" "I was just wondering. My name's Don Watson, who are you?" he asked boldly. "My name's Tom Scotland."

I enjoyed the way Don made himself known to me. We talked on together about our new environment and then fell in line for return to our quarters. Deciding to get to know one another better, we set our bedding close to each other. Then we met Norm.

My immediate response to Norm, was a sense of wonder that such as he had to be thrust into wartime flying. His handsome sensitivity seemed the antithesis of war. Underneath lay a born actor with the ability to make rubber contortions of his finely moulded features. When I commented on his beautifully shaped hands, he confessed that he was a well known musician from the Perth music scene and Radio 6PR. At the word "musician", I understood him as someone from a vastly different world to mine. Norm set out his bedding next to Don and me.

DANCING FEET

For two and a half months we drilled, studied Air Force subjects and swatted for exams. Ming the Merciless welded our group together into a fine marching team, and we received much applause for our display in the Gloucester Park arena.

My first flight came as a passenger in a Hudson bomber. It dived in to drop bombs over the practise range, and surprised me with the stresses I felt in this type of flying. Later, one of the bombers did not pull out of the dive and I lost a boyhood farming friend, John Taylor, a passenger in the plane. I groaned inwardly as I was introduced to the hazards that flying presented.

The day came when the notice board showed the names of trainees and the aircrew category the Air Force had chosen for them. Sixty were listed for pilot training. Would I be one of those? I scanned the names, and there they were; Dunn, Scotland and Watson, selected for training as pilots. Experiencing this very big moment in our lives, we danced and sang, and would not be quieted.

Those selected as navigators, radio operators, and gunners, departed for the next stage of their training in Victoria and South Australia. Of the sixty pilots who were selected, only twenty could begin flying instruction in Western Australia. Forty of us would be going to training bases in Africa, and the list included Don Watson and me. Dismayed at being delayed, I watched, while twenty friends went off to immediate flying training locally. Norm Dunn did not want to break from our friendship, and he elected to join us in going to Africa. His presence stimulated us as we glumly packed our bags and prepared for overseas.

Then December 7th 1941 dawned, and radios hummed with stunning news. Japan had attacked the American Naval fleet at Pearl Harbour in Hawaii. War in the Pacific had begun.

WAR IN THE PACIFIC

We heard the news of Japan's attack on the US in disbelief. Japan declared herself an ally of Germany and Italy and thus we were at war with Japan, and America entered the war against Germany and Italy. The whole globe was now a battlefield. Fear swept over me as I realised that no place on earth would be safe from attacking armies.

War in the Pacific not only took the Japanese on a relentless march southwards through Asia, but also had a marked effect on Don, Norm and me, with the other pilot trainees. Day by day we awaited ship, and day after day we went to Fremantle to load drums of fuel for shipment to the war zone. A forgotten group of forty men amidst a mass of fuel drums and storage tanks, the title Forty Club, gave us painful identity.

A month passed, then official notification came; "No ship available to take you to Africa. Return to Pearce and await your turn to get into flying training in Western Australia." The advance of Japanese forces towards Australia had changed all plans for sending us overseas. But of greater moment to us, a later course of pilot trainees had taken our place and begun flying training. We felt overlooked, left out, disappointed. Begrudgingly, the Forty Club returned to Pearce.

Visiting my home at Nedlands before returning to Pearce, I learnt that another telegram had arrived for the lady who lived with us; her eldest son Tim had been killed by the Japanese in Malaya. With Pat killed in Crete and now Tim in Malaya, their loss touched us all. The men had been like sons and brothers to my family. But, greater than our own sorrow, was that of their mother. Bereft of her family, she brooded alone in her darkened room day by day, and could not be comforted.

ONLY A MATTER OF TIME

The Forty Club moved back to Pearce as British battleships Prince of Wales and Repulse with a screen of smaller ships arrived in Singapore to help break up the Japanese invasion fleets. Then the unbelievable happened. Japanese aircraft attacked and sank the two large British warships, and two hundred thousand Allied soldiers had to surrender in Singapore. The losses in ships and men sent shock waves across Australia, for no longer could Australians look for Britain's help in turning the tide of Japanese soldiers moving southwards. Australian families wept for their men and wondered what greater sorrows could lie ahead.

Indonesia fell, then Japanese forces swept into New Guinea. Invasion of Australia would be only a matter of time.

BACK AT PEARCE

Adjacent to the huts where the Forty Club settled in, US airmen were given quarters. Survivors from American bases attacked by Japanese aircraft and naval ships in the Pacific, they sat with us, and recounted the ferocity of the Japanese attacks. Some even expressed belief that the Japanese were invincible. I experienced my own share of disquiet that crept across the personnel at Pearce.

The urgent need now was for air raid shelters and air raid trenches. The men of the Forty Club took on a new role as construction gangs building defences, something I loathed doing. A personal hatred for the Japs, and what they were doing to us, burned within me.

THERE WILL BE NO FLYING TRAINING FOR YOU BLOKES UNTIL THIS SHELTER IS SO DEEP THAT YOU COME OUT IN THE U.K.

Jim Layton came to say he had joined the Air Force, and wanted to see me before beginning his training in South Australia. I left off digging trenches, and we two friends found a place to sit and talk. The boots of passing airmen crunched on the loose surface of a nearby path, but Jim and I, uncaring of their noise, rode our memories to work again. Around the Swan River and along Mounts Bay Road, those rides, and our conversations then, had meant so much to us in preparation for joining the Air Force. We shared two choice hours, discussing our lives and what lay ahead. Then we parted. Jim's steady gaze, strongly rounded face, serious voice, and firm handshake remained with me long after I saw him board his bus and return to Perth.

DOT IN THE SKY

After seeing Jim off, I returned to digging a survival trench at the edge of the airfield. In pensive mood, I raised my pick to chip away at the solid clay, when an explosive roar crossed the base. I looked up in time to see a dot moving rapidly into the western sky. The dot turned, then headed back towards us. "A fast aircraft," I decided; one very different from any that I thought we had in Australia.

I had read about the Spitfire and Hurricane fighters doing so much to deliver the British from the fury of German Bombers. The plane I now saw coming in, did not fit their description, but what could it be? Our Australian Wirraway fighters on the base could not fly anywhere near such speed. The strange plane continued to draw nearer. "Is it Japanese?" I asked myself worriedly, and then saw the plane's wheels lowering for a landing. Nearer and nearer it came, and for the first time in my life, I saw the blue star marking of the United States Army Air Force. The plane landed, slowed on the runway, turned and headed for the control tower. At the base of the control tower itself, an amazing sight now met my eyes. It had come alive with air force personnel.

I looked again and saw columns of people hurrying along various approach roads and all heading towards the tarmac area where the crowd gathered. The strange aircraft, centre of all attention, stopped, the motor shut down and the pilot stood up in the cockpit.

Rushing to the outer edge of the crowd around the plane, I saw the people surge forward to welcome this visitor as if he were a person from another planet. The pilot, a US Lieutenant, stood in the cockpit of the plane, and tried to communicate with the crowd. In loud, slow American drawl he asked, "Say, can you guys tell me if this is the Maylands Airport?" A hush greeted his words, then a voice responded, "No, this is the Pearce air base, Maylands is 40 miles to the south!" The "man from Mars" had come an unbelievable 40 miles off course, but seemed most unperturbed about it. When asked the name of the plane, he drawled, "It`s a P40." The P40 had also been named the "Kittyhawk," but I had not known there were any in Australia.

Having verified the direction to Maylands, the pilot cleared the crowd from around his P40 Kittyhawk, started his motor, and headed off towards the runway. There, with a mighty roar, he sent his plane into the sky. The cheers of the admiring crowd were loud enough to be heard above the noise of the fast disappearing Kittyhawk, now just a speck in the distance. That US pilot, by losing his way, had just given us all a magnificent boost in morale.

These Kittyhawks were being hastily assembled east of Pearce, tested by U.S. pilots, then flown to Maylands, and transported by road to Fremantle. There, a U.S. aircraft carrier loaded them ready for sailing north to defend Darwin against Japanese attack.

Some weeks later, the aircraft carrier arrived in Darwin, and its arrival coincided with Japanese bombing raids. Amidst the tremendous havoc wrought by the bombs, the carrier became a casualty. Waves closed over the ship and all those Kittyhawk fighters. It was a tragic finale to the dramatic attempt to bring help to Australia's northern town.

DEFENDING PEARCE

Meanwhile, Darwin received its bombing attacks, and the Forty Club worked on at Pearce. Amidst an atmosphere of apprehension about invasion, we dug trenches, built defences, camouflaged huge aircraft hangar roofs and painted buildings.

With my co-worker Norm Dunn, I embarked on building an emplacement for machine gunners as defence against attack by low flying planes. Day after day we filled sand bags and stacked them into defensive walls. Norm's slender musical fingers became increasingly painful, but the wall of sand bags mounted higher until our heads were hidden by them. Amidst putting the last sand bags into place, we heard someone shouting. The voice came nearer, "Whacko you fellows, you can stop work now!" Don Watson came into sight; a huge smile showed his great excitement. "What are you shouting about Watto?" we chorused. "Listen you chaps, you can stop your work. We are going back to studies, then we're moving on to pilot training. What do you think of that?"

There had been so many rumours that we did not know what to think. Such news needed verification. We placed our last sandbag into the wall, then followed Don back to our quarters. Fellows were grouped there, babbling with elated voices. Don and Norm Dunn danced around the hut floor, while I tried to discover the facts. The facts became better than Don's news to us. Not only were we to cease labouring, but also to prepare for immediate removal to the pilot training base at Cunderdin to begin flying.

A shout came through, "Hey! Laurie Greenham has been hurt, they're rushing him to hospital!" "No, not Laurie!" I said to myself, thinking of the big, warm hearted, loveable fellow. It appeared that Laurie had been working at a site containing exploded practice bombs. He had knocked some debris against a live practice bomb remaining amongst the rubbish. It had exploded. Particles of steel pierced Laurie's face and eyes. As we awaited more news of him, our worst fears were confirmed; he had lost his sight, ironically, just when we had received the all clear to begin flying training. Heavy gloom settled over us as we packed for our move to Cunderdin air base.

The night before we departed, there was a concert. The big hall was packed with Australian and US servicemen. We watched proudly as Norm Dunn thrilled the audience with the music of his electric guitar. The concert was a fulfilling send off to the whole Forty Club after our months of painful endeavour on the base.

LAURIE

A short stopover in Perth gave time to visit Laurie Greenham in hospital. I arrived feeling something of the terror that blindness instilled in me. A bright, warm hearted lass met me and I recognised Laurie's girlfriend. She ushered me into a room and pointed to the bandage covered face, "Laurie, it's Tom."

"Hullo Tom," said Laurie in muffled voice, "It's good to see you!" I could not believe such a greeting from one so recently unable to see. The girl stood beside Laurie as he explained that he had indeed been completely blinded. I noticed their acceptance of Laurie's loss of sight. Such a response surprised me. I admired this tremendous courage, and said so. They confided that Laurie's time in the Air Force had finished, but his blindness had not stopped them looking to the future. They planned to marry. I went away from the hospital having learnt a lot about acceptance and courage amidst the sadness of those two brave and beautiful people.

TERROR IN THE MORNING

Eighty miles east of Perth, the Cunderdin airfield encompassed a wide flat area set amongst wheat and sheep farmland, several miles in length. A Tiger Moth training plane could take off and land many times within the airfield boundaries. At the southern end beyond the fence line, lay salt pans and marshy areas that dried in summer. In daylight the heated air over the salt pans boiled skywards giving aircraft a very bumpy boost into the sky.

Our day began at 4.30 am. Bleary eyed, I staggered out of bed to shower, consume my breakfast and then move down to the hangars to help roll out the Tiger Moths for flying. Cunderdin offered about equal time between a lecture programme and flying training. Private study, research, and letter writing fitted into whatever time remained to us.

My first ride in a Tiger Moth filled me with terror. Wally Boud, my Pilot Officer instructor, took off with me in the rear cockpit. We climbed for height and he made the aircraft turn to the left. I chose that moment to gaze earthwards. Overcome by a sensation of falling, I grasped the rim of the cockpit to steady myself. The meagre construction under my fingers alerted me to the fearful possibility that the fragile Tiger was breaking apart in the air. Amidst my overwhelming feelings of terror, a voice came through my earphones, "Take the stick Scotty!"

Hanging on to the cockpit rim with my hands, I tried to turn my gaze to the control stick and to concentrate on it. Gingerly I lifted my right hand and moved it to hold the hand grip at the top of the control column. By this time Wally Boud had straightened the aircraft out of the turn. "See that cross wire ahead of you, keep that on the horizon," he said. "Crosswire, the horizon?" Slowly I focused my eyes on a cable stretched between struts that supported the top wing of the Tiger Moth. Then I looked for that horizon. A vague moving skyline appeared in the distance. "I suppose that's it," I muttered to myself. Then I experienced my big surprise!

In answer to my fumbling right hand, the crosswire and the horizon moved towards each other. The little plane was responding to my touch.

"That's it, hold it there." said the voice. I held it there. "Now put your feet on the rudder pedals near the floor, push with your left foot," droned the voice. My left foot found the gently vibrating rudder pedal. "That's it," continued the voice, "now push with your right foot. Watch the cross wire, see how you've made us dive, pull the stick back, not too much, now forward, there we go in a dive again, level off ..." The instructor's patter went on and on.

Insecurity faded as I became alert to the plane depending on me to fly it. Its response exhilarated me; I was flying at last.

DISCONSOLATE
Conversation between Wally Boud and me came via a piece of hose pipe from his cockpit in front. Whether in the air or on the ground, that speaking tube enabled us to converse from our open cockpits.

I enjoyed the friendliness that Wally offered me. He an officer and I a lowly trainee, he referred to me as "Scotty," and I experienced feelings of warmth in our relationship. But I had a big problem. I flew the Tiger alright, but on coming in to land, I was either too high or too low. When too high, the plane dropped terrifyingly to the ground. The impact shook me so much that I expected the wheels to penetrate up through the floor of the cockpit. On the other hand, when I came in too low, we hit the ground at speed then shot into the air again. I found myself bouncing the plane along like a kangaroo. With every bounce I had to make a fresh attempt to do a landing or else the next bounce would be worse than the first.

HE'S NOT HOPPING, ITS A "SPROG" PILOT DOING HIS FIRST LANDING.

Disconsolate about my landings, I sat on the edge of the airfield, my head in my hands, and watched as other fellows landed. Many did the same as I, and that made me feel better, but others made very good landings, and they were my envy.

Amidst further flying with Wally, my eyes began to focus more accurately. The kangaroo hop gave way to a comfortable rumble of the landing wheels along the ground. I felt jubilant. Then I had the plane to myself. That night I wrote a letter.

9EFTS,Cunderdin, 23rd March 1942

My Dearest Mother,

Well, I told you I'd not write until I cracked the solo, so here it is. I am writing this out on the airfield with slipstreams of aircraft swishing past my ears and the strong smell of gasoline in my nose, and a sense of irresponsibility in my heart. Indeed this has been a great day.

I had a test with my instructor first thing this morning. After landing I taxied the plane to the edge of the drome and stopped. When I saw my boss's safety straps flying in the slipstream and him starting to get out of the plane, I grinned. "What are you grinning about?" he asked. "Just wondering if I am really going solo." He climbed out of the front cockpit, "She's all yours Scotty. Just one circuit now and I'll watch you land. Come and pick me up when you get back." I've never felt so calm in all my life, but I also felt alone. I taxied out, turned out of the wind and checked my instruments with the thoroughness I'd been taught. I turned into the wind again and then gave old "53" the full gun. With a surge of power, my little ship gathered way. "Keep it straight keep it straight" was the whisper. Up came the tail, back with the stick and we were clear of the ground, just No.53 and myself.

"Oh great silver dawn, I pay homage to thee," and I kept the plane climbing right out into the rising sun. "Don't let that wing drop. Keep it up." I could imagine my instructor echoing in my ear. At 600 feet, I flattened out. "All clear, turning left," I shouted down the intercommunication tube and in the great style I had learnt, bringing No 53 around in a ninety degree turn. "Ah, that's what I like"

"And its all day long I sing, the daughter of officer Kelly" I sang. Was I happy? Oh was I happy! After climbing to a thousand feet, I eased the throttle to regulate the motor and continued in straight and level

flight. Right there I felt like doing a loop. This was the flight that I had never imagined myself doing alone in No.53 at a thousand feet above mother earth. To my faithful plane I softly whispered, "You little darling, you beautiful man made creature, how I could hug and kiss you. Where would I be now if it weren't for you. Well who knows for I'm sure I can't think."

On the last leg of my circuit I cut the motor, set the tail trim and prepared, as I determined, for the best landing of my career. Lower and lower we sank, 800 feet, 600 feet, then 400, and 200 and then I was too interested in watching the earth rising to meet us. At what I calculated twenty feet to be, I checked the glide and slowly but surely let her sink, sink, s.i.n.k, s..i..n..k and we settled smoothly as only smooth can be. We came to rest with the motor only just ticking over. I'd made it! I'd done it! Well what of it anyway, this is only the start .... "

IN THE AIR

Day by day, my flying hours mounted, and the times in the air elated me. Between flights I included study on navigation, meteorology, theory of flight, airframes, armaments, engines and aircraft recognition. Exam time drew close.

In the meantime, other pilots made the big step of going solo. Bill, another friend, went off, flew around the airfield then came in to land. His plane bounced so high that he had to open the throttle and get the aircraft to go around the circuit area again and hope for another landing. Round and round he went, trying to land, then bouncing into the sky. On his fourteenth try he must have been very desperate for he just allowed the plane to bounce and bounce and bounce until, miraculously, it came to rest. He alighted from the plane, glad when the Air Force encouraged him to take on something else. He chose to became a bomb aimer. For various reasons others of our mates did not make it as pilots, but went off to begin courses in other aircrew categories. Don and I talked and shared in their disappointment as if it were our own.

The Chief Flying Instructor of the RAAF flew in to check us and to assess our flying. Preparing me for the test, Wally Boud spent time helping me to gain finesse in aerobatics, loops and rolls. He excited me with his loud encouragements, "Bloody good Scotty, do it again!"

REWARD INDEED

Then came my test with the CFI. It was an anticlimax. He requested me to fly my sequences, but said not a word more. We landed. Still he remained silent. Crestfallen, I watched Wally Boud chat to him.

Wally looked serious as he came up to me, and I expected his commiserations. He smiled, "Good show Scotty, he`s given you an above average rating!" It was reward indeed. I had only wanted a pass in my flying test and this rating took me far beyond expectations.

I watched Don Watson go through his flying test. With absolute care, Don took his examiner through the preflight check of the aircraft and I could see that even the phlegmatic CFI loved it. Eventually Don and the CFI took off and disappeared into the distance.

When Don returned, his face glowed. "What are you so pleased about Watto?" I asked. In absolute glee he said, "The CFI has given me a flying rating of exceptional." "I watched you win him right from the start Watto!" I shouted as we danced out our pent up emotions together on the grass of the airfield. Jubilantly we headed away to the lecture rooms to prepare for final written examinations beginning in two days time.

Swotting and examinations went on hour after hour. We tried to put down on paper, those important theoretical aspects of flying that would help to prepare us for what lay ahead. When all was done, I experienced a wonderful feeling of release.

MOUNT BROWN

Wally Boud sent me out flying. "Try to perfect all those things I've been teaching you Scotty!" he said encouragingly. Low flying would not have been one of the things he had in mind for me but I longed to fly low over fences and trees and dams. Wally had warned me about the dangers of flying low without permission, and that I could be disqualified if caught. For some reason, the penalty of disqualification just did not seem important to me just then. A bunch of us agreed to meet at Mount Brown, a hill protruding out of farmland some distance south east of the airfield.

Mount Brown! Six Tiger Moths were there, busily practising their illegal low flying techniques. Aircraft circled the hill like moths around a lantern. A cleft down the middle of the hill offered special excitement as I flew at zero feet and passed wing tip to wing tip, a Tiger flying in the opposite direction. Unknown to us, the farmer at Mount Brown was not amused by all our noisy planes around his farm. A phone call to Cunderdin demanded that the intruders depart. Thus, in due time, a shadow passed over Mount Brown.

Recent arrivals at Cunderdin had been several British Navy Swordfish planes, much faster than the Tiger Moths. One now appeared on a spotting flight, and passed over the seven Tiger Moths still flying at ground level. The eye of every pilot gazed skywards. The effect of that plane was like that of a savage predator over a flock of sparrows. Tiger Moths scattered, their motors at full throttle seeking to escape the all seeing eyes of the instructors. My altimeter read one thousand feet by the time the Swordfish aircraft came up and flew parallel with me. On landing, I received an ominous message, "Report to the CO!"

Wing Commander Norm Brearley M.C., A.F.C., pioneer aviator of Australia, veteran of the first World War, was a CO greatly admired by us all. For me to be called up before him in these circumstances aroused my anxiety to a painful level. I stood as he sadly recounted the taking of my number because the instructor thought I had been low flying. He did not ask me if I had or had not. His eyes fixed on me sternly as he said,

"You need to protect your flying career Scotland. Episodes like this could ground you. That is all, you can go." I walked away from the CO's office feeling stunned by how close I had come to receiving full vengeance from the law. "So," I thought, "No one actually saw me low flying. The CO just had my aircraft number and the hunch that I had been low flying." I respected him for his straight warning.

Another near catastrophe occurred two days later. Melons grew on the airfield, and a group of us loaded them into our planes. We planned to drop the melons overboard and test our bombing accuracy. This seemingly innocent practice was also quite dangerous but it offered much excitement. We discovered only too well that it was difficult to place a melon accurately on a ground point even from a fairly slow flying Tiger Moth. One fellow became particularly unwise. He tried to lob a melon into the town water supply dam adjacent to the town. When the melon went out over the side of the Tiger Moth it overshot the dam and headed towards the main street of Cunderdin. Fortunately no pedestrian or vehicle moved into the path of the falling melon, otherwise serious damage could have occurred. By the time the melon splattered across the road, the horrified pilot had realised his foolishness and headed his Tiger Moth away from town. I decided I had had enough to heed my CO's warning and protect my flying career. I did not embark on further melon bombing runs.

JAPANESE EYES ON AUSTRALIA

While we flew, the Japanese closed their grip on Australia, and focused on destroying Darwin. Darwin had little defence against these high flying raiders until Kittyhawk and Spitfire squadrons were finally assembled and flew against them. But the bombing attacks continued and Darwin suffered.

The port of Broome on our north west coast had few defences when Japanese planes attacked. Seventeen flying boat aircraft, loaded with refugees from Indonesia had just landed in Broome's Roebuck Bay. Seven more big aircraft were at the airport. As the raid progressed, all the allied planes were destroyed, and the number of casualties mounted. Flames from sinking aircraft on the bay added to the horror as people perished, and Broome residents watched the carnage helplessly.

Horn Island off the Queensland coast suffered attack. Then came Wyndham, also Port Hedland, then Onslow, as the Japanese Air Force ventured further and further southward down the West Australian coast. The sense of apprehension about a Japanese invasion of Western Australia, became so strong that once again I could feel the very tension in the air.

The United States sent in air and ground forces, with naval units, to help protect Australia and to make a base for attacking the Japanese. At Cunderdin, American Liberator four engined bombers came and went day by day. Our training planes were well named Tiger Moths for that is how they looked beside the big American planes.

TOSSED LIKE FLOTSAM

The Liberators were behind Don Watson one day as he took off into the eastern sky. I watched as his tiny yellow plane skimmed over the grass and took to the air. Unknown to Don, three Liberator bombers had started their take off run from a mile away on the far side of the airfield.

Don became airborne, and so did the Liberators behind him. The first that Don knew of his danger was his being surrounded by the huge black shapes and being tossed around in the air turbulence from their propellers. Don's Tiger Moth seemed to dance and tilt like a plaything in a giant hand.

I stared helplessly as the perilous situation developed. Even when the planes flew beyond him, the wash of their propellers continued to toss him like flotsam on a raging sea. Through it all, Don fought to save himself and his plane. He aborted his flight and landed, his face pale from the experience. "I thought I'd had it" he said grimly as he carried his parachute back into the flight office.

Much more scary happenings would come to Don when he began flying Catalina flying boats against Japanese forces in the Pacific. But for now such events lay in the future and he took several days to recover.

FAREWELL CUNDERDIN
At last we graduated. Our next step would be to the Flying Training School at Geraldton, 300 miles north of Perth.

WELL SCOTLAND THATS ALL I CAN TEACH YOU. YOU MAY NOT SCARE THE HUN BUT BY HELL YOU'LL SCARE THE POMMIES.

The day came when I was with my Forty Club fellows in a train moving out of Cunderdin railway station for the last time. Rolling along past the boundary of the airfield, I gazed at the wild melons growing along the fence. Were they mocking in farewell, and reminding me I had very much to learn about dropping bombs from an aircraft?

Steaming its way through endless brown stubble of last summer's wheat fields, the train headed towards Perth. I had the excitement of two days leave before catching my next train northwards to Geraldton.

I went up the familiar front steps of our house in Nedlands, and my teenage sister Elsa saw me coming. Now filling out and shapely, with long blonde tresses to her shoulders, she hid her excitement, and in laconic voice said, "Look who's here, where did you spring from?" Her words contrasted sharply with her wild run along the hallway to the kitchen, hair flying out behind her, and shouting, "Mum it's Tom!"

Following her, I saw mother sitting on a stool, making pastry. "Oh Tom!" she exclaimed. "Yes mother, it's me!" I said embracing her as flour scattered over my dark blue uniform.

Slowly we all regained our composure, and I explained about having two days leave before journeying to Geraldton. Then news of absent members of the family tumbled out. Norah was in Melbourne doing secret work in ciphers and signals. Melita, in the Army Nursing Service, expected to be sent to New Guinea to attend Australian casualties from the war against the Japanese. Helen, with her caring attitude for others, had begun nursing training at Fremantle hospital. Pauline worked with Air Force Fighter Control defending Sydney against Japanese aircraft attacks.

Pat, in the Women's Land Army, worked on a cattle station out from Leonora in the desert country. Elsa had settled into secretarial work in Perth.

Feeling deeply moved by all the changes to my family, I went to my room to adjust to being home. How should I spend this short leave?

4

IN EMU COUNTRY

A railway goods van accommodated Don and me travelling on the train to Geraldton. There was little space to set out our meagre bedding; kit bags and cases pointed in all directions as servicemen chose their positions for an uncomfortable night's journey.

In the bumping, rattling, dimly lit van, men talked, played cards or read until late into the night, and then one by one dropped off into sleep. In the early hours of the morning, the train stopped yet once again. Hearing footsteps on the platform and words about pies, I decided, "Ah! A place to eat."

Sleeping bodies lay in awkward array across my path to the door. Near the head of one sleeping body, I searched for a place to put my foot. Something broke. The sound from underfoot was strange, and I could not figure out what it might be. No movement came from the sleeping body, so I continued on, stepping carefully.

Once at the doorway, I heard a groan from behind me, "Aww ... my bloody teeth!" Had I been more awake I would have connected the cry to the sound that had occurred beneath my searching feet, but I moved out into the night to get my pie.

Crunching hungrily on the pie crust, I returned to the doorway of the van, and listened to men breathing. The cry of that fellow came back to me. His words now identified to me what must have happened under my feet. The fellow had taken out his porcelain false teeth and put them by his head, and my foot had found them. My thoughts whirled, "Bugger it, whatever can I do now?" I could not find the chap in the darkness without awakening all the sleeping bodies. I would wait for the morning, and identify myself to him. Feeling more settled, I lay down and slept.

The next thing I knew, I was cold. A weak sun shed light through a window, and the train jerked, accelerating away from just one more stop. I looked around the van. The army men had gone. "They disembarked at the last stop, Walkaway," Don told me. Only airmen remained in the van. On checking around, I learnt that the man I wanted had disembarked. Could I ever forget him? We only had that one strange meeting in the dark, my false step, his false teeth and that cry, "Aww ... my bloody teeth!" I had a painful picture of a toothless soldier trying to eat army tucker.

GERALDTON

The sun rose higher, warming the day; then came Geraldton. Our uncomfortable journey was over. I stepped out on to the platform, rubbed aching limbs, then saw Air Force trucks awaiting us. Lumping our gear, we climbed aboard. The air base was on the outskirts of town. Beyond the base, lay a scene that excited my anticipation of adventure ahead; gently rising terrain backed by distant hills, flat topped, but cut by deep valleys.

Stepping down from the truck, I wearily flopped my gear into the timber and asbestos hut. Our beds were three planks and an empty bag which we had to fill with straw. How could such a meagre structure ever provide comfortable sleeping? Nevertheless, I slept, and soundly too.

BASE ON ALERT

"HMAS Sydney sunk. All 360 crew lost 300 miles off West Australian coast." The startling announcement had been long delayed by the censors, but it had put Geraldton air base in a state of high alert. Responding to the loss of the Sydney, the Avro Anson training planes armed with bombs and guns, flew on patrol from Geraldton daily. Our training had to take second place to the pressing emergency.

Rumours of expected Japanese invasion were rife. Amidst all those rumours and the activities on the base we researched into the theory of bombing, gunnery, gas warfare and the medical hazards of flying, and awaited our opportunity to fly. Then at last, the twin engined Anson was ours. Flying gave us opportunity to get away from tensions on the base.

Now this is an Avro Anson!

The flat topped hills beyond the plains still beckoned me. I embarked on a secret practice of flying along some of the isolated valleys. Emus were there. I thought, "At least we can do some practise for when the Japanese arrive!" The emus seemed surprised by the shattering noise of an Avro Anson coming at them with a gun firing, but most of them survived and the skies around us remained clear of the enemy.

TORCHES IN THE NIGHT

The tempo of flying increased and it exhilarated me. At first we only flew during daylight, and then reported for guard duty at night. Our planes had to be guarded against possible Japanese demolition teams penetrating the coastline and making the air base a prime target. A small team of enemy soldiers could be very destructive. We needed to be ready.

I groaned when I saw my name rostered for guard duty at two till four am, my worst time for guard duty. I completed my day's flying and then retired early to prepare for awakening at two. Prodded awake, just before two, I was still partly asleep, but climbed out of bed. Moving out into the night, I heard eerie sounds around the widely dispersed aircraft; such weird noises. I crept forward to investigate. Strange shadows moved amongst the aircraft. I found that the eerie sounds came from a gentle wind moving some of the surfaces on the planes. The shadows proved to be, just that, only shadows.

Completing my rounds, I sat on a fallen tree near the fence, and looked at my watch: 2.30 am. In another hour and a half I could awaken fellow pilot George Oliver and hand over my duty. But for now I had to be especially ready to challenge the duty officer who had the disconcerting habit of getting into the airfield unseen. I rested my head on my rifle, and waited.

Far in the distance, I heard disturbing noises. "Whatever is going on?" I wondered, identifying the noise as people shouting, and a car horn blaring. Lifting my head, I saw the outline of people among waving torch lights. The rifle was in my hands, and two words shot into my mind, "Duty officer!" Had I been asleep, and not challenged the duty officer? Was he making this noise, and searching for me? I staggered to my feet and moved out of my darkness into his light.

The officer wasted no time. He placed me under arrest for sleeping whilst on duty as a guard. I had undermined the security of a lot of people and a lot of military hardware by my failure to remain alert. I had committed one of the most serious of military offences and would have to report to the CO in the morning to face charges about my dereliction of duty. In the meantime he ordered me back to my tent.

TO PRISON OR NOT?

At nine am, the Service Police paraded me before Wing Commander James Flemming, Commanding Officer of the Geraldton Air Base. I felt terrible, having not slept since being charged by the duty officer. The Wing Commander looked serious. I told him my story, explaining my amazement at having gone to sleep on such an important duty. Then I tried to outline my feelings of tiredness after flying. I thought, "Now I'm in for it!"

The CO questioned me quietly. After some minutes a change came to the severe look in his eyes. Was he softening, or did I just imagine something? He said, "I have been considering your case even before you came in Scotland. I want you to know that I'm going to have pilots removed from the roster for guard duty. I will notify everyone through the Daily Routine Orders. The adjutant will have them on the notice board shortly. Read them; the orders will be important to you. Dismiss!" My throat felt dry, I swallowed hard, and could not believe that I was the person marching free from the CO's office.

Don and Norm Dunn awaited me in the lecture hall. Their faces showed their worry about me. I told them the CO's new order removing us from guard duty. They thumped my back and danced around me, obviously enjoying the fact that for them also there would be no more guard duty. The news raced from pilot to pilot.

Later in the day, I made my way to the notice board. "As from this date, trainee pilots are not required to fulfil the role of guards." The order was backdated to the day before my offence occurred. I felt overwhelmed by the CO's ingenuity; his wording meant I had not committed an offence. I read and reread that order to appreciate it to the fullest. Once again my flying career had remained untarnished. Disciplinary action would have meant I served time in Fremantle Prison. This was reinforced to me later.

PILOT IN NEED OF FUEL

Ray, one of the few pilot trainees with a vehicle, needed fuel. It irked him that fuel rations for private vehicles limited his mileage so much. He decided on a scheme. Drums of aviation fuel sat at strategic places around the airfields at Georgina and Kojarina from where we flew. He would get some of the fuel for his vehicle.

After four days flying, and just prior to our return to the main base at Geraldton, Ray acted. He had a four gallon drum which, at a convenient moment, he filled with aviation fuel. He put the drum in a kit bag, climbed into the Air Force transport with the rest of the pilots, and we set off on our forty mile return trip to Geraldton.

Half way to Geraldton, our transport stopped. Six service police surrounded our vehicle and demanded to search our kit bags. Ray's kit bag soon had the petrol drum extracted from it and displayed for all to see. They charged him with theft and arrested him. We were not able to see him again until he had been safely ensconced in Fremantle prison. He served a long gaol sentence for the theft and suffered dismissal from the Air Force.

Shocked at his fate, I realised that it also could have been mine for sleeping on guard duty. My friends and I visited him in prison. He was shattered by his punishment, but remained positive in saying he deserved it.

WEEKEND OFF DUTY

Don Watson, Normy Dunn and I were joined by two more pilot friends, Jim Mudie and Lindsay Fairclough. The five of us were drawn together with a rich sense of camaraderie as we attempted high marks in our ability to handle the Avro Anson in navigation, bombing, gunnery and radio.

On a weekend off duty, we travelled in to Geraldton town and booked a good bed at the Freemasons Hotel. The evening offered us excitement in meeting local girls and the opportunity to dance. Late into the night I retired to my comfortable double bed at the hotel.

Someone shook me, in the darkness of early morning. A voice whispered, "Tom, can I have your bed, Tom, can I have your bed?"

Shaking myself in disbelief, I saw a pilot friend with his girl. Please, could I hurry, he wanted my double bed. Grumbling under my breath, I stumbled out on to the verandah to climb into the cold sheets of a narrow single bed. Shivering and angry, I thought of my own evening. With so many men in town, I had only been able to enjoy one dance, and had not even met any of the local girls. Yet, here was this fellow enjoying my warm bed, and the caresses of his young lady. What a bad start to a beautiful weekend this was proving to be!

Next morning, throwing off my anguish of the previous evening, I walked with Mudie and Fairclough to the back beach. Our day off duty in glorious sunshine gave us a feeling of freedom and adventure. We had heard of the beach's bad safety record; swimmers had been swept out to sea by the undertow, but we were still keen to swim. Lindsay Fairclough was doubtful about his ability to handle the surf, so Jim and I launched in.

We enjoyed the tremendous waves carrying us to the beach, but failed to notice ourselves moving further and further from the shore. My first sign of trouble came with waves crashing over me and I could not make headway against them. Then seaweed came over me. I felt for the sea bottom with my feet, but could not find it. When I came up for air, I took in water. Jim and I were in real trouble.

Time passed, we swam, we took in more water. "Tom, I can't hold out any longer!" Jim spoke out of great distress. I encouraged him, "Hold on Jim, we'll soon be out of it. Keep your head up, keep swimming over that way!" Next minute I felt myself being tumbled over amongst the seaweed as another wave came crashing down.

"Surely we must get to a sand bottom soon," I thought as I came up out of deep water to get air, "If only we can get across this current!" I felt scared, and began to wonder what drowning would be like. As best I could, I pushed Jim ahead of me. He had obviously taken in a lot of water, for his eyes were glazed, his movements slow, his flailing arms reached out to grasp anything.

"Hey! Over here!" The words seemed only an echo through the sound of crashing surf, but it was a voice. Dimly, I saw a man in the distance. I headed Jim and myself towards the figure. Going deep under water once again in search of bottom, my feet touched sand deep down. Hope rose, had we come nearer to the edge of the rip current, or was it only my imagination? No, not imagination, the crashing waves were less threatening. I kept pushing Jim, and ducking down to find the bottom. It lay just over my depth.

The man was quite near. He locked his arms around Jim, staggered with him through the water, and I followed. Meeting us at the beach, Lindsay showed his own great distress, "I thought you were gone, I thought you were gone!" Touched by the cry, I sat exhausted, and watched as Jim was placed head down on the sand. Ghastly noises as he coughed up water went on and on, then at last Jim's breathing came clear.

Lindsay had seen our danger. At the first sign of trouble, he had run to get assistance. Colliding with a barbed wire fence, which tore his legs, he frantically urged a farmer to come in his truck. Lindsay's care had saved our lives. I watched as he arose, and washed his bleeding legs in the shallow water. A trail of blood flowed out into the waves.

The farmer helped Jim to the vehicle, and drove us to the air base. He took several days to recover from his ordeal, but the overall effect bonded the three of us in a tremendous thankfulness for one another.

DANGEROUS FLYING
Air gunnery was my next assignment that required hours of practise. With the near drowning experience behind me, I gave myself afresh to perfecting it.

Johnny, my fellow pilot, flew the plane while I sat in the gun turret firing my guns and hopefully getting a few shots on the target. We flew run after run at low level, until I had no more ammunition. Johnny stayed low and took the plane hedgehopping. I knew we were too low when I saw the amazed look in the eyes of a farmer opening a gate. We swept on into a valley, "Ping, ping, ping, ping, whine," went the propellers as branches hit the aircraft.

I clambered out of my turret and rushed to Johnny's side. Looking out the window, I saw a branch stuck into the aircraft about the position of the landing wheels. "That was a bloody silly thing to do Johnny. You've picked up a branch." He was tense and shaken. I was furious, but thankful that at least we still flew and did not lie in a crumpled heap at the foot of the valley. Hesitating, he asked, "When we land would you pull the branch off the plane?" I tried to suppress my boiling anger, for he was implicating me. But obviously he had to try and get out of reporting his illegal low flying. I appreciated we were both in a dilemma.

Finally I agreed, "OK, take the plane to the down hill boundary after we land. I'll see what I can do." He was visibly relieved.

We landed out of sight of the flight office, and I stepped into the slipstream behind whirling propellers. There were many branches and leaves caught and I worked to pull them free. Scratches over the underside of the wing showed how close we had come to destruction.

We did lots of other things together, but I never flew with him again. A special appointment would come for him just over a year later; German fighter aircraft would be waiting to give him his last resting place at Rheinburg in the Rhur. It could have been both of us resting together in the bottom of that valley south of Geraldton.

HYPOXIA

Between flights, our lecture programme continued. The medical lecturer fed us fascinating information about flying, emphasising our need to ensure adequate oxygen supplies to our bodies. A rarity of oxygen in the air at upper altitudes resulted in oxygen starvation, or hypoxia, a type of drunken state in which the brain loses its ability to warn the body of danger. A hypoxic pilot endangered himself and his aircraft.

Stimulated by the lecturer's emphasis on the medical side of flying, Don and I became fitness fanatics. Long distance runs helped our breathing to develop. At other spare moments we made our way to the gymnasium for weight lifting to expand our lung capacity. Contests checked our progress, and displayed the ripples we generated in our tensed muscles. Flying together, we checked each other to higher levels without oxygen. Oxygen containers were not supplied in our Ansons because we limited our flying to 10,000 feet, below which, oxygen is not normally needed. Circling higher and higher, we kept checking each other for hypoxia. Eventually the Anson stopped climbing, and I took camera shots to verify our height.

I heard of one pilot flying at height without oxygen. Others in the plane became suspicious when they found him about to land the aircraft on a cloud. Being hypoxic he imagined the cloud as his runway, a highly dangerous thought.

A CO'S WRATH

After four and a half months at Geraldton, our flying programme quickened. Two pilots, returning to base, chose to go low flying without authorisation. They flew too low, hit a sandhill and could no longer keep their Avro Anson in the air. Fortunately for them, a farmer's paddock loomed ahead. They set the plane down on its belly, badly damaging it in the process.

The farmer and his family came home, and gazed in disbelief at an Avro Anson sitting in their back yard. They also saw two disconsolate pilots wondering how they could get back to Geraldton. The farmer returned them to the air base, where events moved swiftly for them. They were arrested and a hastily formed court sat in judgment on them. An ominous tension hung over the whole pilot training programme.

Early next afternoon, the CO ordered the pilots to assemble in readiness to hear his verdict. He strode in. The look of fury on his face told its own story. He stood before us on the raised stage, then walked backwards and forwards, venting his almighty wrath. The two pilots had done low flying without permission; that they had survived their crash was not important, they had destroyed one of His Majesty's aircraft, an aircraft needed in Australia's defence, and needed for pilot training.

"Now for the sentence, hear this," the Wing Commander continued, "The Court has decreed that the two men shall serve twelve months hard labour in Fremantle Prison. Then when their sentence has expired and they recommence flying, they will not captain an aircraft again!"

He dismissed our thoroughly quieted group of pilots with a dire warning. If anyone else flew low illegally they would suffer an even worse punishment. It was difficult for me to comprehend the severity of the CO's wrath, and I felt dazed by it for some time.

WINGS

Our minds dwelt much on the painful fate of our two fellow pilots, but next day we had to prepare for an important event, the Wings Parade. Graduation time had come for us as fully fledged pilots. Because the parade would include official ceremony, we spent our spare moments between flights, practising our marching order.

Then came THE DAY; an excited group of trainee pilots marched to the tarmac area and paraded before the Air Officer Commanding Western Australia. Our footsteps echoed and re-echoed around the walls of surrounding aircraft hangars, giving the occasion a touch of theatre and the Air Officer seemed to love it. He gave an excellent speech, commending us as a group of pilots who had persevered since our induction into the Air Force. No one had ever said kind things like that to us as a group. I glowed within.

It was no secret that the fellows had battled through disappointment after disappointment. Our training had been deferred in order to build trenches, to fill sand bag defences, to paint and camouflage roofs. We had done much more than just flying training. Shortages in aircraft meant we tried to do so much flying with inadequate facilities amidst fear of impending invasion by Japanese forces. Now with our wings about to be presented, the Air Commodore recognised that we had won through something extremely tough. One by one our names were called and we strode forward to receive the coveted wings emblem. With the brevet pinned to our tunics, we returned to our place, conscious that a flying career lay before us at last, no longer trainees to be at everyone's bcck and call. Finally, when all was done, we marched to our huts for a time of gleeful banter. Sewing kits unrolled and our wings insignia became firmly affixed to our tunics.

ONE LAST TRAINING EXPERIENCE

One last training experience awaited us: unarmed combat and self defence. We travelled to the Kojarina airfield to complete a four day course. The instructor's hilarious sense of humour had us laughing about the way we would come face to face with an enemy and try to protect ourselves. But what happened in the process of learning, became no laughing matter.

On the third day, half our number prepared to make an attack on the remainder who represented the enemy. I jumped in from behind my enemy to grasp his rifle and to render him powerless. He turned before I had attacked him. So forceful and so violent was his movement in lifting his rifle, that the wooden stock smacked into the side of my face. I buckled into unconsciousness.

When I awoke, I was lying on the ground, blood poured from my face. I felt for an aching nose and had difficulty finding it, for it sat on an unfamiliar part of my face.

The pilots gathered and eased me into an Avro Anson. Two friends started the plane's motors and flew me back to Geraldton. Attendants lowered me into an RAAF hospital bed, and I felt awful. The nurses worked over me; their neat cleanliness contrasted my bloodied face and feelings of pain and unkemptness. We had been at Kojarina for four days, no shaves and no adequate wash in the primitive surroundings. The doctor came, and decided I had concussion and a broken nose. He sedated me and planned to operate the next day. It was the day I was due to be promoted. Instead, my painful nose and aching head took me into a world apart.

My friends came to visit amidst the anaesthetic aroma of hospital. I listened to their chatter and laughter at the end of the corridor. Jim Mudie came first, "Thomas you've been promoted," he said, "You're a sergeant." "What about you Muddles?" I asked in nasal tones as this giant of a man stood by my bed. "I'm a sergeant too, there's a few got commissions, I forget who." One by one the fellows came and stood by my bed and gradually I gained a picture of who was promoted.

Then the nose operation began. Using a local anaesthetic, the doctor seemed like someone pulling barbed wire through my head. Finally he assured me he had repositioned my nose. I lay back feeling depleted and sore and no longer wanting to talk to anyone.

In the evening, another influx of friends brought more dramatic news. Don Watson had an excited look on his face, "Thomas you old bastard you're going to England!" I looked up at him from my bed. He seemed to be saying, "I wish I were going too!" Through my aching head and blocked nose, I heard myself ask, "So where are you going Watto?" Don looked serious, "I'm posted to the General Reconnaissance School at Cressy in Victoria. I'm going to fly seaplanes and flying boats." I knew that I would miss Don. "So Watto, that's what you get for doing so well in your final flying tests and for having such a love for the sea." Don had spent much of his life on twelve foot long surf skis, riding the waves at Cottesloe. He thought in terms of ocean and wind and would do well in flying the oceans.

Don confirmed that he and I were promoted to sergeant pilot, as were most of our pilots. A few made it to commissioned rank as pilot officers, and the majority were listed for England. I lay on my bed and tried to concentrate on the chatter of my visiting friends. One message was so momentous to me that it kept repeating itself, over and over, "You are posted to England. You are posted to England." What would it all mean, leaving a wartime Australia to go to a wartime England?

FAREWELL GERALDTON

The doctor released me on the third day, as soon as he knew our train departed that night. Jim Mudie packed my gear and by eight o'clock he was escorting me along Geraldton railway platform, alive with people. Everyone seemed to be hugging and kissing. I felt unsteady so Jim took me to a seat in the railway carriage.

A noisy group entered; four RAAF nurses from the hospital. Their banter and good wishes made me love them, and wish I could stay to know them better. Then came my cousin Ron and his wife Doris. He had just completed training as a flying instructor and was now posted to Geraldton. Our friendship dated from the time we were toddlers on the farm, covering our faces with custard at Christmas. Soon the train rumbled out of the station and headed to Perth. We were due for a week's leave, prior to embarkation.

With what mixed feelings did we face that journey? Some of the fellows had married and were in trepidation about a long separation from their wives. Others had become engaged, and were in a dilemma;

whether to marry and risk leaving a widow if they did not return from the war, or to delay the marriage in the hope that they would return. I had just recovered from a broken friendship with a lass, now swept off her feet by the arrival of the Americans in Perth. So I had no love affairs to leave behind apart from my family.

As it turned out, two and a half wonderfully fulfilling weeks would come and go before our ship sailed.

5

CHALLENGE OF THE OCEANS

Perth at last! After being in Geraldton for five months, I felt excited. My mother expressed wonderment at the change she saw in me, but her joy at seeing me mingled with her fear for my future, and she overflowed into tears. Devastated by the tragic news of the war in Europe and the Pacific, she grieved about the cost in lives of the conflict to which I would be going. However, her show of emotion helped me to draw close to her, and gradually she overcame her weeping.

I settled into a bedroom once occupied by our boarders. At morning tea, I talked about my plans and checked with mother about any house repairs she needed. The Japanese had not yet attacked Perth, but I determined to build an air raid shelter in the back yard before I went. The Air Force arranged for me to have a pay deduction sent on to mother. However, despite all my concern, she put that allocation into savings, awaiting my own ultimate return from the war in Europe.

My sister Elsa and I met in town for lunch, and at weekends we had access to horses. Experienced riders, we revelled in the freedom of riding the horse trails in Bold Park.

One day she invited me along to church. The service seemed long and I understood little. However, Elsa had wanted me to go and I valued her asking me.

On arrival home, I saw a white damask table cloth spread over a table ready for lunch, and an aroma from a baked dinner made my taste buds water. I walked into the kitchen. "That smells terrific!" I remarked, and gave mother a hug. "Oh Tom", she said looking very pleased, then looked serious, "After lunch I'm going to be in the sitting room and I would like you to be with me. Will you?" I saw that the occasion meant a lot to her. "I'll be glad to mum," I replied. We were well into the afternoon by the time I followed her to the sitting room.

She delighted in this room. Many items of furniture had come from her Pustkuchen family in Germany and they gave the room character.

I settled into a comfortable chair conducive to our chatting together, and felt relaxed amongst the room's many memories.

AN ENVELOPE

"Tom, I've prepared this envelope for you. Would you quietly read what I have put in it for you?" I took the small envelope, "Read it now?" I queried. "Yes, if you want to." Her eyes searched my face as I drew out several folded pages, and read the words, "Goodbye my son ..." I stopped, realising that I wanted to be alone to take in the sentiments revealed there. "Thanks mother, I'll read this later. I wouldn't be able to talk about it right away," Refolding the pages, I placed them back in the envelope. She spoke quietly, "Take it and open it from time to time while you are overseas?" "Yes I will," I said slowly.

I paused, conscious of her looking at me, seeming to wait for me to respond more adequately, but the words did not come. I knew the importance of being an only son spending this historic moment with his mother, but the moments were taking me back to an event of my boyhood.

In 1934 mother had asked me, a lad of eleven, to accompany her into the city; "I want you to come with me and meet dad." My father had left home, and made a new life for himself. Mother planned this one last effort to get him back.

We met dad on a corner, under the Town Hall clock. I had stood with the two adults I loved, gazing up at them from time to time. They talked on for a long while, far too long and too painfully I had thought. I had longed for it all to stop. Then my mother had thrust me between her and my father saying, "Well, won't you come home for the boy's sake?".

There had come a long pause in which I felt that my mother expected something of me. She needed my support, she needed me to be a man by her side speaking up for her, but I crumbled inside. I had gazed at my father with tear filled eyes and knew I could not meet mother's expectations of me at that moment. Ultimately my father had settled the deadlock by saying, "No, I won't come home even for the boy's sake." In that heartbreaking moment, emotions had welled up in me, but I had no way to articulate them.

That had been 1934, now in 1942, I closed mother's envelope and sat quietly in that beautiful sitting room of our home in Nedlands. My mother was expecting something from me again in the emotion of this moment. She really needed a man's support, but I was trying hard to hold myself together. I felt strong emotions but could not express them. The moments stretched out and then passed. Mother spoke again, "Tom, you know I'm going to miss you, we all are." "Yes, I know that mother." She continued, "I would love it if we could pray together. Will you kneel with me so that we can pray?" I nodded and assisted her in the effort to kneel on the carpeted floor. For a long time we seemed to be kneeling together without speaking. Then her words came haltingly as a cry from her heart, for me, her only son. She came to the words, "Our Father, Who art in heaven ..... " God seemed unknowable to me, far away, a power perhaps, but I joined in the words. I hoped that my being there with mother, fulfilled the needs of the occasion. We came to the "Amen" and stillness gripped us both. Minutes passed, ten minutes perhaps, the ticking of the clock on the mantle piece seemed to grow louder. Then we moved. I assisted her to settle back into her chair. A burden had lifted from her, and her face showed quiet repose.

HUNGARIAN RHAPSODY

The Sunday afternoon passed gently and I felt more free to talk to her about my expectations of flying with the RAF. Elsa came, bringing us afternoon tea. Shadows outside the sitting room window lengthened. It had been some hours since we first entered the room. Finally mother went out to the kitchen to join Elsa in preparing the evening meal.

Left alone in the room, I realised that something important had been accomplished between us. I went to our phonograph, wound it and played a part of the "Hungarian Rhapsody" by Liszt. I loved the music. It carried me away to hills, rivers and people of a distant land.

That evening, Elsa, full of fun, ragged me about some of the hilarious things that I recounted about the Air Force, and we had many laughs, and I noticed mother relaxing and enjoying the fun.

Next day I visited my sister Melita, nursing at the Military Hospital, and soon to be moving north to New Guinea where Australians faced entrenched Japanese battalions. In the afternoon, my sister Helen came home looking lovely with her long curly hair She enjoyed her nursing training at the Fremantle Hospital, and had been writing letters to me consistently. Now she wanted my address in England so that she could correspond with me there.

I reported regularly to the RAAF Embarkation Depot at the historical Princess May Girls High School in Fremantle, and met up with my pilot friends. We were forty three pilots waiting to board the ship, and most of us had some rumour to share as to when our ship would sail.

New adventures came with Jim Mudie and I meeting in town as often as possible, enjoying our opportunities to meet several girls after work, and have them join us in parties and dances.

Four friends joined me at Perth railway station to farewell Don Watson off to Victoria, to the special navigation course that would prepare him for flying in the Pacific area. We walked away from the station and through Forrest Place where air raid shelters dominated the scene. The midday crowd streamed past, unconcerned about those ugly reminders of war.

I returned to Nedlands to continue work on the family air raid shelter. I looked into the sky and wondered how many would survive in Perth if the Japanese did come?

OUR WAITING SHIP

One morning I left home, as usual, to report to the RAAF at Fremantle. On arrival, I received a cabin number and a vehicle transported my friends and me to the wharf where a ship awaited our boarding. By eleven, we were ready to sail. Looking over the ship's side to the wharf, I discerned the blue grey of an army nurse. I looked again and recognised my sister Melita. How she had been allowed there at such a time I did not know. I rushed down the gangway and we had opportunity for an unexpected and brief farewell. I knew that at least my family would get news I had sailed, for phoning home had been forbidden. Wives and sweethearts of others would have to guess that their loved one had moved out.

Our ship, a small Indian freighter bound for Melbourne, slipped her moorings and was ushered out of the harbour. Sailing between Rottnest Island and the mainland, our ship rolled with the swell of the Indian Ocean. I stood by the rails for a last glimpse of familiar Norfolk Pines along Cottesloe beach. Unexpectedly the melodious bells of the lunch call rang out, breaking into my reverie about leaving Perth.

With Melbourne as our destination, we were allocated two watch duties daily as part of the ship's defensive system against submarine attack. For the next seven days, we adjusted and made friends amongst the Indian crew; seeing them daily in Moslem prayers and in ceremonial sheep killing for their meat requirements.

One ship passed us. Late at night, a hospital ship came so close that its red cross illumined us across the water. Next day we arrived in Melbourne and disembarked in preparation for boarding our ship to England.

MELBOURNE

The large metropolis of Melbourne was a world apart from anything I had ever known before. Quartered in the centrally located Melbourne Exhibition Building, we were issued day passes, but needed to be ready to sail at short notice. I made a surprise call on my sister Norah, a sergeant in Air Force communications, but living alone in a nice flat in the city. She met me at the door, "Oh Tom!" Recovering from her shock of seeing me, she welcomed me with surprising news. She had just been married to John Wilkins, a pilot officer who had graduated from Geraldton a little before me. I felt the joy of being a brother sharing with my eldest sister at such an important time in her life.

Wanting to leave Norah a wedding present, I visited her flat for the last time before boarding our ship for England. She was out. I wrapped twenty five English pound notes of those I had received from the RAAF for my use on the voyage, and left the package with a note for her in a convenient top drawer. Later, I had reason to think again about that money.

RIMUTAKA

Boarding ship was without fuss or farewell. The ship moved out and I gazed at an empty, receding, pier. Emptiness and loneliness formed like an ache within me, "How long would it be before I saw this land again?" The ship rolled gently. I moved away from my aloneness and walked towards the lounge with its chatter of many voices.

The Rimutaka was on a regular run to Great Britain via the Panama Canal. Passengers included people from Malaysia and Singapore, fleeing the Japanese invasion. As well as we forty three pilots from Perth, there were eighty others from New South Wales and Victoria.

We soon became a part of the watch, manning the guns of the ship's defences, and practising gunnery. I realised that the most likely evidence of enemy submarines being in the vicinity would be when a torpedo headed our way! Not a nice thought.

Heavy seas in the Tasman made our ship uncomfortable. Cold winds from the south tested our endurance while on watch. When still a day out from New Zealand, a school of dolphins came around. "They always put on a show when we come this way," our steward said as we chatted by the rail.

"Those are the heads of Wellington Harbour coming up," the steward further enlightened us as the ship turned towards high land dimly outlined in the distance. The Rimutaka continued to turn, and there appeared over the ship's stern, distant snow capped mountains of the South Island. It was the first snow I had ever seen. The snows glistened on the horizon and I gazed, captivated.

LAND OF THE LONG WHITE CLOUD

While the Rimutaka unloaded at Wellington, Lindsay, Jim, George and I enjoyed Kiwi hospitality. Captain Cook could not have experienced more excitement as he landed on this Pacific island, and met the inhabitants for the first time in the Land of the Long White Cloud.

I sent a cablegram home, having in mind the censor's reaction to my words, "Have arrived safely, natives are friendly, love Tom." I could not say where I was.

Wellington proved cold and windy, so my friends and I travelled by train to Auckland, where the Rimutaka would reload. Half of Wellington seemed to be travelling to the warmer north. Our being Aussies in uniform proved to be a point of great interest and we experienced the strong camaraderie that existed between Kiwis and Aussies.

Auckland at last! A welfare committee showed their love of West Australians. It stemmed from the fact that New Zealand soldiers en route to the fighting in North Africa, had been overwhelmed by the kindness of the people in Perth.

TAKAPUNA

An offer of hospitality came to Jim, Lindsay and me, from Mr and Mrs Norrie Bell, owners of a sports store in the city. Their home in

Takapuna overlooked an island in the bay. The Bells and twenty year old daughter Marilyn welcomed us as we arrived. Marilyn had two friends, Jan and Gretta who wanted to be in the fun of three Aussies being in the Bell home. Thus, they more or less lived there, and a strong fondness grew up between us all. Meal times filled with hilarity, were lengthened out by our stories of Australia.

One night, three ponies ran wildly through the Takapuna area, trampling on gardens and generally causing concern. I was able to corner one, mount it without saddle or bridle and bring it to heel. The other two ponies followed and soon we had them tethered. It was something I would have done without a second thought on the farm, but here the event gained acclaim, cementing good relationship with the Bell's neighbours.

MEETING THE CASUALTIES

In an Auckland Hotel, we met with wounded U.S. Marines, who had fought the Japanese in the first big battle to retake the Solomon Islands.

The Americans had much to learn about the Japanese in warfare and they sustained very heavy casualties. Day by day I meet with Al, an American officer ripped by Japanese bullets in the upper arm and shoulder. One heartening thing that Al told me; a Japanese invasion fleet en route to Australia had been destroyed. My hopes soared. Possibly, invasion of Australia had been averted.

The Rimutaka, arrived in Auckland, and Mrs Bell made plans to farewell us. She and Norrie organised a dinner at the Takapuna Hotel overlooking the stretch of water we would pass through on our way to the open sea. The girls were there, and their parents. The evening became filled with chatter, feasting and dancing.

We ambled home along a pathway surrounded by shrubs and trees; leaves quite motionless in the still night air enhanced our sense of closeness as we walked. Lindsay huddled together ahead with one of the girls, and slowly disappeared from sight. Mrs Bell revealed that she and the girls planned to be on the shore to wave their favourite tablecloth to us as we sailed through. She just knew our ship would sail the next day, even though ship departures were secret.

At ten the next morning, the Rimutaka glided by Takapuna. Gazing from the deck of the ship across the narrow waterway, we saw them all having a part in waving the huge tablecloth. Tears streamed from Lindsay's eyes as his emotions overflowed. We could only guess the reaction on shore, with Lindsay dropping out of the girl's life, now so near her — yet already so far away.

SAILING THE PACIFIC

The Rimutaka sailed eastward towards Panama, keeping well south of normal shipping lanes where enemy submarines patrolled. In her holds she carried a cargo of refrigerated fruit and meat for the people of England.

Ship life excited me. Our lives were unregimented apart from submarine watch and manning the guns. The warm days were ideal for the fellows to join in the fitness routines I had begun with Don Watson at Geraldton. We followed this with sun bathing, deck quoits tournaments, table tennis contests and runs around the deck. The seas continued calm and the days tropically warm. If enemy submarines lurked nearby their periscopes would have betrayed them. I thought of Magellan in 1520 naming this ocean Pacific because of its calmness, but at least he did not have to contend with the enemy submarines.

PANAMA

Ah! Panama at last. It was welcome change after the continual view of ocean horizons. Yes, shore leave was granted! My anticipation mounted at the thought of putting my feet on the soil of America, the New World discovered by Colombus and Balbao so long ago.

Dark skinned Panamanian officials came on board to set up money changing facilities. The curious thing for me was that I planned to go ashore without any money. While in New Zealand, I had put my remaining English pounds into the keeping of my friend George's money belt. George had come to me late one night in Auckland saying, "Tom you won't guess what happened tonight." "What's happened George?" I asked comfortingly, little guessing the portent of his reply. "My money belt was stolen!"

George explained awkwardly, "I went into a public toilet and hung the money belt on a peg. When I came out of the toilet, I forgot until I'd walked away some distance. I rushed back but the belt had gone." "Have you been to the police?" I gasped, as the realisation of my own loss dawned on me. "Yes," replied George, "I've given them details but they said there's little hope of finding it." Thus I arrived in Panama, and thought it quite hilarious to be travelling the world without money.

We made our way off the Rimutaka and on to solid Panamanian soil. American servicemen abounded as the defence of Panama was of prime importance to the U.S. "Limeys?" a group of U.S. servicemen enquired, thinking we were British. "No, Australians," we called back proudly. "Oh, that's different; Orstralians eh. What's it like over there?" "It's bonzer, terrific, good," we replied trying to find a word they understood. "Yeah, we heard it was good. Orstralia eh!"

The tropical heat of Balbao oppressed us. The night brought no relief. We came into the lighted township and walked along a street lined with liquor bars, like open shops in a bazaar. Fruit stalls were there between the bars offering all kinds of tempting tropicals. We eyed these hungrily, but with the danger of dysentery uppermost in our minds, had to resist the juicy temptations.

The night wore on, and we saw nothing mattered more than to head to our ship feeling glad to get out of the tinsel and glamour and sexual overtones of the night life we had been witnessing. Two of our Australians did not make it back to the ship that night. We feared for their well being as V.D. abounded and the use of knife to rob and kill was ever present, but American Service Police eventually found them.

THE CANAL

By early morning, the Rimutaka had moved into the locks of the canal. The lock gates shut, water rushed in at furious pace, lifting the ship high enough for towing into the next lock. Finally the Rimutaka sailed inland along the canal under her own power. Hills rose on either side. Jungle seemed close enough to touch. The long day wore on, and by nightfall we had come to Gatun Lakes, wide stretches of water filled by streams from surrounding mountains. There in the middle of the Gatun we stopped and anchored. What joy it was to bath in fresh water from the lakes. I luxuriated and felt like a millionaire.

When morning came, locks lowered the Rimutaka from mountain lakes to sea level on the east coast and we tied up to the wharf at Colon.

A day later, we sailed into one of the most dangerous seas for submarine attack. The speed of our throbbing engines increased, and the ship zig-zagged constantly. Our watch doubled. I pictured German submarines hiding behind each swell as it rolled in to lift the Rimutaka.

A tug towing a disabled ship passed by heading back to Colon. "What stories could that ship tell?" I wondered, searching for its tell tale signs of damage. Then I turned my eyes again towards the rolling Carribean swell seeking for that submarine periscope that would signal imminent attack. The skies were overcast and the sea swell increased uncomfortably. Then we came in sight of wreckage from sunken ships.

I breathed more freely when our route took us through the Yucatan Channel between the United States and Cuba. We headed northwards out into the Atlantic Ocean and along the coast of the USA.

With the northern winter upon us, the weather turned cold and watch duty became an ordeal. The balmy tropical warmth of the Pacific Ocean became a dim memory and we used every means possible to stop the cold getting into us.

Like a message carried on the wind, word went around from one to another, "We're going into New York, we're going into New York!" The exciting news became table talk as we planned for our arrival in that great city. Speculation continued all through the next day, then, late in the afternoon, we sailed into New York harbour itself.

A weak glow of sunshine shone through a clouded sky. The shore line white and glistening with snow, reflected the sun's last rays. Calm waters of the Hudson River lapped on the side of the Rimutaka as she made her way along past the Statue of Liberty.

I eyed the statue, smaller than I had expected, sitting alone on an island and isolated from huge skyscrapers, which rose towards the clouds across the waterway. Liberty's raised torch brought me in touch with the anguish of homeless people from across the world. How many millions had passed this way, searching for a place to begin their lives again? I wondered whether they had asked themselves the question I was asking, "What is the future offering us in this world torn apart by war?"

The Rimutaka slowed; its anchor chains rattled then splashed as they hit the water. We friends walked the decks in the cold night air and looked at beckoning lights on New York skyscrapers.

NEW YORK

Morning came. Tugs moved the Rimutaka to one of the great piers that sat beneath Manhattan. Near our berth, an overhead railway carried New Yorkers to work, while beneath the railway, taxis and private cars tried to race each other. Fascinating scents and sounds came to us.

The ship's gangway went down and U.S. officials came aboard. We needed visas to enable us to go ashore. The other fellows changed their money into American currency, then unleashing our excitement, we skipped down the gangway to set foot on American soil.

Our immediate problem proved to be how to cross a road. The traffic moved so fast and it nearly got us killed. A bus came. We were expected to put dimes, cents and nickels into the driver's cash receiver, but what did the terms mean? The impatient driver ordered us off the bus. We decided that New York had no time for fellows like us from "Down Under", but a kindly bus patron saw our need, and we were able to move along the bus to a hanging strap.

SNOW IN THE CITY

Central New York lay deep in snow. Snow ploughs cleared the streets, heaping the snow into mountains eight or nine feet high. Here and there a gap allowed us to see the other side of the street. Jim Mudie had developed a nasty stye in his left eye, so our first need was to get him an eye patch. He came out of a drug store, and New Yorkers turned to stare at this six foot one inch Australian with flyers wings and a black eye patch over one eye— a war casualty?

The Stage Door Canteen, run by entertainers including Hollywood film actors and actresses, educated us about American meals and entertainment, then gave us invitations to functions in the City. The high quality of hospitality made us gasp. A popular love song was worded, "I left my heart at the Stage Door Canteen." We did not quite do that, but we loved being there.

ABOVE THE CLOUDS

The Pennsylvanians were musicians over whom New Yorkers raved. We were invited to a function in the Waldorf Astoria Hotel, and there they were, the Pennsylvanians preparing to delight us with their music. Ted Smith, their accomplished pianist, was said to be going through a life changing experience of dedicating his talents to the service of God. I wondered what that meant?

Making the most of our last day ashore, Jim Mudie and I explored the Empire State Building. Reaching to more than 1000 feet above the roadway, clouds obscured its upper levels. However, the overcast skies lifted, and we gazed over a snow covered New York. Enraptured by the view, we wondered if there really was a world beyond where people struggled for survival through global war?

Returning to the Rimutaka, we read the notice, "All shore leave cancelled!" Our ship had been rearmed and replenished, for the Atlantic crossing. "Were we really ready for enemy "U" Boats?" I wondered.

INTO THE UNKNOWN

Next morning, the Rimutaka slipped from her berth, moved into the main flow of the Hudson River, and passed six new American built landing ships flying British flags. It was a reminder to us that out there, a world really was at war.

Snow on the shoreline made the scene look so peaceful. Large houses faced the water. Adults and children tobogganed down steep slopes; old and young shared tremendous fun together.

The Rimutaka cleared New York harbour. The open sea and a north wind set her rolling. Then it snowed. The after deck became a snow field, and snow fights erupted. This was an exciting world. I had never even touched snow until I arrived in New York, and now here I was having snow fights on a ship rolling in the Atlantic.

Then I saw them! While fights were being won and lost, ships had been gathering around us. Big tankers and smaller freighters were there, with naval ships moving in and out. We had become part of an armada of shipping. It dawned on me that this was a convoy. We were going to England as part of a large assembly of ships sailing in convoy. What a tremendous relief! Other vessels would be near if we were attacked.

ATLANTIC CONVOY

The forty eight ship convoy was an inspiring sight. There were passenger ships, oil tankers and freighters; all being fussed over by eight naval destroyers amongst a conglomeration of merchant ships rolling in the Atlantic swell. Forming into pattern took time, but gradually I discerned ships coming into line.

The Rimutaka pulled in behind a much taller Canadian passenger ship, from whose mast there flew the flag of the Commodore of the Convoy.

The navigation officer on the Rimutaka told us about the Commodore. "He's a retired admiral and an excellent leader. You watch him pull the ships into order; he won't stand for any nonsense."

The Commodore spoke to the convoy by signal flags rising with some urgency to the masthead of his ship. Powerful signal lamps flashed. When black smoke belched from the smokestacks of some of the older freighters, signallers flashed the Commodore's irate warning to desist. Smoke would give away our position to any packs of submarines waiting over the horizon. The freighters could only lessen the smoke by lessening their speed, so our convoy speed lessened. The smoke diminished.

We four friends continued in a cabin together, and enjoyed the helpfulness of our cabin steward, a man who had spent his life at sea. When he had time, he sat and fed our hungry minds with details of the war at sea and attacks by submarines. We were responsible for anti submarine watch at one of the starboard gun positions, from ten at night until six in the morning. The four of us took turn about, two hours at a time.

SHIPS IN THE DARKNESS

Watching for submarines from my gun position in the early morning hours was an awesome experience. As far as my eye could see in the dim light there were ships mounting up to the top of waves then falling as the wave receded. There they were with monotonous repetitive movement, rising, falling, rising, falling, each ship in its own time— all carrying vital cargoes for a Britain at war.

I was due to report any unusual sightings to the chief officer by telephone. I tried to figure out what words I would use to alert him if a submarine attacked. Observing him with his officers on the bridge, I watched as they walked back and forth, their big coat collars drawn up and their peaked caps wedged down over their heads.

Standing beside my Oerliken gun, I felt numbed. The cold bit into me, and the icy wind froze my face. Before leaving home, my family had combined to knit me a balaclava, gloves and scarf. I gladly used them now, but even such good knitting was not defence against the incessant cold.

THE DELIGHT OF BEING WARM

"Anything going on?" It was George Oliver sleepily swinging himself up into the high gun position to take over the watch. "Hullo Olee," I called, "There's not much happening, the wind is getting stronger and the ships are rolling more. I hope you are well rugged against this cold weather, it's going right through me." George rubbed together his gloved hands, "Ooh, it's bloody cold alright!" I began to descend the steps from the gun position, "I'm glad it's yours now Olee. See you later."

I made my way amidships to the galley where the cook had invited us to help ourselves to mugs of coffee, generous slices of bread, and pieces of New Zealand cheese. One by one, those who had been on watch duty, came in, filled their coffee mugs, and then made thick sandwiches, which they held in hands thawing out from the cold.

With the cook already preparing the meals of the day, the warmth of his galley and the flow of coffee gave me an inner glow of contentment. Numb, gloved fingers felt restored. Lingering in the warmth, I chatted to the other pilots, then in weariness, went off for a sleep.

Next afternoon about two, Jim, Lindsay and I pushed our way along wet windy decks, heading towards the table tennis room. We stopped. Our ears picked up frightening sounds. Heavy explosions came from the starboard side of our convoy. We stiffened and grasped hold of railings to steady ourselves against the wind. With each explosion, a reaction occurred on the steel sides of the Rimutaka. It seemed that some giant hammer began to clang resoundingly on the side of the ship.

"So, the German U Boats have found us!" I said to the fellows grimly. A spasm of fear gripped me. I looked at the cold frothy ocean waves that seemed so near as the Rimutaka rolled. I could almost reach out and touch the green icy water rushing by. A torpedo could come rushing in at any time, and its explosion could send us all sprawling into those freezing waters. No one would survive at those low temperatures.

The explosions continued all afternoon. Apparently the naval ships counter attacked a pack of submarines, preventing German torpedoes from finding their mark amongst our convoy. The night wore on, the battle moved towards the south, away from us, and the hammer blows from distant explosions grew less and less. Nevertheless the night passed in uncomfortable apprehension of a submarine getting a torpedo through to us.

Morning came, and I went out on deck. We were in a raging storm. I struggled to save myself from being swept away by strong winds, and gazed in awe as Atlantic waves towered above the masts of the Commodore's ship ahead. Our ship went sliding down one side of a wave, and then the front of the ship rose ever so slowly and took the Rimutaka upward, ever upward, to the white top bubbling high above us. Aghast, I watched this display of wild Atlantic ocean set to destroy us, ocean against ship, ship against ocean.

STORM DAMAGE

The storm raged, mountains of water came at us, waves crashed over the ship. The Rimutaka kicked this way and that. Lunch time stewards had extreme difficulty in walking, let alone trying to balance their dishes for our midday meal. We clung to the sides of tables to steady ourselves and our plates of food. The awkward meal dragged on, and eventually Jim Mudie and I went down to our cabin. The cabin steward, working there amongst other cabins, came over for a yarn.

Suddenly the ship heeled over very steeply and we had to get support, trying to steady ourselves. There came a long pause as though the Rimutaka could not right herself, then she heeled back the other way. It seemed that she just kept rolling. The rugged face of our cabin steward whitened as he gripped the door frame to steady himself. He did not fall, but we were flung helplessly across the cabin. By the time we picked ourselves up, the severe rolling had reversed. We held on again as the ship continued her roll. Then she seemed to steady and the rolls lessened.

I looked at the steward. His ashen face showed concern. "That was near!" he exclaimed. "What was near?" we asked together, looking at the mess of all our goods piled on one side of our cabin. "I've never known our ship to roll like that," the steward said seriously. After a moment, he added, "I'm going to find out what's going on." With that he moved determinedly along the unsteady passageway and disappeared.

Jim and I looked at our gear in disarray across the cabin floor, then we followed our anxious steward, and mounted the stairs towards a favourite lounge room. What had once been a lounge room of warmth and charm now presented a scene of chaos. Items of furniture lay amongst a confusion of people. The piano was on its back surrounded by a pile of broken chairs and tables in the far corner. People huddled in shocked groups, enquiring of each other and trying to help casualties to stand.

Gradually the story came out. The heavy roll of the ship had sent the piano careering on its back across the wooden parquetry floor of the lounge. Like a battering ram, it smashed chairs and tables; passengers had been caught up in the melee and most were painfully bruised. One fellow sustained a broken arm. Reports of damage came in from all over the ship. The worst hit was the galley where my friend the cook had been scalded. The engine room had water and oil sloshing at some depth and the engineers declared themselves unable to maintain the ship at its present speed.

The Rimutaka's distress signal asked the Commodore for permission to heave to. The reply came to not stop but to lessen speed, and make way northward towards Greenland where the seas were not so rough. The Rimutaka slowed, changed course north east, and drew away from the ships of the convoy. We soon missed having the naval ships speeding around us. Their presence had given us a sense of security from our foes beneath the waves. Dusk had gathered by the time the massive convoy of which we had been a part, disappeared beyond the horizon.

Surprisingly, we were not left completely alone. Six other ships had received permission to sail with the Rimutaka. Jim, George, Lindsay and I stood by the windswept handrail and surveyed our tiny group of seven unprotected vessels riding out the Atlantic storm.

Crew and passengers on the Rimutaka worked together in a cleanup operation, repairing damage. Meals were broth and bread.

OUT OF THE STORM

At the end of my two till four watch next morning, George Oliver came. I had some exciting news for him. "George, listen to those thumps on the side of the ship." George listened and asked curiously, "What do you think it is?" I allowed him time to figure out what was going on. "It's an ice field Olee," I informed him triumphantly. In the light of early morning, George had not been able to discern that the Rimutaka sailed through a frozen sea. Great chunks of ice bumped into the ship as she made her way. "Bugger me, an ice field eh!" exclaimed George rubbing his gloved hands together in excitement, and eager now to take over my watch.

With increasing light of approaching day, the scene that met our gaze was of an endless sea of white ice. There were no waves. The other ships looked majestic as they rode steadily through the ice field with us. We experienced no roll to the ship, just steady motion and the "thump ... thump ... thump ... ," of the ice chunks hitting the steel hull. All day we sailed eastward and at every opportunity I went on deck to take in the spectacle of the ships sailing through Arctic ice. The scene excited me and I had to keep assuring myself that we really had survived attack by submarines, damage through an Atlantic storm, and were now surrounded by such an amazing scene of motionless white.

On the following day, when the ice gave way to open sea, Jim, George and I were at the rail of the ship. A call went out from Lindsay Fairclough, "Come and see this!" We moved to the other side of the ship in time to see a Sunderland flying boat with the markings of the Royal Air Force. It circled our group of ships; its signal light blinked out messages. The big aircraft circled around several more times as if to say "Welcome to Britain" and then made off in a south easterly direction. By evening a sea mist had come down.

Next day, rumour had it that we were moving towards Belfast, Northern Ireland. We longed to catch a view of the Irish coast but visibility remained limited. Towards evening, our searching eyes caught a glimpse of land. What feelings of relief came as our steward identified the coast of Ireland, and we discovered we had crossed the Atlantic.

A shout went up, "Periscope to Port!" I thought, "Oh no, not now, not when we are so near to England!" The periscope was clearly visible in the calmer waters of the Irish Sea. On and on it came. My heart seemed to jump out of my chest in apprehension, as I awaited a call to action stations. No call came. I watched, goggle eyed, as out of the depths arose the conning tower of a submarine. It continued to rise and the hull came into view. "Ahh! It's British!" a voice called.

The object of danger now turned into something of great relief. Seeing the peaked caps of two officers appear out of the dripping conning tower, we speculated about the sub and its crew. Was it a crew returning from patrol in German waters up in the North Sea? We discussed for a while some of the hazards that must accompany submarine warfare.

Breathing a sigh of relief for our deliverance, I turned around in time to see the lengthening shoreline of Ireland emerging out of the distant haze with just a faint indication of a distant city. "That must be Belfast," I decided, wondering if I would have opportunity to tread Irish soil. When our anchors went down we were in the outer harbour, and there would be no shore leave.

SOUTHWARD TO BRISTOL

Early next morning, one by one, we gazed from our porthole to a distant land. Our cabin steward brought an early morning cup of tea, and informed us we journeyed through the Irish Sea with views of the Isle of Man and of the Welsh Coast backed by mountains rising up to over 8,000 feet. I was thrilled to at last see something of the British Isles. It signified the word courage to me as I thought of Britain's survival against terrible punishment since bombing by the German Air Force began. Our eyes strained to pick out details of this land soon to be our home. It was now our eighth day at sea since leaving New York.

Later in the day our informative cabin steward said, "We are now in the Bristol Channel lads." "What does that mean?" Lindsay Fairclough asked. "It means," said the steward, "To the north of us is Wales and to the south of us is Somerset. We're heading into the port of Avonmouth to unload the ship." "And what do we do there?" asked Jim Mudie in the midst of reading a book. "You catch the train to London from there. Avonmouth is the port of Bristol. It's all been badly knocked about with the bombing, but the trains were running alright when I was here last."

The further we sailed through the calm waters the more we realised that Avonmouth was a busy port. Behind the town, grassy slopes rose steeply towards higher land and the distant city of Bristol. At last the Rimutaka tied up to the wharf. Excited chatter bubbled out the words, "England at last."

The cabin steward came to say farewell. After being together with him for two and a half months a fondness had grown between us. He came with a whole bag of apples rescued from the Rimutaka's New Zealand cargo. "You'll need them lads," he urged.

I hoisted a small kit bag containing daily needs to my shoulder and joined my friends in marching down the gangway to actually put my feet on the soil of England. Standing on the wharf, we looked high up to the decks of the Rimutaka. The cabin steward stood by the rail to shout, "Take care lads!" We waved to him acknowledging our appreciation of his care during the long sea journey from Australia.

With George, Lindsay and Jim by my side, I trod the gritty road that led upwards from the wharf and away from the Rimutaka. Beginning to absorb the sights, sounds and the smells of Avonmouth, I felt overwhelmed by a sense of wonderment, "Muddles, we really are in England!" Jim's eyes sparkled as he fixed me in his gaze, "Scotty, I wonder what the sheilas are like?"It was New Year 1943.

6

BOURNEMOUTH BELLES
AND BERLIN BETTY

Seated in the fast moving train of the Great Western Railway to London, I gazed on small fields and hedges sweeping by. How strange it all felt, after our travel on board the Rimutaka, covering thousands of miles of ocean.

Hour after hour, the train raced eastward through cold wintertime farmland and towns. I visualised the bare, uncomfortable carriages in which I often travelled in Australia; so different from the warmth and speed I now experienced. Nearing London, the centre of Britain's scattered empire, wonderment gripped me. The very name London, invoked drama and history in my mind. I was excited. What would I be seeing?

Outer London came and I seemed to be level with row upon row of chimney pots. Roofs of buildings were a sea of chimney pots. My mind staggered as I tried to assess the amount of coal needed to provide warmth for such a multitude of London homes in this English winter. Then our train drew in to the largest covered railway terminal I had ever seen. We had arrived at Victoria Station.

Carriage doors opened, passengers streamed out, and amongst them our one hundred or more Australian flyers. Standing on the platform, and waiting to greet us, was a tall, distinguished Air Vice Marshall. He made an impressive speech, thanking us for coming to help the RAF. He represented an England determined to overcome the enemy that had brought war to the doorstep of nearly every home in Europe. He then outlined some of the RAF's plans for us as we settled into England. I felt uplifted by this caring officer spending his valuable time in welcoming our travel worn group.

The Salvation Army hostel in Westminster provided overnight facilities for us. The rooms were austere and the mattresses hard, but sleep came to me that night without any problem at all.

I awoke to the smell of burning coal; my introduction to a distinctive aroma that I would encounter all over wartime England. Breakfast came with wartime sausages, a mixture of meat combined with a little bread. Toast and marmalade followed, washed down with a cup of tea; a "cuppa char" the RAF steward called it.

BOURNEMOUTH

Our final destination lay southward at Bournemouth. The train drew in to the platform, and entranced us with its small locomotive, glossy black, and with brass fittings all gleaming. Bournemouth, a town of 156,000 people, encompassed the valley of the Bourne river meeting the sea on the south coast. Ideally situated as a coastal resort, Bournemouth's wide sandy beaches offered a warmer climate than other places in this land of great climatic contrasts.

Our first English home had steep narrow stairways and many tiny rooms, and went by the thoroughly English name of White Hermitage Hotel. I entered our room, and sat on the bed to survey my surroundings. We had finally arrived, and I felt exhilarated. I walked around the room and then stared out the window. My gaze went across the roof tops to lawns and gardens in the distance. I had discovered the Bournemouth Gardens, a place that I decided I must visit.

We forty three pilots from Western Australia fitted snugly into the White Hermitage, like a close knit family. I assembled with some of my friends in front of the hotel and asked Johnny, one of the pilots, to take our photo. At least it would show my folk at home that we had arrived. Then the air raid sirens sounded.

The wailing noise went on mournful and long; an alert that prepared us to move quickly to an air raid shelter if Bournemouth became the target of the attackers. A long fifteen minutes ensued and then the "all clear" sounded, short blasts and mournful wail. We sighed in relief and proceeded with our camera shot.

Word came later that the air raid had been on Southhampton further along the coast. We could see the Isle of Wight on which were located much of Southampton's defences. Only the English channel separated us from France, and I pictured German squadrons there, planning their attacks against England. Bournemouth, situated on high cliffs above the sea showed little sign of bomb damage, but every sign of being well defended. As far as my eye could see along the wide sandy beachfront, there were barbed wire entanglements, gun emplacements and warnings of explosive minefields.

THE GARDENS

My first visit to the Bournemouth Gardens came sooner than I expected. As Jim, George, Lindsay and I went for our first meal, we found we had to walk through the gardens to get to the RAF cafeteria in Bournemouth's bowling alley. We strode into the huge building as its timber floor echoed to the eager tread of hungry young men, flyers from Canada, New Zealand and Australia.

After our meal, my friends and I donned great coats, gloves and scarves, and walked in the Bournemouth Gardens. Its broad sweep of grassed areas amongst gaunt leafless trees, led us to steps up embankments where well kept gardens were still garbed in the drabness of winter.

The routine of going to the Bowling Alley for our meals became our time of meeting with fellows from across the world. We lined up with them to receive our meal, and then sat with them at one of the hundred tables. As an extra bonus, the WAAFs who staffed the cafeteria, were our first contact with young English women. They were full of fun, and able to enjoy their role. Friendships developed with the girls quickly and easily and when the day's work finished, a few free hours together with them in the evenings, meant closeness. Romance blossomed.

TRAINING SCHOOLS

Four steps lay before us in changing from Australian conditions to flying with the RAF.

Step one:-Bournemouth would provide lectures to give us insight on how the RAF co-operated with the British Army and Navy in fighting the war.

Step two:-A flying school would help acclimatise us to difficult flying and weather conditions in England.

Step three:-A further flying unit would enable us to form a flying crew as preparation to flying big bombers.

Step four:- A conversion unit would familiarise us with flying the new big bombers before we moved into a squadron.

My first training school in Bournemouth was run by the Royal Navy. It brought an echo of my boyhood dream of becoming a naval officer. I learnt naval tactics, ship recognition, code methods in communications and air force/navy co-operation. Week days were filled with study and on weekends, I was free to relax.

A month passed, then Army training began. A group of us travelled to the north of England to Whitley Bay, near Newcastle on Tyne. The Army had us crawling through the night amidst mud and thorn bushes, gunfire and exploding hand grenades. After experiencing the hazardous insecurity of a soldier in action, I gladly returned to Bournemouth, and nursed a sprained ankle that had me limping for weeks.

LADY IN DISTRESS

On our first morning back in Bournemouth, Jim Mudie and I perched ourselves comfortably on the railing pipe fence around the gardens. Enjoying rays of sun peeping out from an overcast sky, we watched the people of Britain walk by. A lady saw us, stopped, then confronted us with a question, "Do you really think that we British are too proud?"

To say that I felt surprise, was an understatement. I hoped she wanted Jim Mudie to answer, but she looked straight at me. Well dressed, attractive, under forty I thought, but under strain, even though she seemed composed when she spoke.

"Yes," I said, "I do find the British are different to talk to, ..." I searched for the word, "You are more, ah, reserved than we Australians and Canadians. Why do you ask?" She hesitated for a moment, then told us how a Canadian had attempted to "do a line" with her and she had brushed him off. Her quiet rejection of his overtures caused him to blurt out, "You British are too damn proud." The retort had really stung the young woman and she brooded over it as she walked. By the time she came to where Jim and I relaxed near the footpath, she just blurted out her question.

The ensuing conversation became an education to me of how this British woman was trying to cope with the invasion of her land by colonials from Australia, Canada, and NZ. She was like so many others with sons and husbands in British services overseas, and vulnerable to the overtures of overfriendly young men. I could see how change had begun for this woman and thousands of others without their own men folk around. She went on her way with a warm, "thank you for listening to me." I thought about the conversation for days afterwards.

COFFEE, OF SORTS

Feeling peckish after our surprising encounter, I said to Jim, "I'm hungry Muddles?" "Let's have some coffee Scotty." Jim was only too ready for our morning regular. Inviting others to join us, we ambled to a small restaurant in the main street. "Yes," said the young waitress, "I can get you coffee and also welsh rarebit." So mid morning found us sipping coffee, of sorts, and nibbling welsh rarebit: grilled cheese on toast. This type of food echoed British rationing, severe because huge supplies were being lost at sea as a result of German submarine attacks.

We chatted and enjoyed the warmth of being Forty Club friends together around the table. Jim, Lindsay, George and myself with Norm Dunn our guitarist, Alan Forrester a farmer, and Normy Carr, Max Hubbard, George Ives, Kev McKnight and Arthur Berryman, all from Perth.

Sipping my coffee and gazing out the open doorway, I noticed a slight touch of colour had come to the drabness of the Bournemouth Gardens, and a distinctive scent wafted pleasantly into my nostrils; the scent of an early English spring. Such delight gave no opportunity for us to consider that this may be the only English spring many of us would enjoy. As events unfolded, before a year was out, the graves in Europe's soil would claim eight of the eleven who sat there together.

BERLIN BETTY

Towns along England's south coast continued to be targets of the German Air Force. All too often, the air raid sirens wailed their "alert" and then came "all clear" signals. But listeners to Germany's English broadcast over Radio Berlin, twigged that Bournemouth must soon be on the receiving end of an attack by the German Air Force. The female announcer on Berlin's English programme had a most attractive and cultured English voice, and she became popularly dubbed "Berlin Betty".

"You Australians there in Bournemouth," she said over several evenings, "We are coming over to visit you soon!" This announcement caused consternation to the Aussies, for how did she know we were at Bournemouth? Berlin Betty's broadcast turned to news about German gains against the British and Americans in the Mediterranean area and against the Russian Army on the Eastern Front. A favourite female vocalist rendered "Lily Marlene". The German forces would also be tuning to the song.

German aircraft did visit Bournemouth. At ten o'clock one morning, the sirens sounded and in they came, low and ferocious. One of their targets, the Central Hotel, had become a favourite drinking place for the Aussies. The hotel collapsed like a pack of cards. Bombs continued to explode elsewhere and a tall spire of the Anglican Church in the centre of the city crashed into the square. When the explosions and gunfire died away, Berlin Betty's promise had been fulfilled.

The planes raced away leaving behind wreckage in Bournemouth and a question, "How did the German Air Force know that the Aussie's congregated in the Central Hotel?" One mistake they had made; in attacking at ten o'clock in the morning, they chose a time when Australians were not likely to be in the pub. Had the attack been at ten in the evening, then, it would have been a huge tragedy. As it was, the hotel fell into rubble and people died, but no Australians.

WANTAGE

Jim Mudie and I received our posting to the next stage of our training in England. Situated near Wantage, an ancient Roman and Saxon town along the London to Bristol Railway, was the RAF base called Grove. Jim and I packed, said farewell to others of our Perth "Forty Club" friends, then headed off.

Spring time flowers surrounded the Grove air base as we settled in. Amidst their scent and the buzz of hungry bees, we began to fly. Lew Moncrieff, an instructor, put on an excellent aerobatics display to show us what our plane, the twin engined Airspeed Oxford could do. Although it was a passenger plane, Lew made the Airspeed Oxford look like an aerobatics special.

After six hours, with the instructor, I flew mostly solo, doing my own navigation and radio work. Flying went on day and night, as I adjusted to the difficult and changeable flying conditions of England and

Europe. The countryside seemed to be continually covered either with clouds or with smog, and navigation was very difficult if I had no view of the ground.

FOR YOU NEW ARRIVALS THIS IS A MAP OF THE UNITED KINGDOM. HOWEVER IF YOU GET LOST AND CANNOT SEE IT JUST LOOK FOR THE NEAREST CLOUD AND LET DOWN, THE U.K. IS BOUND TO BE BENEATH IT.

One day I flew north into the industrial heart of England. Smog hid the terrain from my searching eyes. On returning south, in limited visibility, I had not been able to identify landmarks for some time, and I was convinced I had lost my way. Espying a landing strip, I landed, and came to a halt near the flight office. A squadron leader explained that it was an airfield called Kalscott. Pinpointing Kalscott on my map, I discovered to my chagrin, that my navigation had been accurate, and had I continued flying, I would have arrived at my destination.

Phoning the Grove Air Base, I received the necessary permission to become airborne again. My flight commander chuckled about my poor navigation, and then awarded me the week's goof medal, "The Order of P.O. Prune". That quite fictitious Pilot Officer Prune, nitwit of all flyers, had a big wooden medal struck in his honour. I wore the ungainly thing, and became the butt of many jokes about my misfortune. However my friends had their turn at making mistakes in the air. As a result, they too suffered when the flight commander awarded them, one by one, "the Order of P.O. Prune". How well I knew the indignity.

CITATION. FOR "WHILST ON A TRAINING FLIGHT, LANDING TO ASK YOUR POSITION," THE AWARD OF THE P.O. PRUNE MEDAL.

HEADACHE FOR JIM

One stormy evening, when flying had finished, Jim and I made our way to the local pub in Wantage. It was one of those old world buildings erected centuries before and it offered us a place in its ancient atmosphere to relax. On this night Jim did not want to play our usual game of darts or snooker. "What's up?" I asked searching his face. "Scotty, I'm worried," said Jim seriously, "I'm dinkum, I really am worried. Janette told me she's going to have a baby. What will I do?"

Jim's piercing blue eyes bored into mine. Janette was Jim's find, in Wantage. She was a lovely strong looking country lass, desperately fond of Jim. She and Jim had found a haystack where they could enjoy some of their evenings together; the result being that now she thought she was pregnant.

Jim, delightfully open about it all, explained his worries. Now that she was pregnant, his heart ached for her and for himself. The unexpected thought of parenthood overwhelmed him. "However will I cope?" he asked, "Do you think that Janette and I will need to get married? I'd have to do that wouldn't I, WOULDN'T I Scotty?"

Ever the hopeful one, I encouraged Jim, "Give Janette more time. It may not be just what you think." I had in mind that some girls pretended they were pregnant, when in reality they were only trying to hold on to a very exciting love affair. Jim went through a week of agony.

He came home late one night when I was in bed. It did not matter to him that I was tired after a day of flying, and slept heavily. He shook me, "Scotty, Scotty!" I sat up and stared into a pair of piercing blue eyes. "Scotty, it's OK with Janette. It's OK. Can you believe that? Oh I've been so worried." In his excitement he could not wait till morning. He sat on my bed with a beaming smile and expressed his absolute relief.

WHERE ARE YOU BILLY SWAN?

With the worry lifted from Jim, his face shone like the sun and he gave himself to his flying. On a cloudy day in May, he and I with two other pilots set out to fly to Exeter in south west of England. There were Jim, Hoodge, Billy Swan and myself. We went in separate aircraft on a navigation exercise that included returning from Exeter to land on Salisbury Aerodrome and then fly a devious route back to Grove.

Heading south west to Exeter, I thrilled to flying under a clouded sky and over changing patterns of fields, roads, forests and rivers. Exeter, with its tall cathedral, appeared in the distance. I turned eastward and completed the journey as far as Salisbury. Heading the plane to a parking spot near the control tower, I saw Jim and Hoodge waiting. The fourth pilot, Billy Swan had not arrived. Time passed and we could wait no longer. We flew off and landed back at Grove, expecting to see Billy there, but he had not yet arrived.

Red haired Hoodge came to me asking, "What do you think might have happened to him Thomas?" "Well," I replied, "I saw Billy's plane heading to Exeter, then the clouds came lower and I lost sight of him. Are you worried that he may have pranged Hoodge?" I had spoken the words of my own foreboding. Hoodge answered, "I'm bloody worried Thomas, let's go and ask the instructors about him."

We entered the instructors' office and saw Lew Moncrieff looking very concerned. He told us that the RAF in London had information that an aircraft had crashed at Taunton, a town we had passed on our way to Exeter. Later identification at the crash site confirmed that Billy Swan, our Rimutaka friend from Melbourne, had crashed into the Blackdown Hills south of Taunton and been killed.

Billy's body was given a place in the cemetery of St. Mary at Taunton, a lone Australian amongst English dead. His death brought home to us the hazards of flying in Europe's rain, cloud and smog. We mourned his loss amidst increasing intensity in our flying programme.

LANDING IN FOG

The RAF established a special type of flying training school near Cirencester in Gloucester. Selected pilots were seconded to go there, and I was one of them. For a week I flew with a hood covering my head, and navigating purely from readings on the plane's instruments. An instructor rode with me as my eyes, to check that I did not bump into anything. He had to be courageous!

One day I flew in towards a fog bound airfield and landed the Airspeed Oxford on the runway, without seeing anything but my instruments. We stopped. I lifted my hood and looked out; how eerie it felt, being on some unknown airfield, and surrounded by intense fog.

To actually land on a runway guided only by a few flying instruments and signals from a radio beam, was a magnificent experience. The reality of this dawned on me as a wonderful culmination to the flying course, and I felt ecstatic at having completed such a landing. I then faced the reality of having to repeat it.

I turned the plane, pulled the hood over me, then made my take off run, once again directed by instruments alone. Becoming airborne and climbing through dense fog layers, I heard my instructor speak of seeing a building emerge ghostlike from the shrouding fog then disappear below us.

What an exciting flight this was proving to be. I lowered the landing wheels and prepared for a second landing. Trusting the instruments and radio signals to tell me that I was approaching the runway, the minutes ticked by. The aircraft flew lower and still lower. A loud beeping signal made me jump; we had passed the boundary of the aerodrome. I waited for the landing wheels to skim the runway. With the wheels rumbling along the bitumen, I kept responding to instruments so that the aircraft ran central along the runway, then flew off again. I thought, "Bloody terrific!" I had come in touch with something of the ultimate in flying.

DARK SHAPE

Returning to Grove, thrilled with the added confidence I had gained at the Instrument Flying Training School, I had the job of duty pilot waiting for me. It involved my being aerodrome controller during night flying exercises. One night, the task became particularly heavy. Planes were taking off and landing on the one runway and I sweated, working hard to cope with them all. Radio communications had shut down, so I used a powerful Aldis signal lamp by which I controlled the landing sequence of aircraft.

Pilots flashed identification letters on the white light attached to the plane's belly, indicating their desire to land. If it was clear for them to circuit and then land, I signalled a green but if the runway was already booked, I flashed a red. Aircraft coming in for landing needed to receive my green signal a second time. If the runway had not cleared, I gave plenty of time for the pilot to receive my red signal, and take the plane into a climb away from the runway.

One plane had run out of battery power, and so could not signal me. The pilot showed no lights on his aircraft, and was unable to lower his landing wheels for landing. I had a terrible shock to see his dark shape coming in lower than the aircraft to which I had given the OK to land. In desperation I flashed red signals to the unlit aircraft and the one above. Both aircraft climbed away for another landing approach. For a moment they were both white shapes reflecting the glare of the runway lights. I gasped. They flew dangerously close together and neither would see the other. Then they flew on into the darkness.

Searching the sky for that mystery plane, I now gave a red "NO" to each aircraft requesting permission to land. But with so many aircraft in the sky, I missed one. I saw wing lights of a plane coming in on a landing approach. The pilot had obviously not seen my red signal. I decided to let him land while other aircraft circled the base.

Just then, below the lighted aircraft I saw HIM, the unlit plane I had been seeking. The pilot above would not be able to see HIM below and HE could not see the one above. "Heck, this is bloody dangerous," I shouted to myself. I raised the signal lamp and flashed RED RED RED RED. The signal lamp should only be seen by the one pilot above, but both pilots may have seen it. I desperately wanted only one pilot to act on the red and take his plane away and wanted that unlit aircraft to land. I waited.

The higher plane with lights visible, seemed to hesitate, then very slowly lifted its nose and began climbing away. My eyes scanned the darkness for sight of the unlit plane. Ah, there he was, just a shape sinking lower and lower, coming over the entrance to the runway. Was he too low? What happened next, caught me completely unprepared.

The aircraft, nose first and without landing wheels in place, ground itself into the runway surface. Sparks peeled out behind it. The runway lights glinted on it as it flashed by. On and on it went, seeming loath to stop. It finally came to rest at the far end of the airfield, an ugly glow exploding out of it, and lighting up the whole airfield.

I stared at the flaming plane, fearful for the safety of the pilot. But the fire unexpectedly flickered, lessened, then died. Fire tenders were there pouring on foam. I danced my feet, feeling tremendous relief, "Bloody good show."

A profusion of aircraft were now signalling for permission to land, and I signalled a rash of red refusals. Parts of the runway still had to be cleared of debris. Most pilots would have seen the fire from crashed aircraft but would they understand the present delay? I cursed the fact that our radio link was out of action, giving no way of informing pilots how long the delay might be. Twenty minutes passed. A red flare shot into the sky indicating a plane in a new emergency.

Duty officer Lew Moncrieff came racing back from the crash site in his jeep. Soft light from his vehicle outlined his small stature and the twitch of his moustache on a worried face. "It's OK Tommy, the runway is clear, the crashed plane is well away from the main runway, let the pilot land." I flashed several green signals to the distressed plane, and urging the pilot on, "Come on fella bring it in!" Lew sped away to meet it. I watched the lights of the distressed plane as it turned in to approach the runway. My steady green signal flashed out. On it came, wing lights speeding in from the darkness, over the airfield boundary it flew and in towards the runway. Landing wheels screeched on the paving. What a beautiful sound it was after the ripping, tearing, rattling sounds of the previous emergency!

A relieved Lew Moncrieff returned from the plane, and explained that the pilot had exhausted his fuel, but now having landed, his emergency no longer existed. Lew pushed his peaked cap to the back of his head, "Phew, what a night Tommy." "It's not over yet either," I said as I signalled other aircraft to come in and land.

Planes flew in from their darkness and I pictured the relieved faces of pilots. Soon the airfield was alive with noise and lights of aircraft on the move. Wing lights showed planes heading towards their parking bays while others continued to descend on to the runway.

When all were down I gazed upwards, and drew deeply on the night air in wonderful feelings of relief. Sensing a kinship with the stars in a night sky of unbelievable brilliance, I thanked them. They had become my friendly fellow travellers shining out their strength from a boundless canopy of space.

TO MANCHESTER AND BACK

Next morning I awoke early. The CO had asked me to fly him to Manchester on business at an airfield belonging to the Avro Aircraft Factory. He also wanted to assess my flying as we went along. I thought, "This is an interesting way to do a flying test!" The three hour round trip to Manchester also gave me opportunity to learn from the CO as he shared some of the wisdom he had gained from his flying experiences.

My flying went well until smog around industrial Manchester, made it extremely difficult to check my navigation. I was a most relieved pilot when I looked down and saw Avro's aerodrome and we could land. I parked the plane on the tarmac beside the factory and within a few moments one of the new type of big bombers, a Lancaster, taxied in and parked a short distance from us. I gazed wide eyed at the black painted aircraft beside us, and hardly noticed the CO disembarking.

For twenty minutes, I intently gazed at the big plane, amazed at its size, and wondering if I would ever have opportunity to fly it. Then the CO reappeared. He had two RAF Officers with him and he introduced me, explaining that he had offered them a ride with us back to Wantage.

We became airborne and smog again hindered visibility. I complained to the CO about the factories creating this blanket of fumes in the sky. He maintained that he was willing to put up with the smog in the light of what the factories were doing to help win the war. The workers had kept production going despite heavy air raids night after night, when German bombers had attempted to cripple British industry.

The visibility continued poorly, but we flew on southward and gradually it improved. A tree lined river Thames came into view and then a little further to the south, near the Bristol to London railway, I recognised the town of Wantage and not far away, the runway at Grove air base. It thrilled me that my navigation worked out, especially after getting myself lost earlier.

PILOT IN THE BLACKOUT

Having landed and disembarked the senior RAF men, I parked the plane and hurried to my billet to change. Night approached and Jim Mudie and I were taking our two young ladies to a dance on the base.

As our evening ended, Jim took his lass home and I escorted my young lady, a farmer's daughter, to her house out beyond Wantage. It had been a beautiful evening and she and I rode cycles to her front gate where we spent time saying our fond goodnight.

I only noticed how lonely and very dark it was when I started my journey back to the air base for I had no cycle light. I kept my bicycle on the road by looking at the sky between the trees that partly met overhead. No lights showed anywhere in the night, so I rode, guiding myself by looking above, not along the road.

A West Country voice spoke from out of the darkness, saying, "Hoi therrre," and then came glaring light from a torch. It was no doubt someone having fun. A friendly voice on that lonely country road would add to my appreciation of a lovely evening. I slowed, half dismounted, and voiced my Australian response, "How are you cobber?" "Stop, in the name of the law!" he shouted. Imagine my surprise when the cobber turned into a constable, and he thought I had been calling him "copper", not "cobber".

I could not believe the unsmiling seriousness of his face as he looked at me through the glow of his now subdued torch. His pocket book came out. Seeming to enjoy having caught me, he read out my charge: "Riding a bicycle without a light." Was my evening of dance and closeness about to be wrecked by this silly confrontation? I remonstrated, "But we're in blackout, no lights anywhere and I'm an Australian pilot just getting used to English conditions. How am I to know that I'm supposed to have a light in a blackout on a lonely country road?" The constable, equal to my remonstrations, replied, "The law's the law sir. Will you give me your name and address. You'll hear more about this." Further objection seemed pointless. Eventually he pocketed his book, then rode off into the night saying, "You must obey the law, sirrr."

Several months later I heard from the police about my grave offence. The CO at my airbase called me to his office and he became witness to my receiving from the "Law" my summons to be tried by the Court at Reading for my cycle offence. The court fined me two shillings and sixpence which I duly paid, still angry at the English police for their unfriendly attitude towards an Aussie cobber. After all, was I not there in England helping them win the war?

AIRBORNE INVASION

Next day, the Army invaded Grove air base. They arrived in massive Horsa gliders towed by big bombers. The gliders cast loose, and floated into the airfield, descending at a very fast rate. Surprised by this invasion, I watched their heavy landing on the grass. Khaki clad figures flowed out of the now stationary gliders and lined up on the airfield. Each glider seemed to carry about thirty armed soldiers. When the bombers flew back over the runway to drop their tow lines, snake like coils plummeted to the ground, landing with a loud thud. The tow planes then landed and their crews began a process of hitching up the big gliders again, ready for take off.

Standing next to me and watching proceedings was my pilot friend George, who had shared watch with me on the Rimutaka. "Tom, how would you like to tow one of those gliders?" he asked. "It's not for me George, that's dangerous work towing those things." I assured him.

The soldiers re-entered their gliders and the take off became more fascinating than their landing. Each glider trailed behind its tow plane gathering speed, then left the ground to climb well above the runway until its tow rope strained at the tail of the tow plane, which continued to lumber along the runway until it finally struggled into the air. We watched them head eastwards, and wished them well in the dangerous work that lay ahead. This spectacular exercise helped to prepare them for landing their gliders in Allied attacks on German Forces in Sicily.

As for George, he went on to pilot planes towing gliders into Europe!

FAREWELL WANTAGE

Instructor Lew Moncrieff came to me one morning, "Tommy, here's your log book. You must have pleased the boss when you took him to Manchester; he's given you a good assessment in your flying. By the way, you are being posted away to Abingdon to fly Whitleys. What do you think of that?" Lew had just given me good news and bad news. I paused, pained at the thought of flying Whitleys, "Bugger the Whitley. I'd hoped it would have been the faster Wellington." Lew held up his hands, "It's nothing to do with me, I can't change it Tommy." A strange feeling of acceptance came over me, "Ah well, thanks anyway for all your help in teaching me how to navigate around England. It sure has been very different from Australia." "Let's celebrate on it tonight eh!" said Lew.

We planned our evening at the Wantage Arms Hotel. A night of farewells lay before me for I was the only pilot from Grove posted to Abingdon and I would be parting from some wonderful friends.

I had grown fond of the country lass with whom I went dancing, and I set aside the last evening to say farewell to her. Our friendship had blossomed, and I found it hard to say goodbye. I had explained to her as much as I could about my steps into wartime flying so that she would understand our friendship could not last. I was the first Australian she had met and our friendship had opened a new world to her. I knew that other Aussies would follow me at Grove and she would be interested in meeting some of them. But she remained unconvinced, for she didn't want OTHER Aussies!

WHIN COTTAGE

Next morning I packed my belongings, collected my leave pass from the adjutant, and headed off to "drop in" on my uncle and aunt at Beaconsfield, near London. My aunt met me at the door. I was struck by her grace and beauty, and I introduced myself. She overcame her shock at seeing me arrive uninvited and taught me lesson number one in English custom. "In England you do not just drop in." However, she invited me in, and I sensed her increasing warmth towards me as a relative from Australia. She invited me to stay for a week.

I settled into a room that belonged to son Peter, then she took me for a short walk and a talk as we went around Beaconsfield. Returning to Whin Cottage, we saw Uncle Will arrive from the opposite direction. A captain in the Royal Navy, he was heavy with naval gold braid. I went to him and shook his hand. My aunt was indignant, and gave me lesson number two in English custom. "Why, even his sons salute him when they meet!" The two sons were officers, son John, commander in the Royal Navy, and son Peter, a lieutenant in the Royal Marines and shortly to take part in the invasion of Sicily and Italy.

Somehow I seemed to forget to salute my gold braided uncle in my excitement of meeting him. However, we became used to each other and sat together under a large window sharing the newspaper and conversing about the war. At five, we walked to the Beaconsfield Arms to enjoy a pint of English "bitters", and in the evening, daughter Betty came home. A Red Cross nurse in a nearby hospital, she quickly changed the home's quietness into animated conversation reporting the day's happenings at the hospital.

HOUSEHOLD EMERGENCY

At the end of a week, we had our last evening together. Betty and I were chatting and washing dishes when aunt screamed, "He's dying!"

The "he" turned out to be the cocker spaniel lying motionless. Betty and I rushed to him, and I thrust my hand down his throat to try to discover if something blocked the air passage. Sure enough, a bone had caught and I released it, a loathsome action because the dog had a fetid breath. We worked on the dog to regenerate its breathing, and I admired the way Betty endured it. At last the spaniel arose unsteadily to its feet, and we all joined in aunt's cry of relief at seeing the family pet restored to life.

That night I received an open invitation to return and spend more of my leave times with them at Whin Cottage. However, for now, I was going to Abingdon to fly Whitley bombers and to meet the men who would train with me as a crew to operate the plane.

Soon after my arrival at Abingdon a letter came addressed to me. It was from my aunt. She commenced, " To my hero ..." I pictured her in her long graceful dress, sitting on the large lounge and grateful for my encounter with the foul smelling throat of the cocker. Her letter made me feel rewarded indeed.

7

ST ELMOS FIRE

Within sight of the spires of Oxford, that great university town of England, the RAF vehicle turned off the main road, and drove in the entrance to the Abingdon air base. It stopped at the administration building, and I alighted to gaze at groups of aircrew, new arrivals like myself. Searching the faces of men talking together, I recognised none, nor did one dark blue Australian uniform appear amongst the blue grey of the RAF. I felt very alone.

Needing to report my arrival, I mounted steps that led towards the main office. A large RAF transport drew to a halt nearby, and I watched as aircrew fellows stepped out — more new arrivals. A figure in the front seat of the vehicle caught my eye; an Aussie in familiar dark blue uniform busily conversed with the WAAF driver. After a moment or two, the figure turned, and I could not believe that I beheld the broad smile of Alan Forrester, whom I had last seen at Bournemouth. Alan recognised me, bounded out of the front seat and we met in a hug. Then we danced, oblivious to the amusement of our RAF audience, who must have thought they witnessed some sort of corroboree peculiar to the Aussies.

That first week at Abingdon saw Alan Forrester and me gradually become acquainted with other aircrew.

Our study programme began immediately, involving us in understanding the intricacies of the aircraft we would be flying. The Whitley had been an RAF front line bomber, smaller than the Halifaxes and Lancasters now being produced, but still needing a crew of five to operate it. Unravelling the mysteries of this aircraft demanded hours of reading and lectures on its engines, airframe, navigation, bombing systems, its hydraulics and electrical workings, defensive guns and methods of emergency escape for the crew. Alan and I competed for top results in our knowledge of it all.

The first day of the second week was set aside for crewing up. This democratic system gave aircrew themselves the right to form a team and the pilot as crew captain to have final word of approval on who came into the crew. I entered the large room where a mass of RAF grey, mixed with a few Australian dark blue uniforms. I wondered where I could start to choose out men with whom I would fly.

NAVIGATOR

I put my hand on Alan's shoulder, and asked, "How are we supposed to select a crew out of this bunch of guys?" We talked about the task, but in the midst of our talking I became aware of a pair of eyes boring into me.

Looking towards those eyes, I saw a sergeant navigator returning my gaze, and waiting to converse. He stopped in front of us both, and introduced himself to me, "I'm Derek Hopper and I'm wondering if you need a navigator?" I was startled by the sight of his cap that sat on his head most awkwardly. "Hullo Derek" I responded introducing myself. I saw beneath the cap, a reserved, sensitive Englishman with generous mouth and steady eyes.

We chatted for a while, then Derek explained about himself, "I did my flying training as a navigator in South Africa. Actually on arrival there, I was carried off the ship with a raging fever, and the South Africans could not do enough for me. After I recovered, they gave me excellent training and I came away with absolute praise for their kindness and friendship. Back in Britain, I had to acclimatise into flying conditions here, so the RAF sent me to Scotland."

Derek paused for a moment, then he became quite animated, "I've just come down from Scotland. My, it's cold there. I've been permanently frozen, uughh, it's cold. You know the navigator's table in the Avro Anson?" "I sure do'" I replied. "Well, our aircraft leaked when we were flying and do you know, that water on my table actually froze?" I looked at Derek in disappointment about the cold conditions, for I had looked forward to visiting Scotland.

We returned to the subject of navigation and I explained, in all my previous flying I had been my own navigator, but now I would welcome having Derek in the aircraft fulfilling that role, "I'm glad you spoke to me, and I'll be glad we can team up together. Can we shake on it?" I put out my hand. Australian pilot and British navigator met as man to man in that moment.

BOMB AIMER
Derek moved away, and a short time later he returned saying, "Tommy, I'd like you to meet Edgar Riley. He and I have been talking together and he tells me he'd be interested in becoming a part of our crew." I looked up and saw a skinny British sergeant with blue sparkling eyes and straight rebellious blonde hair poking out from beneath his RAF cap. His winged brevet showed him to be an observer/ bomb aimer.

"Hi Ed," I said as the three of us met in a small circle. I thought Ed looked half starved. His thin body made me wonder if the RAF had been limiting him to half rations.

Having registered my first impressions, I asked him about his training and experience as a bomb aimer. Ed responded at some length but I had difficulty following his accent. However, as my ear tuned to what he said, I became impressed. An ex draughtsman, Ed's experience in drawing and assessing plans had been a great asset in map reading and navigation; a decided attribute in filling his role as a second navigator and bomb aimer in our crew. I recognised an integrity about Ed, and my opinion of RAF men took a considerable leap forward as I talked with him.

Later I shared a little of my own background and I noticed a beguiling twinkle in Ed's eyes. His face became a picture of amazement as he listened to my Aussie speech. He admitted that it had given him a shock when Derek wanted him to meet an Aussie. I was a Colonial to him, and he explained, "I wasn't sure whether I was about to meet a kangaroo or a stockman with horses and stockwhips." All he had known of Australia he had read in books about our cattle stations and bushranger Ned Kelly.

"Cheeky bugger," I thought as I warmed to him, "He's going to keep his eye on me to see how this Colonial ticks." To Ed I said, "I'm glad to meet you Ed, welcome to the team."

EACH TO HIS OWN DIALECT
By the end of the day, I had discovered not only the navigator and

the bomb aimer, but also two other men who would fly with us: Aussie radio operator Wes Weekes from Queensland and air gunner Bill Smith from the Midlands of England.

The five of us stood in a circle discussing our first flight together. Ed was sure he had seen my name listed for flying next day and said, "Whey aye Aa'm reet!" I eventually discovered that he said, "Of course I'm right!" His words highlighted my need to come to terms with differences in dialect. Both Derek and Ed spoke the dialect of geordies. Air gunner Bill Smith had an accent from the Midlands and Wes Weekes and I brought with us the language of the Aussies. We all spoke a type of English but each very different in expression. "How am I going to cope with all these different languages?" I wondered. Next day, Ed Riley, sensing my dilemma, handed me a hilarious sketch expressing our language problem.

DO YOU THINK HE SPEAKS ENOUGH ENGLISH TO BE ABLE TO ORDER THE BEER

Entering the names of each man into my pocket book, I felt thrilled at the prospect of flying together as a team. No longer would I be alone in taking an aircraft long distances through darkness and storm; these men would be there to share in overcoming the difficulties.

Derek Hopper waited for me to complete my list, then we walked together. I soon felt at home with him and called him Hoppy! Tall, handsome and serious with strong sensitive lines to his broad features, he would have loved it if the RAF had at least tried him as a pilot before training him as a navigator. However, his ready chuckle covered any feelings of hurt. His major concern seemed to be the welfare of his parents and sister, and I noticed how absorbed he became as he talked about them.

RADIO OPERATOR

Next morning, I sat with our radio operator Wes Weekes. He was strong, like the trunk of a tree, broad shouldered, not tall, and aptly nicknamed "Shorty". "I've worked amongst trees all my life Tommy," he said. Hauling logs down hazardous mountain slopes to timber mills on lower ground had proved to Shorty that risks had to be taken in earning a living. He spoke a Queensland drawl with words quaintly clipped, but articulated with the assurance of one who made decisions for himself in a rugged life.

IN THE EVENT OF THE RADIO GOING U/S WE CANNOT SEE YOU HAVING MUCH SUCCESS IN TRYING TO SIGNAL BASE WITH THAT DIDGERIDOO.

Shorty had completed his radio training in Australia. "But I'm not a good radio operator!" he assured me as he undervalued himself. According to Wes, nothing he ever did seemed any good. But to me, he appeared ingenious, practical and one who would remain calm in the midst of emergencies. I had no doubts about his ability to handle radio.

THE WHITLEY

Learning to fly the Whitley bomber, Alan Forrester and I had the guidance of an experienced Whitley bomber pilot for two hours and forty five minutes. Then we had the plane to ourselves, and much more to learn about flying it. Far bigger than the zippy Airspeed Oxford, the plane was slow and cumbersome, like handling a large sluggish beast. But it had motors more powerful than any plane I had flown before and I loved having access to that power.

Hoppy, Ed, Wes and Bill Smith kept their thoughts to themselves about flying with an Aussie pilot who had only two hours and forty five minutes experience of flying the Whitley. But I had no worries, the main purpose was to enable us to harmonise as a crew, and I felt more than ready to do that.

LESS OF THE GET ABOARD YOU B----- POMS. DO YOU FLAMING COLONIALS KNOW HOW TO MAKE THIS THING WORK.

STANTON HARCOURT

Forty miles of winding roadway lay between Abingdon and Stanton Harcourt. I warmed to the sight of this quaint old world village with its centuries old thatched roof houses and their white plastered walls. The main road twisted narrowly between the houses and out beyond the village to the duck pond and the village pump, while further along the road lay sleeping quarters, stark, corrugated iron Nissen Huts. Stanton Harcourt had an airfield from where we now flew to build up our flying hours.

Near to the huts, a high fence guarded an orchard that had tempting mouth watering apples. At the earliest opportunity we risked all in wriggling under that fence, and proving the apples tasted as good as they looked. I had not tasted such apples since the steward on the Rimutaka had filled my pockets as we disembarked at Avonmouth.

On our third flight from Stanton Harcourt, we flew low level out over the Irish Sea. Low level flying delighted me; so much more interesting than flying three and a half miles above the earth. On this occasion, a heavy layer of fog covered the ocean and we skimmed along just above it. For some minutes I observed unusual specks above the layer of fog and Ed, from his forward position in the nose of the Whitley, noticed them also. We closed in. The specks grew into long sticks, then the truth dawned. Those were not sticks, but ship's masts above a fog layer.

That we were about to fly right over a large concentration of ships sailing down the Irish Sea towards Bristol, I had no doubt. One thing I had learnt from the Royal Navy at Bournemouth, "Never fly over a convoy!" Sailors had lost too many ships to German Bombers to wait and ask questions of intruding aircraft. They shot the planes down even if they were British. "Hell," I called, "We're flying into a British Convoy. Let's get out of here!" With that, I pulled our plane around and headed away from the forest of masts and away from danger that moved below the blanket of fog. "Ye gods!" exclaimed Ed, "that was close!"

During our next flight around England we flew in cloud and mist with only here and there, a view of the ground. Near Peterborough, a huge defensive balloon came streaking out of the mist and swept past our starboard wing. That balloon spelt trouble. Sausage shaped balloons, floated high over the industrial and manufacturing centres of Britain. They were tethered to the ground by long cables, and were there to prevent low flying German bombers from getting too close to the cities. I was flying deeply into a trap that a concentration of balloons now presented.

Another balloon appeared out of the mist, and I cursed having turned down my alarm that would have bleeped at our nearness to this danger. Adrenalin surged through me. My heart pounded. I forced the Whitley into so steep a climb that the airspeed fell off rapidly and the plane stopped climbing and began falling. What an awkward stall turn manoeuvre; it headed us to earth with gathering speed, but turned us away from the balloons.

Eventually my instruments indicated we had distanced ourselves from Peterborough, and I saw the balloons no more. The experience had given me a fright, and it took me quite a while to settle down. However I gained a renewed respect for the hazards of flying in Britain, and determined to be more watchful.

Our homeward journey included flying over the bombing range, where Ed dropped our practise bombs. His accuracy would be assessed by RAF personnel on the ground. As we made our turn off the range, what should appear but Alan Forrester's Whitley going in to bomb. I waggled our wings in farewell and headed for home.

The Forrester crew and the Scotland crew had been in healthy contest from the start. It was a matter of great elation when we were one up on one another. We flew in separate aircraft but our rivalry stirred us to strive for accuracy in direction and timing as we flew on long navigation trips, night and day. Sometimes we flew in formation and then competed for accuracy in practise bombing after an arduous flight. Our competitiveness had now reached an exciting stage. When my fellows shared about our flying amongst the balloons, Alan and his boys delighted in making us the butt of many quips.

BLACK OIL

An emergency of a different kind occurred on a return flight from Scotland. On nearing Stanton Harcourt, the starboard motor of the Whitley had crankcase failure and it spewed oil in a long black stream behind us. The main problem was I could not "feather" the propeller to stop it rotating. The temperature gauge rose alarmingly, showing the danger of fire. That rotating propeller also acted as a powerful air brake, forcing us to lose height. I called the crew, "This is an emergency fellows, I must get this plane on to the runway quickly!"

For some reason, my pilot's radio to the control tower at Stanton Harcourt went dead. "Wireless operator" I called over our intercom, "contact the control tower and let them know that Foxtrot Tango is in trouble and we're doing an emergency landing." Shorty came back to me in quick time, "The flying area is cleared skipper and they wish us luck."

The quickest way to land the plane was downwind; dangerous

because the plane's speed and the wind speed become added together. I made a diving turn onto the runway, adding further speed to our landing, nearly a fatal error. I flew over the entrance to the runway alright, but at too great a speed.

The wind behind pushed us along, and a cushion of air kept the big wings flying above the runway. The Whitley just would not sit its wheels on the ground. We floated on and on, and I could see the far end of the runway coming. "Oh God!" I cried, and in desperation pulled the control column back into my stomach and tried to break that air cushion beneath us.

My violent action broke the air cushion alright. The wings lost their lift, and the Whitley sank on to the runway. It overran the end of the bitumen, and we raced towards a strong fence, beyond which lay ditches and trees, and calamity! "Those brakes have overheated, they can't stop us now!" I exclaimed to myself. But with a slow release of brake on one wheel, I managed to slew the Whitley into a left hand turn. Round we went, the starboard wing tip coming within feet of the fence line.

In the midst of this forced left turn, I fully expected the juddering crash of a collapsing undercarriage. The sharply turning aircraft exerted colossal weight on its wheel assembly. But the crash did not come.

The Whitley's impetus had to be exhausted eventually and the plane came to rest in a cloud of dust and smoke from the dud engine. I looked out the pilot's window. We were surrounded by three fire tenders; the crews gazing at us. I felt so relieved that we had not given them a job of extinguishing burning pieces of Whitley scattered across the airfield.

Quietness reigned and then I noticed the pounding of my heart. I took a deep breath then looked back along the fuselage to Shorty still sitting by his radio set. "Good show Shorty, " I called. Shorty gave one of his great big grins, "I didn't do much." he said. "But what you did, I needed," I replied.

We emerged from the Whitley carrying our gear. The crew members of one fire tender walked around the plane and one spoke in broad Lancashire, "It's good to see you down safely. You did a nice chubb (job)" Just then a crew transport vehicle arrived and the WAAF driver, in broad London cockney said, "Group Captain Adams is waiting to see you and he wants me to take you to him." She pointed out the CO waiting on the tarmac. "I wonder what he wants?" I asked her with some trepidation.

The driver stopped near the CO and I alighted. "That was a tremendous landing you did," he said in a well cultured Scottish accent, adding, "I saw your smoke trail miles out and worried you'd catch fire in that dud engine. I want you to bring me your report and your Flying Log Book. In the meantime I'll be commending you to the Air Ministry."

The expression on the CO's face showed his appreciation of the incident, and added to my sense of amazement at what we had been through as a crew after only a few weeks of flying the Whitley.

I took my report and Log Book to Group Captain Adams. He wrote:-

EXCEPTIONAL FLYING SKILL.

Flight Sergeant Scotland carried out single engine and right hand circuit and force landed. No damage to aircraft. In view of limited experience on this type of aircraft, pilot put up an excellent performance and took all necessary precautions.

Signed Group Captain Adams, Commanding No.10 OTU, 30th July 1943.

Air Ministry Authority, 91G/1405/293/P1

I think the CO was just so relieved that he had not lost a Whitley bomber, nevertheless I felt wonderfully encouraged by his words.

PUNTS ON THE THAMES

Following our emergency landing, Alan and his boys invited us to join them in a walk to the Thames River, less than an hour away. The peaceful summer evening looked most inviting, so we agreed to hire punts and include a jaunt on the river.

With Alan's team in one punt and we in another, our two crews poled our way with the slow current of the River Thames. For half an hour water slapped the wooden sides of the craft and we relaxed in the serenity of the evening. Then Alan gave a call, "Let's go boys!" His crew turned their punt, paddled hard, and headed away from us. Not to be outdone, I yelled, "Come on fellas!" I pushed our punt into a turn, then let out an Indian war cry and the fellows grabbed boards and anything else loose in the punt that we could use as paddles, and we headed after Alan.

In the excitement of contest, we shortened the distance to Alan's boat and filled the air with shouts. As we neared the landing, the noise and commotion brought out the punt owner, "Hey therrrre! Hey therrrre!" His voice only added to our excitement. I steered our punt towards Alan, hoping to slow him by battering tactics.

We collided. Alan and his boys went sprawling into the river. Our punt filled with water and Ed, Hoppy, Smithy, Shorty and I splashed into the Thames. The relaxing cushions and the loose boards of the punts floated away. Amidst shouts for retrieval of floating objects, and calling to one another in hilarious glee, and "Hey therrrre!" from the owner, the whole scene became one of utter confusion.

In the midst of the melee, I called, "Ed, Hoppy, can you give me a hand, I've hurt my ankle." The two men supported me until I could lie on the ground at the water's edge. Gradually, they collected everything, dragged the punts to shallow water, and emptied them.

Breathing hard and nursing my ankle, I watched Alan placate the irate owner. Alan was so gentle with him, and eventually a price mollified the outraged man. Alan came to me for help to make up the money. By this time everyone lay on the grass, drying out in the warmth of the evening. In typical fashion, Alan's articulate radio operator, "Big Time", described the race, and caused further glee. Our closeness as two crews became cemented in warm appreciation of one another as we lay there on the bank of the Thames.

After a while, Ed reminisced and showed us a side of himself I had wondered about. He had a deep hatred of the enemy and a much more than average desire to smash Germany and finish this war.

He told the story of his long drawn out journey to South Africa and then his flying training there as a bomb aimer and observer. After graduating, he had a most devastating return journey to England in the Queen Mary. Ed, with lilting geordie voice, explained.

"Whereas it had taken us three weeks in the Dutch ship Volendam to sail out to South Africa, the Queen Mary went from Capetown to Glasgow on the Clyde in ten days. On the way to England we passed through wreckage from an Atlantic convoy that had been attacked by submarines. I can still see them now, those men on the rafts waiting to be picked up and we couldn't pick them up. It was awful. The captain of the Queen Mary dare not stop as submarines could still be in the area. On the contrary, he opened up the engines and the Mary went like the clappers of hell."

Ed fell silent and then continued, "We had to leave those men behind. It was terrible to see them, terrible. I hated those submarines for what they had done." These were sombre moments. I could see why the experience had kindled in Ed a smouldering anger against Nazi Germany.

The evening grew late. It was time to leave the banks of the Thames, and I needed help for my painful ankle. Hoppy and Ed came to my rescue. With my arms firmly about their shoulders, we made the hour long walk back to Stanton Harcourt.

BOOST TO MORALE

Next evening, as my crew and I enjoyed the long summer daylight, the sky began to fill with aircraft. "Bomber aircraft heading out on attack somewhere," we conjectured, "But why are they so low?" Next morning, our CO explained what it was all about.

Five hundred RAF bombers had streamed low over London on their way to Germany. They had flown from bases as far north as Yorkshire and for half an hour the roar of aircraft had continued overhead.

Londoners flocked out of their houses to witness the incredible spectacle of their planes streaming out from England at roof top height to attack Germany. The bomber crews flashed "V" for Victory messages to groups of people in London streets, and the Londoners loved it; responding explosively with cheers and shouting. Britain had suffered terribly from German bombs, and now these people were having a part, with an armada of RAF boys, in taking the war to the heart of enemy industry. What a morale boost it proved to be, to a Britain wearied by war.

The whole of Europe, apart from neutral Switzerland, Spain, and Portugal, lay under German domination. The RAF and US Air Force were alone in challenging German control over hundreds of millions of people.

But the air war had slowed. The U.S. Air Force had suffered very high losses and the Americans were regrouping their bomber force and rethinking their strategies. Bomber Command of the RAF, operating at night, had insufficient heavy runways to take the Halifaxes and Lancasters now coming into the squadrons, so the changeover from the older Wellington and Whitley bombers had not proceeded as quickly as was hoped. Continual rain had slowed down airfield construction. The war seemed to be dragging on endlessly, so the RAF had given British people that wonderful show of its strength.

INTO THE AIR AGAIN

Two days later, I still limped but felt fit enough to fly off into a sunny afternoon, heading for the north of England. Fluffy clouds floated over the picture book scenery below.

Ed occupied his forward position in the nose of the Whitley, where the transparent perspex around him gave a clear view below and ahead. "I love it when we skim over the tops of those clouds," he called. As assistant navigator, he pinpointed objects on the ground and identified them on a map to assist Hoppy. As bomb aimer, he had the task of guiding me over a target so that we could drop our load of practice bombs on to a ground objective.

Ed's third responsibility was assisting me on "take off". Standing beside me in the aircraft, he held the throttles to full power, while I concentrated on getting the plane off the ground. I also needed Ed to learn to fly the plane for the emergency of my being disabled or killed in the air.

Having flown now for two and a half hours, I decided to answer a call of nature. "Ed" I called. "Yes Skipper" he replied. "Come up here and take over will you. I've got to go to the toilet." Ed duly appeared; I climbed down out of my seat and Ed climbed up into it. He appeared apprehensive, so I coached him along a bit and then left him to it. We were above oxygen height, so I unplugged my oxygen mask, walked to the toilet at the rear, and proceeded to unzip myself.

Someone tapped my shoulder. An agitated Shorty directed my attention forward, where all was not well with Ed. The deck along which I had walked now sloped steeply upwards. The nose of the plane pointed far too high and the plane rolled from side to side. I began a tortuous climb up a precipitous walkway.

'I CANNOT SEE WHAT YOU ARE WORRIED ABOUT

Being without oxygen, it was hard work, but shock from Ed's dilemma gave me added strength. I had visions of a stalled and spinning Whitley, with myself jammed to the side of the aircraft by centrifugal force unable to get back to the pilot's position. The pilot's cabin at last! I struggled to Ed's side, saw our speed at stalling, and the Whitley juddering. Giving the engines full power, I then reached over and pushed the pilot's control column forward. The control column seemed floppy, but I watched as ever so slowly, the nose of the plane came down from its steep climb. Increasing air speed whistled around the cabin, sounding to me like music.

The plane returned to level flying, and Ed climbed out of the pilot's seat. "What went wrong?" he asked. "I should have warned you that my body weight moving to the rear of the aircraft would effect the flying of the Whitley. It's my fault!" Still shaken by the experience, I viewed England on this warm summer day, and thought, "All this peace and beauty, but none of it could help us in our emergency."

Two hours later we landed back on "terra firma". My crew gathered around. Ed looked glum, and the rest of the fellows pleaded, "Skipper, don't ever do that again to us, please!" It intrigued me that no one suggested how I might solve my toilet needs!

ST ELMO'S FIRE

A week later, in mid August, a violent storm covered the north of England. We flew into it as we navigated northwards at night, along the west coast of England. Clouds closed in and lightning flashed around us. Thin ice formed on our wings and intense air currents tossed us. We turned eastwards and neared the centre of the storm, where the bumpy air quietened and our aircraft flew more smoothly. Ice formation ceased. We still flew in cloud but the air was quiet and peaceful.

What happened next took me completely unawares. From the area of outer clouds a faint green aura surrounded our aircraft, and tinges of green shadow pervaded my cabin. The whole aircraft reflected an eerie green, in ghostlike variations off the clouds swirling around us. Then the propellers of our Rolls Royce motors became alive with incandescent green. The glow intensified around the motors and then flowed towards me. I myself became enveloped in a mass of strange shapeless green. My gloved hands were enfolded in a ghostly green, then the instrument panel, the throttle levers, and my whole cabin glowed. Our aircraft was invaded with spectral green from outer space. Some strange unknown seemed to be hovering over us.

"Saint Elmo's Fire!" The words sprang to mind. History books spoke of a green mass that had clung to the masts of sailing ships. Sailors of the twelfth century called it Saint Elmo's Fire and to them it was an omen.

"Fellows, this is Saint Elmo's Fire" I called on the plane's intercom, "It's a rare occurrence and nothing to be scared about!" I felt nowhere near as calm as my words. We flew spellbound by the invasion for a long ten minutes, then the green lessened and disappeared. Storm clouds swirled around us but the eerie glow had gone, vanishing as mysteriously as it had come.

We continued to fly through towering cumulo nimbus storm clouds and Hoppy and I had already begun to worry about our position, for Ed had not been able to give any ground navigation checks for some time, nothing by which he could verify our position. Shorty worked hard to get a check on a radio beacon but heavy static made it impossible to get useable information. We were a crew tossed by a giant storm, with no way to check our position. The aircraft flew on, time ticked by.

Half an hour later, Smithy called from the tail turret. Storm clouds had parted long enough for him to read the letters of a beacon flashing miles behind us on the ground. The RAF had installed such beacons to assist crews in night navigation.

Smithy read the letters, "Dah dit dit dit ... dit dah", the letters "BA". Searching our maps, we found beacon "BA" located on the coast, a hundred miles north of our estimated position. What was more, we were now out over the North Sea and heading towards a watery grave.

We checked our compasses and our gyroscopic instruments. The truth then dawned on us. Our green invader had left with us a signature. The directional instruments, by which I flew a set course, had been altered through powerful magnetic forces. The Saint Elmo's Fire had seriously affected our compasses and destroyed Hoppy's facilities for accurate navigation. "Smithy," I called, "You're a genius. Thanks for reporting that beacon!"

Assessing ourselves on various directions of flight, Hoppy calculated a course that would take us southward to Stanton Harcourt. Continual checking showed that the excessive magnetising effect of the Saint Elmo's Fire gradually faded. At two in the morning, we landed out of the storm, and a greatly relieved crew sat to enjoy a steaming mug of tea and a return flight meal. Next morning, Ed expressed his feelings about our near destruction in the North Sea. As became his usual form he presented me with a humorous drawing and there, central in it, trying to solve our navigation problem, was Hoppy.

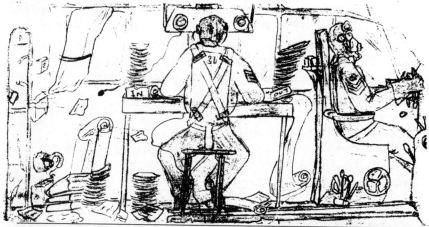

TROPHY

Our days of flying Whitleys at Stanton Harcourt and Abingdon drew to a close. Written examinations concluded with Alan Forrester and me still competing. The day arrived for a trophy to be awarded for the "Best all round crew". All crews assembled for the big announcement of course prizes. The name read out for top prize was Scotland. We were jubilant, and I felt so very proud of the work each one had put in, Hoppy, Ed, Shorty and Smithy. Alan Forrester and his boys came to congratulate us, but I could see that he was disappointed as he and his boys had really worked hard for the prize. But they were all there to cheer us when we had our photos taken and to celebrate with us.

We now awaited our being appointed to fly one of the big four engined Halifaxes in preparation for our part in the air war on Germany. The nearer we came to joining a squadron, the more pressing became the sobering question of survival over Europe.

ESCAPEES

The next step took us to the Driffield air base near York, not to fly, but for training as an escapee from Europe. If ever we landed in occupied Europe, we needed to know how to make our way back to Britain.

After weeks of training, we faced our big test. We were driven out into a foul rainy night, dumped together as a crew in a mountainous area; the time was near to midnight, and we had no idea where we were or what direction to take.

Soaked by the pouring rain, we crossed a farmer's field and came to a disused fowl shed. It seemed a good opportunity to sleep, and in the morning the sun would give direction. Five bodies curled up under the fowl house roof, only to find it already occupied by myriads of fleas. Grumbling and stumbling out into the rain, we left the accursed place, and plodded through a field of leafy vegetables. I pulled at one - a turnip. "Turnips boys! Let's have some breakfast while we can!" I had never seen my boys look at a more unwelcome breakfast food. It was cow's fodder, but I munched one and as we walked, they all, one by one picked their turnip.

Daylight came, but the cloud and rain continued so that we still could not determine our direction. Cold and wet, we came on a well trafficked road and followed it for miles, passing farm after farm, hamlet after hamlet. The terrain became less mountainous and we recognised Yorkshire country, estimating that Driffield lay about thirty miles away.

Dressed in motley uniforms that made us conspicuous, we needed to get back to Driffield without being caught by the police. By three o'clock in the afternoon we were numb and beyond feeling. The country was flat, and we passed through small towns, where people eyed us curiously.

Very late in the afternoon, we came to a large town, too big to walk around. A friendly "Hullo," came from behind us. We turned. A constable was approaching, gazing at our unusual clothing. When he walked alongside us, I whispered to Ed, "Do you want to run for it, we don't want to get caught at this stage!" He replied, "It's too late to run, let's bluff our way through."

But the constable would not be bluffed. He stepped in front of us saying, "You are from Driffield aren't you!" We had no heart to avoid the question further. He opened his pocket book and entered our names. "Scotland from Australia eh?" he asked looking doubtful about my name. He departed, closing his pocket book, and shaking his head.

Having been caught, we waved down an army truck. The soldiers were only too happy to take us. They were an experimental group testing heavy trucks in crossing rivers in preparation for the Allies invading Europe.

Darkness had fallen by the time we reported in at Driffield. Other crews were straggling in and sharing their stories. The adjutant came to me with some interesting news, "Scotty you and Forrester are posted. You are to proceed to Marston Moor to begin flying Halifaxes. I've already told Forrester." "The big planes at last!" I said to him as I thanked him for going out of his way to let me know. I felt thrilled that next day we would leave the muddy conditions of Driffield, and fly again. When I told my crew, Hoppy, with unusual exuberance exclaimed, "Marston Moor here we come!"

8

MIRACLE OF DEVILS GLEN

The air base at Marston Moor! It lay forty five minutes drive west from York, and we arrived there on a cold, foggy, Yorkshire day. Our billets, Nissen huts amongst a grove of trees, well away from the main buildings, could only be reached by following a narrow winding track. In less squelchy weather, the setting would look very pretty, but on our arrival, the huts looked pathetically alone in a sea of sodden earth and dripping wet branches, drooping in the dense mist.

Several letters had arrived for me. I sat on my bed to read one from my mother. She began by saying, "Tom I know this will come as a blow to you but Jim Layton is dead. He crashed in Victoria whilst flying through a storm and he has been buried at Sale, east of Melbourne. I know .... "

I read and reread mother's account of Jim's death. It was difficult to grasp that he had gone. The letter hung from my hand as I recalled our growing up together before the war, our cycle rides to work, our joint decision to be flyers as our contribution to the war, and our last meeting at the Pearce air base. His mum and dad had written an inscription for his gravestone, "Tranquil he lies, his knightly virtue proved." How apt, I thought.

The second letter came from Jim Mudie. He and Lindsay Fairclough were together but they were missing our good Aussie friendship. "When can we meet and spend some time together in London?" Jim asked. Then came another blow, "Norm Dunn has crashed in Devon and been killed."

I sat holding Jim's letter feeling stunned. I saw Norm, loaded with his gear, guitar slung across his shoulders, a smile on his face and a dancing sparkle in his eyes. I had loved his music, his fun and his friendship. Why did such a fine, sensitive person have to fight in this war? Norm's Lancaster must have iced up. Upper atmosphere storm clouds continually presented the flyer with the hazard of destructive icing.

LETTERS TO WRITE

The death of my friends, and incessant foggy weather, kept me in sombre mood. I knew that I must write to Jim Layton's parents and to Norm's mother. It depressed me that neither friend had seen active service against the enemy, yet their lives had been lost. Putting pen to paper and expressing my sorrow, helped me to do something with my own utter dismay.

The cold ate into me. Puddles along the roads that froze overnight, thawed in early afternoon. I could not work out which I liked better, the mud and slush of the thaw or the cold of the freeze. I felt shut in by the fog and I longed to fly to get above it all, but our aircraft were grounded by the weather.

A sad note arrived from Mrs Dunn replying to my letter, and sharing her grief. Her inscription for Norm's grave read, "Our Norm, a lover of music and loved by all who knew him." Letters of condolence had flooded into her home from hundreds who had known Norm or had listened to his music, especially on radio 6PR in Perth. She treasured the caring letters. At Marston Moor, I experienced my own sadness, and then the fogs lifted. Flying began.

TAMING A GIANT

The Halifax looked a giant; its six foot high wheels supported a massive fuselage standing twenty feet off the ground. The great wings spread so wide that I found it hard to judge if their tips cleared those of the plane next to me. Power from its four great motors started it moving, and when I had the wheels rolling, the weighty aircraft seemed to never want to stop. The wheel brakes were controlled by a hand grip on the pilots flying column, and emitted loud hisses of air when released. The noise of air brakes amidst the vibrating roar of four motors made it like some great monster that we had to take into the air and tame.

A MONSTER TO TAME

After three hours and ten minutes flying with a staff pilot, I found myself given command. Alongside flying, our study took us into the principles of operating the Halifax. Day after day I pored over the details until I knew what to do in emergencies.

One morning I awoke, breakfasted, and saw a marvellous sight. The early sun shone on our enclave of huts amongst the trees, and I felt exhilarated. We had a clear day ahead. I rode my cycle into the sunrise, and headed to the main buildings on the air base to prepare for flying.

On entering the crew room, I heard my name called. A young RAF sergeant asked, "Is your name Scotland?" "Yes it is." "The flight engineer leader asked me to see you. He said you needed a flight engineer." The softly spoken sergeant gazed steadily at me, and I listened closely to his Glasgow dialect. "Yes we need a flight engineer; and you are one," I said, looking at the "E" brevet neatly sewn on his tunic. "Aye, I've recently arrived from training school in Wales. My name is Bob Lewis," he said nervously.

The sergeant's youthful appearance surprised me and I thought to myself, "Is the RAF recruiting boys for this work?" His soft appearance, bright red lips and milk like cheeks matched an extremely light build. While shaking his hand and enquiring about his qualifications, I thought, "However will he handle the toughness of this war?" I looked around the crew room for a quiet place in which we could talk further, but noise and chatter seemed to fill every corner. I suggested we talk somewhere else. "Aye" replied the sergeant preparing to follow me.

We walked out on to the tarmac. Two Halifaxes stood near the control tower, their noses pointed proudly skywards. An officer stood on the balcony of the control tower watching a Hurricane fighter roar along the runway. It looked so tiny compared with the great outspread wings of the Halifaxes. The Hurricane took its noise into the sky and then I turned expectantly to the young Scot.

He spoke about working as a ships' chandler on the Glasgow docks before joining the RAF. He had also been a soccer player for one of the Glasgow teams. Then I discovered he was older than me. His soft white skin and youthful appearance had belied his age.

I saw him hold his head at times. "A bit of a party last night," he said, "Too much whisky!" He added that he always drank whisky, it was far superior to the Englishman's beer. I sympathised, for I found English beer less attractive than Australian beer. We walked on. A cold wind cut into me. I looked at the lightly clad Scot, oblivious to the cold. How did he do it? No doubt his Scottish upbringing had hardened him, but the icy darts pierced my layers of Australian clothing, and I shivered.

Despite the cold, I warmed to this youthful Scot. His serious demeanour made me long to hear him laugh, but I could not deny the rock solidness about his committal to the work ahead as a flight engineer. He would make a staunch and reliable crew member. "Well that sounds bonzer, I reckon you ought to come and meet the rest of the boys!" "You mean, you want me as part of the crew?" he asked in surprise. "Yes, too right I do!"

We walked back to the crew room area and I found my crew sitting in the lounge reading and writing letters. I introduced the Scottish sergeant saying "Fellows, meet Bob Lewis. He's joining us as flight engineer." I turned to Bob and pointed out each crew member, "Ed - bomb aimer; Hoppy - navigator; Shorty - wireless operator; Smithy - rear gunner; Bill Butler - mid upper gunner. " Bob Lewis became the seventh member to join our crew. The sixth member, Bill Butler, had joined us earlier. A man of the earth with a ready grin, he came from a farming environment in Devon. He and Smithy were making the most of being gunners together. I watched them welcome Bob into a seat. Camaraderie spread over the group and they began telling the stories that flyers tell.

OVER BRIDLINGTON BAY

A sergeant pilot appeared at the door. Fred Annan, newly arrived at Marston, spoke in lilting geordie. He dropped in to see Ed from time to time, and they enjoyed some good geordie talk together. "I believe I'm flying with you today Scotty," he said to me. "Yes Fred, our instructor is going to show us how to make the Hali fly on one engine." "Ay maan," nodded Fred.

I called out, "Bob, you could fly with Fred Annan and me, and start getting used to the Halifax. Oh by the way, Fred, this is our flight engineer, Bob Lewis. Bob this is Fred Annan, he's a geordie, so, nuff said!" I looked at the Geordie meeting the Scot, and thought of their heritage, ancient enemies sharing a common border. "Och," replied Bob "It's good to meet you." He spoke soft Scottish brogue, and I was impressed by his gentleness and the quiet way he voiced his words.

They all began talking. I listened, enjoying the language, and chuckling under my breath at their unbelievably quaint phrases.

Bob Lewis took up the flight engineer's position behind the pilot's flight deck. He had an observation window by which he could see the pilot and the array of instruments covering the pilot's flying panels. But he also had his own set, engine indicators from sensors in the four big motors that powered the Halifax. He also had controls for our fuel supplies, facilities for directing fuel from eight big fuel tanks carried in the one hundred foot wings. If the tanks were damaged in battle, there were electric pumps to transfer fuel to other tanks.

The instructor arranged for me to do the take off, flying into a cloudy Yorkshire sky, above green Yorkshire fields. I flew out over Scarborough and Bridlington Bay; stopped one motor and then another. The Halifax kept me busy as power decreased, and three motors were stopped. Speed dropped off alarmingly. Flying on one motor, I pointed the plane's nose high into the sky, and managed to maintain slow speed. It seemed that at any moment our plane would cease hanging there, and head downwards into Bridlington waters.

The most difficult flying came when I stopped two motors on the same side. With all that power on one side, the Halifax wanted to keep turning and it needed the full force of my foot to maintain the rudder pedal in a position to keep the plane flying straight and level.

Fred went through the same procedures, then on our return to

Marston Moor we flew low over the Wharf river at York. In the glow of a low afternoon sun, Fred followed its beautiful broad sweeping curves to Marston Moor and Boston Spa. We enjoyed the sight of the picturesque river flowing between hedgerows and green fields of sugar beet and potatoes, and at last our wheels rumbled on the thick concrete runway of Marston Moor.

A month after that flight, we lost Fred and his crew. In freezing and snowing conditions, Fred's aircraft left the runway, gained height, but went over on one wing and disappeared into the deep, dark waters of this same Wharf River. The crew had no chance of survival. Fred's body was laid to rest near his home at Hexham, Newcastle on Tyne.

HURRICANE FIGHTERS

Crew training proceeded in earnest, with practise bombing, navigation day and night and then came the Hurricane fighters simulating attacks on us. With their camera guns flicking away, they tried to get gun shot photos of us and we did our best to avoid their cameras.

I became used to having my foot on the plane's rudder pedals, awaiting the command of our gunners that a Hurricane was coming in on a practise attack. I learnt to use my strength to pull the Halifax into an evasive diving turn the instant I heard their command. The gunners, Smithy and Bill Butler and myself co-operated, learning to trust each other's judgment to weld us together as a team. Bob Lewis became another set of eyes to detect those fighters.

Bob battled with air sickness for a start. At times he became very quiet, setting his mind to concentrate on his work, but he looked like death when we landed. The only one in the crew who seemed to be plagued with it, he battled through courageously until one day, we noticed he was no longer air sick.

LONDON

In order to have a break from our intense programme, Alan Forrester and I received a few days leave with our crews, and headed for London.

Having leave in London meant a hotel room with the enjoyment of fresh comfortable beds. We found a nearby basement where women steam pressed our crushed uniform trousers. While waiting trouserless, we chatted with men of varying ranks and nationalities, and read names on the walls covered with signatures. One name made the ladies particularly proud; Ike Eisenhower, the Supreme Allied Commander for the invasion of Europe, had stood there while they pressed his trousers.

Feeling smart, our next goal became the Covent Garden ballroom and its magnetic draw of music and dance. Alan and I walked there and I chuckled, thinking of the girls heading to the ballroom, worrying about their hair, whilst we fellows worried about the appearance of our trousers. Pride took various forms.

The Covent Garden Opera House had been turned into a ballroom. Well known dance bands from the United States and Britain, gave us thrilling music, and we had opportunity to dance with partners under a huge revolving and scintillating ball suspended from the very high ceiling; the ceiling that had once echoed to the voices of opera.

My partner, a lass who worked in an aircraft factory near Oxford, had come to London to be with her parents for the weekend. She worked on the construction of the new high performance fighter called "The Tempest". Bigger and more powerful than the Spitfire, it would help to prepare the way for allied armies to land in France.

I felt a satisfying sense of teamwork with this lass. Young women in factories across England, provided planes and equipment needed to carry on the war. They worked hard in helping to turn the tide of battle towards victory after years of defeat.

The theme of the Symphony Pathetique, by Tschaikovsky, became music for a song entitled, "This is the Story of a Starry Night". I loved it. It fitted the scene of the Covent Garden ballroom magnificently. The orchestration with female vocalist echoing across the packed dance floor, became a majestic experience for me. My partner responded to it. We waltzed through the romantic movements and the high, glittering, rotating ball flickered its starry reflections across the dancers flowing and moving like a glimmering rolling sea in the ultimate experience of dance.

BOOMERANG CLUB

After our long night at the ballroom, Alan and I slept till well into the morning. I left him and made my way to the Boomerang Club, that section of Australia House set aside for Australians in wartime England. I had arranged to meet John, the pilot husband of my sister Norah.

I approached the Club through the business district where air raid shelters and sandbag walls, dozens of them, protected fine looking buildings from the blast of German bombs. The burnt out wreckage of Saint Clement Danes Church designed by Sir Christopher Wren in 1690, straddled an island in the Strand. Broken buildings and sandbags were all reminders of how much London suffered as enemy bombers pounded away at this big city.

At the entrance to the Boomerang Club I negotiated past sandbagged blast walls, and walked into a generous hall with a very high ceiling. "Tommy Scotland!" The voice came from my brother in law, hidden for a moment. Then I saw him ensconced in one of the comfortable brown armchairs. He arose and we moved towards each other. I noticed how John's bulky frame sagged at the shoulders, and his face looked more lined than when I had last seen him.

We spent the afternoon together at the Club, chatting, discussing Aussie newspapers and meeting other air force fellows. Voluntary lady helpers handed out the enjoyable biscuit and a "cuppa". I listened to the chatter of many Australian voices finding it incongruous that I had to retune my ear to hear Aussies after my sojourn amongst British dialects.

Evening came, and with it, our desire to find a suitable bar before dinner. We headed over the street, dodging taxis as we went. Then the air raid sirens sounded. At first only an alert, then they wailed out their mournful warning of the real air raid. I had never before experienced such claustrophobia as walking in that narrow London street in an air raid.

The population of London seemed to flow underground and into air raid shelters. John said in his casual voice, "Let's go in here Tommy." Here, turned out to be a bar that opened off the street. The barman saw us coming. It was illegal to not seek shelter during an air raid, but the barman ceased making his hasty exit to the shelters and said, "Why not!". Those words of determination helped John for he did not feel he could take to an air raid shelter. The barman reinstated himself and took our order.

"Listen!" I said as distant explosions came nearer. John looked out the door wearily as I drew his attention to them, but we gradually settled into our pre dinner drinks. John began sharing about his last three months flying Wellington Bombers over Germany. "There's no future in it Tom!" he said emphatically, referring to the losses of planes and their crews.

I could see that the experience of "ops" (operations over enemy targets) had greatly shaken John and made him glad to be finished. He had done twenty three trips on Wellingtons including seven gardening trips. "Gardening", was the RAF word for dropping explosive mines into enemy shipping lanes and "vegetables", the mines that they dropped.

Amidst the engrossing tales of John's experiences on ops, the "All Clear" wailed. My feelings of discomfort at being shut in during an air raid began to ease. After the air raid came dinner, but not much choice; smoked mackerel, potato and brussel sprouts. The coffee that followed the meal helped and I enjoyed the restaurant atmosphere.

John shared news about Norah travelling by train across to Perth, for a month's leave with my mother and sister Elsa. We talked of home after the war and the things we would like to do. The hour grew late and we parted. I had spent time with family, and that meant a lot to me.

Next day, life went on as normal. Alan Forrester and I went to the Houses of Parliament in Westminster. The devastation of the House of Commons by bomb blast had to be seen to be believed. Big Ben in the high clock tower now rang with one bell cracked. Saint Pauls Cathedral stood surrounded by vast areas flattened by German bombing. In other streets we saw damaged buildings, others flattened or missing altogether. But Londoners carried on, accepting the pain, and hoping for victory.

Feeling much benefit from our visit to London, Alan with his crew and I with Hoppy and Ed, alighted from the bus at Marston Moor, ready to tackle the next stage of flying Halifaxes.

HALIFAX WITH NO BRAKES

Next morning, briefed for a navigation exercise, we boarded a vehicle taking us to our plane. It waited like some great bird, and beside it we seemed like grasshoppers.

With four big motors roaring, I finished the preflight checks and headed the plane out towards the runway. Then the brakes failed. What could I do to stop this lumbering aircraft? Leave the taxiway? That would mean sinking the aircraft in boggy ground. Continue to the runway? That could take me into the path of a landing aircraft. Ah! A heap of crushed rock used for runway surfacing. I headed the Halifax there. The huge wheels rolled up the incline, up and up they went, faltered for an instant and then stopped.

In utter relief I sat there breathing deeply for some moments and then called the control tower for a spare aircraft. Painted on the side of our next Halifax was the letter "J". A surge of power from its four motors sent us on to the taxi way once more, and soon, lined up on the runway, we began our take off.

Today we flew south to Oxford and then turned northward towards Bridlington Bay. We searched the sky, expecting simulated attacks by Hurricane fighters giving our gunners practice in being under attack.

"It's minus thirty four degrees centigrade outside the plane," called Hoppy. "You don't have to tell me it's cold," I called back, "I'm dancing my feet on the floor of the flight deck here to get them warm, can't you hear me?" "No" replied Hoppy dispassionately, his mind concentrating on his next navigation task. The heating of the Halifax was erratic, if I wanted heat in the pilot's area, the flight engineer cooked, so I had no heat.

Ed shared the forward area with Hoppy and radioman Shorty. Sometims Ed sat beside the navigator checking over charts; at other times he lay on his stomach in the transparent nose, and observed the world below so that he could follow the map location of our plane. Carefully fitted in line with his eyes, he had his bomb sight. A highly technical instrument, it remained level even when our plane was not.

We flew over the bombing range, where Ed soon sighted the target arrow on the ground, and dropped our practice bombs. I was now free to descend to Bridlington Bay and warmer air. It was something the gunners eagerly anticipated, to fire their guns, test their accuracy, and let their noise and shouts of glee echo through our intercom. Ed and I then map read our way across Yorkshire until the winding Wharf river led us home to our runway.

REQUEST FOR PATHFINDER CREWS

A Lancaster landed after us. It was unusual for a Lancaster to call in at Marston Moor, although our past CO, Leonard Cheshire, now with a Dambuster squadron, had dropped in from time to time to revisit Marston.

Parking near the control tower, I switched off the motors. The propellers slowed to a stop, and I watched the Lancaster come from the other side of the parking area. From my high perch nearly twenty feet above the ground, I studied the crew of the Lanc. The pilot wore on his tunic the gleaming gold Pathfinder eagle. My heart did a leap for the Lancaster came from Eight Group, the RAF Pathfinder group in Huntingdon. I wondered what drew such a specialised crew to Marston Moor?

The Pathfinder crew were in fact visiting on a recruiting drive to select out crews for a Pathfinder squadron to be set up in Italy. At Marston that afternoon a meeting went on behind closed doors and decisions were made choosing out crews who would begin Pathfinder orientation at Upwood. I learnt that my crew and I were amongst those recommended for selection for the new squadron.

HISTORICAL CITY OF YORK

Saturday evening came. Alan Forrester, in exuberant mood, burst into my hut to see if I was ready to go into York. He and I planned to spend an evening in that historic town. York at night, was the meeting place for aircrew from squadrons and training bases flying Halifaxes and Lancasters in Yorkshire.

A bumpy bus trip, took us into its cobbled streets. Complete blackout meant that Alan and I had to make our way in dim light shed from a darkened sky. Footfalls of aircrew fellows descending from the bus, clopped on the cobbled pavement. Ahead of us, a "clip, clip, clip," of many more walkers echoed out of a dark mysterious distance.

We found our pub. Its familiar interior, arrayed with British, Canadian, New Zealand and Aussie flyers, warmed and invited me, and I looked for opportunity of getting news of friends. A hum of voices, low at first, rose in intensity from time to time. Chatter about the air war intensified through the evening. Warning signs, "Beware, the enemy listens", did not stop the stories as groups bunched together to share secret things more and more as the hours wore on.

Alan came to me with news of a dance nearby. "Let's go eh?" he said. "Too right," I responded looking over the crowded rooms of the pub. The thought of a dance attracted me and buoyed up my anticipation of meeting some of the local girls.

We headed out of the warmth and into the cold of the narrow cobbled street. York entranced me. Its ancient brickwork seemed to breathe out the annals of past ages. Historic walls enfolded me until I could picture myself as a person living in some past age.

There it was, the sound of dance music! We followed its beat, and mounted stairs over a group of shops. On entering the hall, Alan and I surveyed the scene of swaying couples. Two girls stood together. We caught their glance, and they responded to our invitation to dance. Becoming part of a moving sea of dancers, I swept my partner enjoyably across the floor, and then we introduced ourselves. She was a teacher and her friend worked in the Borough Council. In the thrill of dancing and chatting, the evening stretched on until early morning. Alan and I walked the girls homeward, then ambled back to the town centre.

Buses to Marston Moor had long since ceased, and everywhere we enquired, the same answer came, "Sorry, we have no spare beds!" Disconsolate, we entered the waiting room of the York railway station, and found two long, cold, wooden seats. "Could there be anything more uninviting?" I wondered.

The early morning hours wore on. "Are you awake Alan?" I called. Alan mumbled something out of his sleep, then I heard him say, "I'm too bloody cold to sleep. How are you going?" "I'm freezing," I replied, gritting my teeth to stop them chattering. Perhaps the shivering warmed me, for I awoke to the noise of an early morning train. Alan had found a newspaper, wrapped himself in its pages, and still slept.

I shivered, and longed for a hot drink, something to warm me. Walking out of the station, I searched for breakfast. The Salvation Army hostel served "bangers" (sausages) and a "cuppa char". Sipping the hot tea, I warmed to its flow, and then went to get Alan to join me in the breakfast queue.

TROUBLE FOR AN AUSSIE

In the months we were at Marston Moor, the two girls in York were there to meet with us and go dancing. However, we made sure that we did not miss our last bus to the base. Our railway station freeze had lifted our value of having warm bunks at Marston.

One night the four of us had been dancing and getting quite hot. Taking a breath of fresh air out on darkened pathways, we saw passing faces loom out of the darkness. Taken up with cuddling close in with the lass next to me, I suddenly heard Alan call, "Don!" It was his rear gunner. "Whatever's happened to you?" We gathered around to better appreciate Don's plight. Dishevelled, with blood on his face, he talked about having a fight with six young RAF Officers. We were amazed at how foolish the sergeant had been.

Don, fancied himself as a boxer, and the fact that he had landed blows on officers was disastrous, for he could be court-martialled. "They recognised me, what will I do now?" he wailed. Nothing more remained that he could. Alan said grimly, "You'll just have to bloody well tidy yourself Don. Go back to Marston Moor and face your medicine. The CO might not be hard on you, and I don't want to lose you, you're a bloody good gunner."

But what did Don do? He left us, searched through York until he found the same officers, then restarted the fracas. Service police arrested him. He insisted on them taking him to the dance hall to get Alan and me. We were horrified at his more battered appearance. "Whatever have you done now?" we asked. But Don seemed only to want us as his excuse to escape the RAF Police. He tried to make a dash out a door, but they waited for him at every exit. Eventually they sat on him and handcuffed him. But Don was made of ingenuity. At the Courtmartial he managed to have his sentence reduced to a fine and reprimand, and Alan retained his "Bloody good gunner."

DEVIL'S GLEN

Boxing Day 1943, we flew off in Halifax "J", and headed for a rendezvous with a Hurricane fighter. We had arranged to meet the fighter over the mountains to the west of Leeds where our gunners could practise shooting at an attacking aircraft.

For half an hour the Halifax climbed and dived to avoid the attacking Hurricane amidst heavy cloud patches high above West Yorkshire. Our gunners shouted instructions to me as they worked to protect us from the simulated attacks. From time to time a heavy vibration went through our plane like a wave going from nose to tail. I worried about it, but could not detect the cause.

At the bottom of a high speed dive, I pulled the plane back up into a rapid climb through clouds. Then it happened! A loud rumbling, shattering, rattling noise shook the plane. The Halifax flew awkwardly through a series of bucking movements I found hard to control. Out the left window, I saw devastation; the left wing had been ripped open and parts were flapping loosely. A motor had torn loose, its propeller blades disintegrated, and the motor itself swayed at a crazy angle.

A further shock! Flames licked over the stricken motor. Fire could collapse the whole wing. Muscles tightened around my stomach. I would have to get my crew out. "This is an emergency fellows, parachute, parachute, jump, jump!"

Wind roared into the aircraft. I looked down the flight deck stairwell towards the navigation deck, and a gaping hole met my gaze. Hoppy had unlocked the forward escape hatch and was making his escape. Others followed. Then, just one face stared up at me: Shorty! He gave me a grin, a thumbs up sign, and disappeared. I was alone.

The plane vibrated, and gave strange bucking movements, but I was still in control. I reported by radio to Marston Moor base. Back came the reply, "Bale out, bale out!"

Setting the controls, I started to move out of my seat, but where was my parachute? Normally clipped to the wall of the aircraft, it must have been snatched by one of the gunners; his was still there in position near his turret. My view through the gaping escape hatch now gave me a view, not of mountains below, but of houses and factories. I was flying over a city. How could it be? Was it Leeds or was it Bradford?

I groaned, flicked my eyes towards the flames licking over the wing to the left of me, and regained my seat. I had to find somewhere to land the plane.

The aircraft flew lower, less cloud now, more factories and houses, more houses and factories. A curl of dust rose above the floor near the hole through which my boys had gone. I watched a cyclist ride away from the gates of a factory; he looked so casual, so different from the feeling of jeopardy that gripped me as the plane came lower.

In the distance, amongst the houses, I saw a green area. Hope came; I had a place to head for. The plane sank lower. The field drew nearer. Hope turned to despair! Heavy power lines stretched across the area of green. A smaller area appeared to my right, away from the power lines. Hope again! I turned the plane low over the tops of houses and down into a small valley.

Down, down, down, I sank. Would the plane finish up amongst the houses surrounding the valley. I lifted the nose of the Halifax to miss a road. I felt so peaceful. What would death be like?

The plane crossed a road, hit overhead cables, then exploded through a stone fence. Noise and flames were all around me. On and on, bumping, ripping, tearing, "This thing isn't going to stop," I thought. Trees and houses rushed towards me. I braced myself. It was the end!

The Halifax did stop; or all that was left of it did, and I was alive. Flames roared high.

The pilot's escape hatch lay high above my head. I stood on the pilot's seat and pulled the release, but no movement came. I pulled the release more strongly, still no movement. The whole aircraft seemed engulfed by flames. The fury of them did much to strengthen my struggling hands. Giving an almighty heave on the release handle, the hatch came away. I climbed to the top of the cabin and jumped. Twelve feet down, I hit the ground. Pain shot up my back. Someone led me up a steep slope. The noise of the crash still echoed in my head and my back ached horribly. "Where am I?" "You've just come over the Leeds to Bradford road and landed in Devils Glen," said a Yorkshire voice.

Devils Glen! People appeared from houses all around. I sensed danger, for the petrol tanks were due to explode. "Get back! Get back!" I shouted, trying to make them hear above the noise of exploding bullets from the gunners' turrets.

CAN I HAVE THE TAIL

The Yorkshireman standing near me kept emphasising, "Eeh, you did a foin landin'. I'm glad I could be of some 'elp." I tried to respond, but my mind remained on the expected explosion. He asked, "Eeh, will you be alright now? I must go. My wife's 'avin' a baby." Another voice said, "I'll stick by him, you go." I looked to see a tall man with kindly face, "I'm Herb Umpleby." he said, "I saw your plane coming in."

Before I could speak, a small voice pleaded, "Say mister, can I have the tail?" A cheeky faced ten year old gazed up at me. The tail, the boy had said? My eyes searched along the length of the burning Halifax and I found myself thinking, "Where is the bloody tail?"

Downwards from the burning and then out across the valley, my eyes searched. Then I saw it, lying broken and alone, the large tail jagged and torn still had its gun turret. It must have weighed several tons and the boy wanted it.

"That tail is too big for you!" I said bending down to look the boy in the face. Pain wrenched my body as I did so. I pressed my hand around my back to help myself.

A clanging fire bell announced the fire brigade. In a moment, a uniformed fire chief walked into the arena formed by people gazing at the burning Halifax. "Anybody else on board?" he asked quietly. "No." "Any bombs on board?" "No." My anxiety about the crowds of people getting too close, showed as I said brusquely, "You must get those people back. The petrol tanks are due to explode!" "Leave it to me!" That was all. Firemen rolled out their hoses.

"Could I get some details from you sir?" I looked around to see a police sergeant with open note book. He waited expectantly. "Details," the word seemed to echo in my mind as I thought back to the events preceding my crash. I felt rotten. I just wanted to lie in a hot bath and rest my aching back. "Can I do something for you sir, you look done in?" The police sergeant asked. "Yes, I'd like a hot bath." My request must have seemed ludicrous from the middle of a plane crash, but the law was unruffled, "Let's go back to the station sir and we'll see what we can do." I nodded.

Crowds increased. The Boxing Day holiday gave factory workers a free day and they would not be able to view a burning Halifax every day. Black smoke drew them from miles around. The man called Herb said quickly, "I'll drive you to the police station." He and the sergeant led me to a car. Herb explained that he managed a local factory, and I could travel with him in the firm's car. I entered the vehicle conscious of stares from a myriad of eyes that made up the crowd.

The Police Station had a tall steep roof and the sergeant assured me that under the roof, on the third floor, they had a bathroom. The police sergeant's wife prepared my bath while I answered routine questions. Then at last I was free. I slowly mounted the stairs as the sergeant phoned the Marston Moor air base. Marston Moor seemed to be part of another world. The sergeant's voice faded into faint echoes.

A bath of hot water! It felt luxurious, a balm to my aching body. "Hullo!" A round faced man appeared at the door and came into the bathroom, "I'm a doctor." He handed me a tall glass filled with fluid. "Drink it down, it'll do you good." It was whisky and it was a welcome offering. He said, "I'm here to check you over, how are you feeling?" I handed him the now half empty glass and clambered slowly to a standing position. "I'm sore."

The wet nude Australian pilot took the whisky again and the doctor began his examination. "You'll need to get that back seen to when you return to your base; you've got a nasty bruise there, it looks quite deep." I gave him brief answers as I sipped at the huge glass of fluid. Eventually he took the now empty glass, and I returned to the warm water. His cheery voice and retreating footsteps echoed down the narrow stairway.

The alcohol was sedating me. I began to laugh at the unique way I was spending Boxing Day in England. Herb appeared at the door. "How are you getting on Tom?" I told him about the whisky and the doctor's report.

Encouraged by his care, I told him I felt guilty about having asked for a hot bath in the midst of wartime coal rationing. Herb was vehement. "Tom, these people feel they can't do enough for you. Enjoy your bath; you've earned it." In measured Yorkshire tones he queried, "How many crew members did you have on board? The police say they've picked up four of your boys." "There should be six, Herb. I hope they're OK, can you let me know when the others turn up?" "I'm sure they'll turn up. Don't worry, I'll let you know." Herb said, then added, "I want you to come home with me when you are ready and we'll have a bite to eat. Take your time." With those words, he disappeared down the stairs.

Now well anaesthetised by the whisky, I felt relaxed. The police sergeant came with the news that a number of police stations had phoned in to report the safety of my boys. All were awaiting transport.

I joined Herb driving to his home, high up on the hill. Night had come. He described how he had seen my plane in trouble as I turned near his house to crash in the valley. "Devils Glen," he informed me wryly.

Mrs Umpleby welcomed me, and ushered me to the table prepared for an evening meal. A six year old daughter eyed me off as I sat in the appointed chair. I smiled, and she ran to find the security of her mother, but still her eyes remained fixed on me.

A tasty meal proceeded with conversation about the afternoon's events. Afterwards, Herb and I walked a few doors along the road to the Hunsworth Pub. It seemed that everyone there had intentions of buying "their Aussie" a drink so that I could tell the story of the crash. Beer after beer came my way.

REUNION

Late in the evening an RAF vehicle arrived from Marston Moor. With my back very stiff now, Herb Umpleby helped me out of the warm atmosphere and into the cold December night to meet the RAF lass who had already collected the rest of my crew. Being reunited with the six fellows gave us exciting moments together. "However did you survive?" they chorused as they recounted the police version of the crash.

The lass stood back observing our reunion, then quietly asked if we could get going because we had a long night drive ahead. Headlights on vehicles in wartime Britain showed minimal light; night driving became a slow business, and would be especially slow through the nearby city of Leeds. The driver eased me into a comfortable seat and off we went.

ED'S ADVENTURE

The fellows had become uncharacteristically quiet, still shocked by the suddenness of their parachute jumps. With some prodding, Ed began to share his experience.

Coming down through the clouds on his parachute, Ed saw that he headed for some coking ovens. To avoid the structure, he pulled the lines on one side of the parachute and went floating towards a nearby roadway. A courting couple stood on the roadway, wrapped in each others arms, and were in the way of Ed's feet. "Bloody hell," he had muttered.

The couple did not notice Ed, neither did they see the parachute deposit him well down the slope on the far side of the road. Ed would not share what he heard as he passed over the couple, but he was proud of his memento of the jump: the "D" handle of his parachute release.

DARLING, I'M SURE I HEARD A VOICE SAY "BLOODY HELL"

HOPPY'S JUMP

"What happened to you Hoppy?" different ones asked. Hoppy had been the first out of the Halifax. In carefully enunciated tones, he said, "I recall lifting the escape hatch cover in the passageway behind my seat. I sat on the edge of the gaping hole facing the rear with my parachute clipped on to my chest, my legs dangled in the roaring slipstream. On looking down to the country far beneath me, I thought, `What a lot of nothing lies between me and the ground. I don't recall if I counted to ten or whatever. My harness tightened like a vice, then came peace. I did think I'd clipped on my parachute harness too casually, and now it bore all my weight. I wondered if I'd been too casual."

"I drifted towards a tree. Did I need to curl up, and crash through it? The parachute caught in a branch, and like a giant spring, it broke my fall. I landed just outside a golf course and almost at once a group of golfers surrounded me. Shaking my hand, one said he was a parachutist, and had never seen a better landing. He did wonders for my morale."

"At a nearby house, the lady gave a slap up tea, while the twelve year old son kept gazing at me as a superman. Then the police arrived, and I couldn't believe they had disentangled the chute without tearing it; an amazing effort. They took me to Wakefield police station."

THOUGHT TO BE A SPY
These were special moments for each one of us reliving the events of the past nine hours. "Come on Shorty, what about you?" said Ed. I added, "You were the last one out of the Halifax Shorty, giving me the thumbs up and then your grin." Shorty drawled, "Well, I let go of the escape hatch, and I swear I didn't pull the ripcord. I felt a terrific jerk and there I was, the right way up and floating on a parachute. The Hali disappeared into the distance but I didn't see your parachute Tommy, and I felt worried about you. I landed in a paddock and my left leg seemed to be driven up into my body. Then the wind dragged me."

"Finally my parachute collapsed, and I looked up to see a crowd staring down at me. I couldn't understand their lingo, and I guess my Aussie accent didn't help me. They seemed to think I spoke a foreign tongue, and was a spy. Then someone in the crowd said I wasn't an enemy. A little old fellow, well whiskered and well whiskyed, shoved his face into mine, and shouted, 'We'd a shot yer if yer wus a German.`
"

TWO GUNNERS CAME DOWN
Voices carried clearly into the upper air where Smithy floated on his parachute. Village children talked excitedly about the man in the sky, and he heard it all. He landed on a railway line, and was momentarily knocked unconscious. Villagers rescued him, and his only reminder of the incident was a slight bruise and a headache.

Bill Butler's parachute lowered him over electric power cables. The canopy caught for a moment in the wires, and then dropped him. His body felt seared by hot irons, as long stinging nettles penetrated his flesh. He had fallen into a gorse bush, and tried to laugh about it, but it was obviously very painful.

LONG DRIVE HOME

Leeds to Marston Moor seemed an endless drive, but at last, in the early hours of the dark morning, the RAF lass deposited us at the air base hospital. She wished us luck saying, "Considering you have just crashed you are the happiest group of fellows I've met. Thanks for the entertaining drive I've had with you."

A very tired medical officer checked us over. One by one, the fellows went off to bed, and I remained, resting on the white sheets of an examination table. "You seem to have had a gruelling day, I'm glad to check you alive and not as a corpse," he said seriously. "Thanks Doc," I responded, wondering about the compliment. He checked for internal injuries and then warned me about my back. "You'll need to be very careful with that back of yours, you've had a nasty blow. Come back in daylight, and we'll start some treatment."

Thorns in your rear quarters may entitle you to the Purple Heart in the US Air Force but here you get medicine and duty.

DEVILS GLEN AGAIN

During the days that followed, XRays and treatment went on for my back. Bill Butler also attended the hospital, where his daily tally of gorse nettles were extracted from the cheeks of his bottom.

A letter arrived from Herb Umpleby. There were things about my survival in the crash that mystified him, and he invited me to have a holiday in their home so that he could talk about it. In due time I was able to be with Herb's family again. We chatted together, late into the night, well after six year old Margaret went fast asleep in her chair determined to not miss a word that I spoke. Next morning, we walked around Devils Glen and I listened to Herb reconstruct the events of Boxing Day.

I relived the crash as Herb led me through the big gap in the stone wall and continued into the glen. "You hit the ground here and went skidding across the creek, then all the way up the side of Devils Glen towards that row of houses and trees." We walked over rough ground, crossed the water course and moved up the steep side of the glen to the trees, where my skidding plane had stopped.

Herb stood beside the fire blackened earth and pointed to the trees and houses, "Look Tom, you were so near to wiping out all these; it's a miracle you are still alive." Wonderment showed in his face as he tried to drive home the fact that the Halifax had stopped only a little short of death for me. I recalled the moments of approaching death and for a long second I seemed to be in touch with some eternal over-riding power, then my strange awareness faded.

Picking up an electrical fitting from the crashed plane, I walked with him down the rain misted valley back to his car. A question remained in my mind, "Had there been some Eternal Hand operating in my affairs that day?" The question would return to me as the war progressed.

AFTERMATH

After my return from Devils Glen, I penned a letter home, "You will be glad to know that the angels looked after me on Boxing Day." What my family made of the statement, I never heard.

The CO sent a message for me to report to his office with my pilot's log book. He wanted to discuss the crash. I duly entered his austere office, bare floor boards, a desk in the middle of a big room and a hard chair which he indicated was for me.

As I sat, I saw that he had my crash report, and he asked for my log book. Opening it, he grunted, "You've already had one commendation for your flying. Well done." Flicking through the book, he looked up saying, "Did you know that I am to write a commendation about the way you handled that crash?" The CO's words surprised me for I had been feeling bad about having destroyed the Halifax.

He sat back and discussed the performance of the aircraft and my impressions of it after the crash. I assured him that my confidence had not altered. Then he asked, "Have you been told that you and your crew have been selected for a new Pathfinder squadron to be formed shortly in Italy?" "Yes the Wing Commander mentioned it," I replied. "Good, it's all very hush hush you understand, but we want you to be informed about it. You will do your PFF training with Group Captain Don Bennett at Upwood, and I don't want any of this talked around."

He chose a page in my Log Book and wrote in green ink:-

Halifax JB788   26th Dec. 1943.

F/Sgt Scotland, by excellent captaincy avoided casualties to his crew and by making a skilful forced landing instead of himself abandoning the aircraft saved himself and possible damage and casualties to civilians.

By order of Air Officer Commanding 4 Group his log book is hereby endorsed in green for good captaincy.

> *M.V.Delap, Group Captain.*
> *C.O. RAF Marston Moor, Yorkshire.   6-1-44*

THE BATTLE OF MARSTON MOOR

The day came for our last training flight in navigation and bombing. At night, high up in the sky over the Helmsley bombing range, we would observe the techniques of the Pathfinders as they simulated an attack on an enemy target. I looked forward to a rewarding trip.

During the afternoon, Bob Lewis wanted to talk about our selection as a Pathfinder crew. "Tommy it's scary to be asked to join PFF. Are you sure it's what we ought to be doing?" "How about we talk about it Bob? We've got time before our meal. Let's go for a walk." "Aye," replied Bob, "I'd like that."

Walking beside the road to the village of Rufforth, we shared about the future. I explained to Bob my expectations of working with the Path Finder Force (PFF) in Italy. We would train as Pathfinders at Upwood and then fly to the squadron out in Italy. At the same time, Pathfinder instructors from England would go to Italy and give Pathfinder training to selected bomber crews on 462 squadron which had already made a name for itself in North Africa. Out of all these crews, a new squadron would be born, called 614 Pathfinder Squadron.

Engrossed in our talking, I became aware of a cold wind, and tightened my scarf. My gaze lighted on a large monument standing alone in a field of sugar beet. Bob saw it too. We left the road and read its marble inscription. "The Battle of Marston Moor, 1644." It informed us that the ground we walked on, had run with the blood of fallen warriors. Just 300 years before, two opposing armies had fought here, battalions against battalions, units against units, man against man; thousands had suffered and died. The result: democracy was established in England under Oliver Cromwell. We could almost hear the battle, clashing swords, shouting victors and cries of the vanquished.

Bob turned to me, and by the look in his eye I wondered if the Battle of Marston Moor had now become for him, our battle in the air. Was Bob facing his own possible demise? Deeply moved, he said, "Tommy, we go on leave tomorrow. How about coming to Glasgow with me and meet my parents? There's not much time left now and later might be too late." "Sure Bob, I'd love to come!" I said.

Bob explained, "There's a bus leaving the base in the morning." I felt enthusiastic about visiting Scotland and I added, "Hoppy has invited me to spend some time with his folks too. I can drop in on him at Newcastle on the way back from Glasgow. That'll be great!" We retraced our footsteps to the air base. The monument, with its ghosts of 300 years, receded into the distance behind us.

PATHFINDERS SHOW THE WAY

We flew off from Marston's well lit runway into a dark, stormy night. Flying at night in England, had a deep sense of mystery and intrigue for me. We had the weather factors to consider, but also the danger of attack from German night fighter aircraft. On this night, we criss-crossed our way through the British Isles, in a difficult final exercise of navigation, carried along by 100 miles per hour winds, our first encounter with "jet stream" effect in upper air.

We flew in towards the simulated target at Helmsley. The Pathfinders were there right on time before us. Their coloured markers lit up the night sky like showers of red and green rain, then hit the ground, and spread out into a circle of glowing colour. The circle would be an aiming point for bombers over an enemy target. I was spellbound by the display and said, "It won't be long before you are doing this yourself Ed. What do you think of it?" "Ye gods, it's awesome!" said Ed, then added, "The falling colour gives quite a beautiful effect though." I listened to Ed, and thought, "We'll certainly get plenty of colour when those German guns start firing."

I could see that Pathfinder work would be demanding, with concentrated accuracy of flying, navigation, and careful bombing. The challenge stirred my adrenalin and made me feel proud of my team of seven men, drawn from different parts of the world, and now like a family to me. Returning to Marston, our wheels rumbled on the runway in our final landing.

OFF TO GLASGOW

Next morning I did some hasty packing and joined Bob on the double decker bus going to York. The flat Yorkshire countryside spread its winter greyness around us as we swept along the road. At York, the powerful, green locomotive of the London to Edinburgh express pulled in to the long platform. The carriages were warm and cosy and we joined Hoppy and Ed going as far as Newcastle. They explained the places we passed as the countryside rolled by. I was entranced by our view of Durham with its great Cathedral and battlements, high on the hill. Here it was that the Scots and English met in battle long ago. Newcastle came into sight and time to farewell Hoppy and Ed. I looked forward to returning there in two weeks time.

At Edinburgh, the train terminated and Bob and I caught a bus. Enjoying its warm interior, we sat back and gazed over the receding metropolis of Edinburgh, and the gigantic Firth of Forth rail bridge, then headed into Scottish countryside. All seemed sodden and muddied by the icy rains of winter. By nightfall we had arrived at Glasgow. I was in the land of my Scottish forbears. How exciting!

DENISTOUN AND A COOPA TAY

Near the centre of Glasgow, is Denistoun, where Bob's parents lived in a block of flats. His mother met us. A pleasant small boned woman of Bob's height, she showed her joy at meeting someone with whom her son would fly. She soon had us seated and sipping at a "coopa tay".

After the excitement of meeting Mrs Lewis, we set off into winter darkness to find the bar Bob's dad frequented after work. Bob caught sight of his dad walking slowly along the footpath carrying his leather lunch case, and swinging it as he walked. He saw Bob. "Howee Borbie?" "Aright" said Bob then, "Dard I'd like you to meet my pilot from Osstreelya, Tom this is me dard." With greetings over, Lewis senior said, "Wul ya huv a whusky Torm?" All who drank there seemed to be drinking whisky, so we sipped whisky.

Bob's dad, a warm hearted man, worked as a tally clerk in the busy Clyde River shipyards. I discovered that the yards formed a very important part of the Lewis way of life and conversation. Numerous air raids had been aimed at the shipbuilding area, and I was amazed at the casual way these people talked about the German bombers coming over night after night.

Over the meal that night I thanked them for sharing their home with me. Bob's dad responded, "Torm lud we're so glud to meet yue und to harv yue und Borbie home fer a time." A new note entered the conversation when Mr Lewis spoke of Will Fyfe being in town. "Whuully", Scotland's entertainment idol, brought overflow crowds to Glasgow, and Mrs Lewis had tickets for us. The next afternoon Bob and I made our way to see "Whuully". The adulation of the Glasgow audience was overwhelming. They laughed, they cried, they stood to cheer, they bowed in silent reverie. Will Fyfe entertained through many changing emotions, touching heartstrings about Scottish history, its love songs and its pain. Then "Whuully" sang "I love a lassie, a boony heelan lassie, she's as swit as the heththerr on the muuur ..... " The entranced audience rose as one, to cheer to clap and to cry.

At the meal table that night, the enthusiasm of the Scottish audience still rang in our ears, and we recounted the events of the afternoon. Scottish hearts in the Lewis home reverberated afresh with appreciation of their idol.

Bob and I had our photo taken. "Och ya luke foin yue und Borbie," said Mrs Lewis eyeing off the photograph as I walked out the door to catch my bus. "Borbie's torld us a lo' aboot ye. It's bin gud ta huv ye in oor horm." Her last words were of the gladness they felt that their

Borbie could spend these days with them before going to war.

Journeying eastward to Edinburgh, I looked at the rain pouring down on Scottish countryside, and recalled my warm stay in the Lewis home. Bob had introduced me to friends at some fast Scottish dances where I had enjoyed meeting the local lasses. Then there were the shopping sprees and our joking with shop assistant girls as I tried to understand their "burrr", and the wonderful afternoon with Will Fyfe. All had touched something in me of my own Scottish heritage.

AT HOME WITH HOPPY

Arriving at Newcastle on Tyne, I met up with Hoppy. My stay in his Geordie home delighted me. Their language heritage left by Viking invaders from Norway centuries ago, was tantalising, lilting, with distinctive words, foreign to my untrained ear.

On my long walk with Mr Hopper senior, he said, "Tom, how long do you think this war will go on?" I sensed his anxiety about his son. "Well Mr Hopper," I replied, "The German army has been defeated in North Africa. The Allies have landed in Italy, that's an important turning point in the war. Your own Prime Minister said on radio, 'the end is not in sight, neither can we see the beginning of the end, but, we can now see the end of the beginning.'"

Silence remained between us for awhile, then I said, "I really appreciate flying with your son. He's a great navigator." Mr Hopper responded, "Is he indeed, I'm glad to hear you say that Tom. Have you met his young lady?" "Yes," I replied, "He's chosen a lovely girl. Derek and Olive make a fine pair together." They certainly did; he tall, dark haired, serious, and she shorter with flowing blonde tresses and full of fun, I enjoyed seeing them together."

I continued, "I know that we are in for some tough times in our flying, but Derek will tell you that we've already had some emergencies in our plane, and the crew have handled these with excellent teamwork." I sought to comfort Mr Hopper but he knew that war was able to destroy even the best."

One evening I chatted to Olive and said impulsively, "I'll see that Hoppy gets home safely." Olive looked at me gathering in the import of what I said. In her spontaneous way she reached up to me and gave me a warm caring kiss. I loved that but had reason later to wonder at my ability to carry out my promise.

TO JESMOND

Exploring my own father's home at Jesmond in Newcastle on Tyne, I found the big home of Doctor Scotland, and still it was called Windsor Place, although now a part of the University of Newcastle.

Nearby, my father and his brothers had frolicked as boys in Jesmond Dene, where the deep, tree covered valley, carried the river Tyne through Newcastle. I tried to imagine him going off to fight in South Africa, then migrating to manage an Australian cattle station in the isolation of the great outback. I was born when he had become a wheat and sheep farmer and people recognised his ability as a practical vet. We had scant need for a doctor to tend our ills. He sutured us after accidents as well as doing the same for our horses and cows. My reverie about him ended with a sigh. I was conscious of a gap in my life since he had separated from us as a family.

TO UPWOOD AS PATHFINDERS

Returning to Marston Moor, I met Bob Lewis arriving from Glasgow. The holiday had done him good. He looked a much happier person now as we collected our bags, and journeyed southward to the RAF base at Upwood near Cambridge for orientation as Pathfinders. "Since you and I talked about PFF, I have felt so much better at the thought of our being Pathfinders," said Bob. We had been appointed to a PFF squadron whose purpose would be to go ahead of bomber squadrons on attacks from southern Italy into Germany, France, Austria, Hungary, Rumania, Yugoslavia and northern Italy.

9

"GET TO KNOW THE STARS"

Six crews from Marston Moor settled into the Pathfinder base at Upwood east of Cambridge. There to welcome us was Group Captain Don Bennett who had met us on his visit to Marston Moor. An Aussie from Queensland, he had founded PFF as the Pathfinder Force had become known. Small of stature, piercing eyes and a commanding voice, his lectures were more like a chat, but his discussions with us about the dynamics of the war in the air were very powerful. He had been a man of international fame as a pilot, navigator and radio operator and he set us a high standard of training right from the start.

He had been chosen to launch PFF in August 1942, with the goal of finding and marking out targets in German occupied Europe so that crews in heavy laden bombers could drop their bombs more accurately. PFF had developed expertise in leading a bombing force across Europe at night; a difficult task needing close teamwork, precise navigation, and the will to carry on to mark out a target in the face of strong enemy opposition.

Don Bennett spent hours lecturing us and sharing his insights on how to accomplish his expectations of us as Pathfinders operating from Italy. Out of his experience in navigating by the stars, he urged us, "Get to know the heavens, get to know the stars!" We did that and gained kinship with the stars, basic to our navigating across continents.

But PFF orientation was much more than getting to know the stars. We had to be effective in operating new electronic air navigation aids, airborne radar and another code named "Gee". It required hours of airborne experience; interpreting electronic information and reminding ourselves that crews in following aircraft would be depending on our accurate navigation.

Airborne radar had many faults. It could fail at a vital moment. Nevertheless this brilliant invention enabled us to fly above cloud at night and yet gain a picture of the earth below us. The picture on the screen generally gave confusing patterns of green textures that had to be interpreted, but sea shores and edges of lakes were very clear. Cities were like blobs, but on closer inspection we saw that the blobs had shape. We interpreted the shapes from special maps. Later we were able to enlarge the scale and even identify parts of a city.

Ed became adept at making the equipment work despite its faults. Miraculously he turned meaningless fuzz on the screen, into vital map reading points.

H2S, airborne radar had been invented in an exciting break through by British scientists in 1942. H2S was a shortened version of the words "Home Sweet Home". It would help night flying crews to guide their aircraft home. H2S also identified the scientific lettering for a gas emitted by rotting vegetation. So H2S became the confusing code name selected by the inventors to trick the enemy.

TARGET INDICATORS (TIs)

An important tool for Pathfinders, was the Target Indicator, the TI. The TI was a large container built in a bomb shape to give an accurate fall from the aircraft. A built-in barometer exploded the fuse at 3,000 feet above the earth so that the pyrotechnics would fall like rain on to the target below. The following bombers identified the target by the TI's falling into a pool of colour on the ground.

While at Upwood, a Lancaster returning from an attack on a target in Europe, exploded while losing height in preparation for landing. Some undetonated TIs remained in the bomb bay, causing this tragedy. When they exploded, the Lancaster and all its crew were destroyed. Don Bennett took up this matter of the exploding TIs, and applied it to the dangers of our taking a plane in too low to bomb a target. Later I recalled his warnings in my temptation to dive too low over an enemy target, with TIs in our bomb bay.

NEWMARKET RACE COURSE

Because Upwood had its own full flying programme, we flew our aircraft from land adjacent to the Newmarket race course, one of the top horse racing venues in England. On a popular race day, the war seemed to stop. Our Halifax became one of a variety of planes circling to watch an exciting race of the Newmarket Calendar. With eyes glued to binoculars we encouraged the horses as they raced around the Newmarket course. Our aircraft were either Halifaxes, Stirlings or Lancasters. We enjoyed the variety and also the relaxed living that our PFF training offered. The six crews became close buddies, comparing results and encouraging one another.

On February 8th 1944, we took delivery of a new Halifax and prepared to join our squadron in Italy. My whole crew went to work checking the new aircraft, its compasses, radar, radio, guns, and bomb switches. Bob Lewis and I gave special attention to the instrument calibrations of our fuel tanks and motors. It meant hours in the air and hours of ground work.

Finally, we flew our aircraft to the Hurn air base, near Bournemouth. Loading it with fuel and spare parts for our squadron, we made ready for our flight to Italy via the Bay of Biscay and Africa.

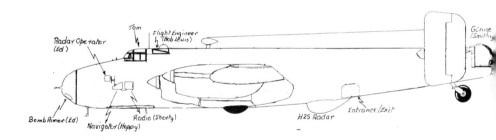

TO AFRICA WITH THE STARS

With the goal of reaching Africa in the morning, we flew off on a dark, cold, windy night. Secrecy surrounded our time of take off due to German fighters patrolling the Bay of Biscay near Spain. We flew out over Bournemouth now just a blacked out city below us. I gazed with appreciation on the town — my first home in England. Nearby, Barton on Sea had given me the Newman family where Jim Mudie, Lindsay Fairclough and I had received warm family hospitality while on leave. I whispered my farewells to people I had come to love, and turned the nose of the Halifax towards Africa. It was 1.00am.

At fifteen thousand feet, with the shores of England disappearing behind us, I switched in "george", our automatic pilot. We had a long trip ahead, and I needed all available eyes to scan the sky for enemy aircraft patrols. German Junkers 88 long range fighters had been successful in intercepting some of the British aircraft flying south from England and we did not intend being another shot down statistic for them on this night.

Gazing from my pilot's position on the flight deck, I noticed an ethereal beauty about us beneath a cloudless, star filled sky. Such beauty gave me a sense of awe, a feeling of affinity with creation. Group Captain Don Bennett had urged us at Upwood, "Get to know the stars." So the past six weeks had seen me studying star positions in the sky and their attributes for navigation. I now warmed to their presence and welcomed them as friendly fellow travellers across the canopy of space.

We had been flying for two hours when Smithy jolted me, "Aircraft approaching from astern, a long way from us yet, at about ten o'clock high, hold steady!" Was this the enemy? We were far from possibility of rescue if shot down over the Bay. Smithy kept to his patter about the aircraft, "He's still coming in," he called. It went on until I chipped in, "Smithy, I'm taking a look!" With that I swung the Halifax round in a tight turn, its great wings silhouetted against the sky. I fully expected to run headlong into an attack, but Smithy's aircraft was a star. The motion of our long flight, had given him the impression of a fast moving aircraft coming in. The event helped us all become aware of strain on Smithy's eyes in long hours of watching from the cramped gun turret.

Had I imagined it? Some strange movement in the flying pattern of our Halifax alerted me, "Yes, there it goes again!" Some fault in "george". At irregular intervals, he waggled the controls. I checked and rechecked but could not discover what his antics were about.

Then "george" went wild. He had the Halifax diving towards the sea, and in a moment he changed and had the plane flying steeply towards the stars. I had a fight on my hands. Eventually, sweating hard,

I regained control, cursing in the realisation that for the rest of our flight to Italy I would be flying the Halifax manually.

We flew on into coming morning and increasing light. Cape Saint Vincent, the most southerly point of Portugal, lay below. Here, the Atlantic Ocean began curving in to meet the Straits of Gibraltar. In this area, two hundred years before, Lord Nelson had helped to lead the British Navy to victory over the Spanish Fleet in what history calls the Battle of Cape Saint Vincent. I wondered what it was like to be living in a neutral Portugal not involved in war.

Exercising tired limbs, I saw we had been in the air for five and a half hours; another two before refuelling at an RAF/US base on the west coast of Africa. At last a coastal strip came into sight. It showed signs of green, fairly flat with creamy brown beaches, but not much sign of habitation. Southwards lay our first stop, Rabat Sale in Morocco.

Hoppy called, "Rabat Sale should be coming up in five minutes time." "Thanks Hoppy," I replied feeling glad at the thought of being on the ground again. But below us was sheer desert; not a patch of green appeared anywhere. Then shimmering in the distance I caught sight of the runway. "It's a huge runway," I called to my crew. Air traffic from America landed here with troops and materials for the Mediterranean area.

The wheels of the Halifax skimmed the runway surface and a loud rattle ensued. The noise came from the long steel interlock sections, laid down over desert soil. The more the runway took our weight, the louder grew the rattling and clanging of interlocked metal strips. It sounded like our Halifax falling apart. We slowed and the noise grew less. At the end of our run, the noise ceased. I turned the plane on to a taxiway and noticed some steel sections turned up at the ends. They could slice into an unwary pilot's tyres and I made a mental note to check our tyres carefully.

With the Halifax parked, the heat of Morocco became oppressive. Our overnight flight to Africa showed me that England had softened my Australian toughness for hot conditions. I looked at my watch. It was still some time before nine o'clock in the morning. So I did not dare think of what the midday heat would be. I wondered how the rest of the crew were coping. All were weary, and looking forward to sleep.

Arranging for refuelling and a thorough check of our tyres, I enquired about repairs for our automatic pilot. "We can't look at it until tomorrow," the engineering officer told me. I decided that Rabat Sale would not be a good place to wait for repairs. Smithy gave a call, "Here it comes." A vehicle had arrived to transport us to our quarters.

Arab men provided us with a meal and then one fellow led us to our sleeping quarters. Arab chatter and Moroccan desert conditions were all around us. I lay on the bed resenting the heat and dust, and regretted having left England.

ALGIERS

Next day, we flew off from the long steel mesh runway at Rabat Sale. Flying the Halifax eastward towards Algeria, we gained a good view of the Sahara Atlas Mountains to the south. To the north of us lay the Maritime Atlas mountains and the Mediterranean Sea. We flew between great ranges of mountains and over the Plateau of Shotts and the Hauts Plateau. Our altimeter read six thousand feet above sea level, yet at times the plateau rose up to meet us and we raced along close to grasses and small trees, thrilled at our sense of speed down low on the plain.

No sign of life appeared on the plains until straight ahead I saw them, ten or eleven large but lowly slung tents all clustered together. There was a boy, a shepherd to a herd of goats. Our four engined Halifax bearing down on this lonely, isolated group, must have been a fearsome sight for the lad. Grabbing a sling from his side, he twirled it about his head. He now stood between us and his herd, a defender to the last. My eyes were transfixed on the twirling sling going faster and faster. An object sped towards us, and I waited for it to hit.

By Allah I must have hit
it, it did not take any
of my sheep or goats

Shorty stood near me watching the boy. He ducked his head momentarily saying, "He missed!" I hoped he was right. "Ed, did you see if that stone might have hit us?" I called. "No," replied Ed, "I don't think it did." "Well you are in the best position to judge" I replied, then added, "I will just check with the other fellows." I called Bob Lewis in the mid plane area and Smithy in the tail turret. Neither had felt or seen anything.

I chuckled, "We've just been under enemy gunfire on the Hauts Plateau, think of that!" The humour of the situation had me chuckling for some time after we had passed the shepherd boy. I pictured his excitement as perhaps right at this moment, he was telling his elders about his close encounter with a roaring beast out of space.

Ahead of us we saw a tall pinnacle of rock, several hundreds of feet in height rising out of the plateau. A giant pillar, it must have remained through timeless centuries of erosion that this area had experienced. We flew lower than its tip and admired its resistance to destructive elements of wind, water and blowing sand. Rocky cliffs appeared and I climbed the Halifax to a greater height to clear them.

Eventually the Hauts Plateau fell away below, a track crossed a dry river bed, a more defined road stretched into the distance, then the green of agriculture brought us to a large coastal development. Distant white buildings gleamed in the sunlight, Algiers! The city stood out against a backdrop of Mediterranean blue. While we circled the city, the control tower at nearby Maison Blanche Airport gave landing instructions. My ear phones rattled with radio calls from numerous other aircraft flying in and out from this busy centre for air traffic across the Mediterranean.

ONWARDS TO ITALY

Next day, heading eastward from Algiers, we flew over Tunis and the mountainous Cape Bon. For me, recent events came alive as I pictured Allied armies battling German forces along this coastline. The war had moved from here, up through Sicily and now the battles raged in Italy. Thoughts about the battles touched me and I struggled with the grim picture of men killing each other, and I could not determine what the killing would produce in the end.

Turning out over the azure blue of the Mediterranean, I headed our plane towards Sicily. The very name excited me. Well out into the ocean, we flew over the island of Pantalaria recently captured from its German defenders. I gazed down on an expanse of island, then "Whooooomph". Something exploded within our aircraft. I thought, "Oh no, the bastards are shooting at us!" Then I remembered that the battle for Pantalaria had been won. Something else must have happened within the aircraft to cause the explosion.

"Calling all crew members, search your part of the aircraft for damage," I called urgently, and at the same time I gazed out of the pilots windows for any damage to our wings. One by one the crew reported their area of aircraft undamaged. Ed, in nose position had turned his face to search across the underside of one of the Halifax wings and then the other. He called, "Ye gods! It looks like the starboard tyre has burst, there are bits of it hanging below the wing."

Looking out the starboard observation window, I recognised the truth of Ed's report. My thoughts went to Rabat in Morocco, where the interlocking steel mesh strips had made such a noise when we landed. I had been concerned over some steel strips, bent up and jagged and what they could have done to our tyres. The tyres on the Halifax were six feet high. To land with a burst tyre meant that we faced a hazardous arrival in Sicily.

Hoppy, Ed, Shorty and I discussed our dilemma and decided that Shorty should radio Catania in Sicily and advise of our problem. Catania control replied, "We will have tenders standing by for your emergency. Call again later for landing instructions." The message sounded so casual, too casual for my feelings of apprehension.

Two more hours of flying brought us over Catania. Heavy clouds gave sign of approaching storm. A voice from the control tower said, "Land on Runway 010, call again when making your final approach." I asked Bob Lewis to close cooling vents on our motors ready for landing, and then join the fellows in crash positions where Ed remained in communication with me.

CATANIA

On our final approach to the runway I called up the Catania tower to advise them I was coming in and at the same time I eyed off a group of waiting fire tenders at the end of the runway. Then a Yankee voice, presumably from an American DC4 transport plane flying near us, said, "Control, that British aircraft still has his trailing aerial extended!" Had Shorty, in the pressure of the moment, omitted to wind in his trailing aerial? If so, nearly three hundred feet of steel aerial cable would be whipping the air behind us. I gave the Halifax full power, climbed into the sky again, and called Ed to let me know if Shorty had wound in his aerial.

My mind went back to an event in Western Australia when a pilot in an Avro Anson had made a mock attack on an army camp. Flying low, his trailing aerial flailed out behind the plane and whipped the head off an unfortunate Australian soldier. I now had visions of our trailing aerial decapitating one of the men on the fire tenders waiting for us on the end of the runway.

I reported to Control about my further circuit of the airfield then noticed the motors were overheating due to closed cooling vents and hot Sicilian conditions. "Oh hell!" I exclaimed to myself remembering that I had asked Bob to close them. I could not reach the vent controls as they were operated by the flight engineer. I was in a dilemma between thoughts for the wellbeing of my crew and thoughts for the wellbeing of our motors. I did not want to get Bob Lewis to come up and operate the vents because that would mean I needed to do another circuit and give us even more delay in landing. The crew had been through enough tension already; we had a war to fight, there would be enough tension for them then. I decided to risk the overheating and get on with the business of landing.

Our motors roared taking our Halifax struggling around the circuit, with wheels and flaps down. Temperature gauges were well into danger level. I breathed, "Come on, just a little further, just a little further, ..."

I kept leaning over to glance through my window at our shattered landing wheel. Every time I looked, I felt confirmed in my plan as to how to hold that wheel off the ground in landing. After what seemed an age, I once more advised Control, "I'm on final approach for landing!" Everything looked OK as we approached the runway. To the fellows in their crash positions, "This is a good approach, hold on, I'm all set for the landing." I hoped we were set for a good landing and believed that my talking to the fellows would help allay their anxiety, for they had been waiting in their crash positions for quite a while.

We flew in over the fire tenders. The runway came up to meet us. The port side wheel touched the surface. It touched smoothly and began to take the weight of the Halifax. I felt encouraged. My work now was to hold up the starboard wing and to not allow the shattered wheel to grab the ground and dig in.

The slower we went the more that disabled wheel wanted to drop on to the runway and the more I gave power to motors on that starboard wing, trying to keep it high off the ground. But the shattered wheel had to touch ground eventually. When it did, something like a giant hand gripped the plane and started to twist it, forcing the Halifax to skid sideways. Tremendous forces drove me against the side of the flight deck.

Then came the sound I had been hoping would never come, an awful "crack", then a rumbling sound. The huge landing gear gave way beneath us and I had a falling sensation. Then came a heavy jarring thump as the full weight of the loaded Halifax hit the ground. We continued to turn in a sideways skid. From deep underneath me somewhere, thudding and banging accompanied our slewing and spinning motion. Then flames flashed along the wings as ruptured fuel lines spewed fuel.

My thoughts leapt to the escape I had made from the flaming Halifax at Leeds several months before. Was I now in a sad repeat? The noise ceased, petrol fed flames leaped high, the plane became motionless.

Out of the corner of my eye, I saw fire tenders, foam, and men moving with hoses amongst a sea of white. They must have followed us as we skidded down the runway. The fire teams surrounded us in foam. Flames disappeared. Only an ominous spiral of smoke rose from the ocean of white. Quietness reigned. We had arrived.

Someone emerged through the escape hatch on top of the aircraft. I heard Hoppy shout, "All there is, is a bit of smoke. What an arrival!" Other fellows stomped about making a noise in the rear of the plane, and I knew then they were at least able to move.

I climbed slowly out of my escape hatch and sat on top of the plane. One by one my other crew members emerged through their escape hatch. They were all there, sore and shaken, but alive. Our skid had taken us well clear of the runway. At least the Halifax would not be a hazard preventing the continued operation of the Catania air port. I checked amongst the fellows and found many bruises but no broken bones. Hoppy chortled, "Shot at in Morocco and now shot down in Sicily. We've really been in the wars Tommy."

WELL, IT HAD WHEELS WHEN I TOUCHED DOWN.

An RAF ambulance awaited us. The driver was very solicitous about our bruises and urged us to take it easy until we had rested up a bit. He gave me time to collect a few things and then drove me across the airfield towards the Administration block to make a report. The remainder of my fellows loaded themselves and their goods on to a second RAF vehicle.

At the wreckage of a large hangar, my eyes lighted on the unmistakeable burnt out remains of a German Stuka dive bomber. Behind it were heaped up spars and wires of other wrecked German planes. Not long ago, the German Air Force had operated out of Catania.

The administration officer met me and gave me a chair and table for writing my report. I felt stiff with pain down my back and left side and I sat to rest and tried to write a sensible report. I was responsible for our freight getting to the squadron in Italy and signing over the papers to the Commanding Officer. I urged him to arrange its early despatch northwards. With the paper work completed, the ambulance took me to a US Army hospital where a doctor checked over me. I was bruised. My back troubled me but he thought I would be right within a week or so. Finally I was deposited at an RAF hotel in the main street of Catania where the rest of my crew had already settled in. We had ten days of freedom in which to recover from our ordeal.

Next morning, feeling sore and tired, we began to explore the city. A few months previously, warring armies had rolled through here and left behind shell craters, rusting tanks and personnel carriers. We took advantage of the warm mornings to relax on seats and view the people of this interesting city. The winking eyes of prostitutes passing by gave us something to talk about. But high in the distance beyond Catania, the snow capped slopes of Mount Etna beckoned.

Catania, rich contrast to the harsh austerity of wartime England, was colourful, abounding in the products of a Mediterranean climate. From time to time, I journeyed to the airport. Our broken Halifax looked a sad spectacle out on the airfield and I fretted about our misfortune in having to leave it there. I urged the RAF administrator to get us a flight to Italy, but instead, in his wisdom, he arranged for us to have five wonderful days on Mount Etna. At the Albergo Etna, caring staff helped our restoration through daily activities out on the snow fields. I loved being there. When the RAF finally phoned to say we had a flight to Italy, I vowed one day to return to this haven amongst the clouds.

ONWARDS TO ITALY

We bade farewell to Sicily, and two and a half hours later the plane landed on the main aerodrome at a town called Foggia, in southern Italy. This historical market town, centre for agriculture on the Foggia Plain, showed signs of being recently recaptured from the German Army. Destroyed buildings and wrecked tanks still lay where they had been halted.

A vehicle drove on to the tarmac. The driver would take us out from Foggia towards the east coast, where our squadron's Halifaxes were located. It was one of the many airfields being hastily constructed for the air offensive against Germany.

Rolls of thunder came in from the north. The persistent noise had to be gunfire. Not far away was the battlefront, where the ebb and flow of battle raised its thunder and then died down. It frightened me to picture this battle of the nations, Allied and German Armies meeting head on in desperate struggle, something I was soon to experience personally.

We bumped through flat plain country along a rough road eastwards, then our vehicle slopped along a boggy track towards an array of tents. Behind us, some distance beyond a line of trees, I caught sight of the proud nose of a Halifax. We had come to the end of our journey.

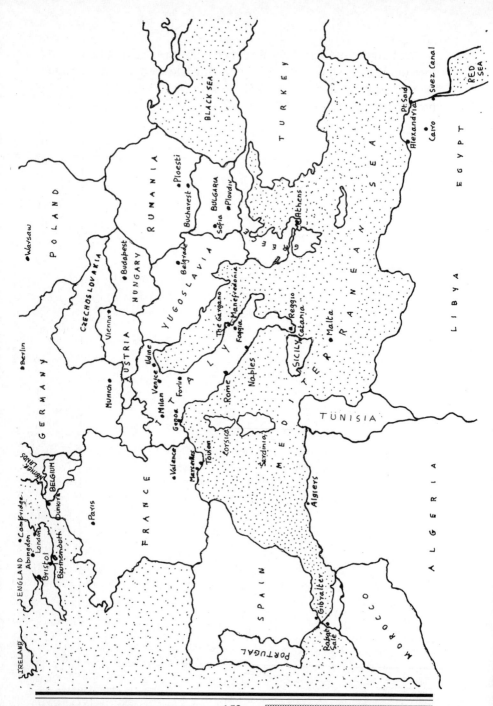

10

UNDER THE SHADOW OF GARGARNO

The RAF vehicle drove off the Foggia to Manefredonia road, sloshed along a boggy track, and stopped beside a large marquee. We had arrived at the squadron administration office. I reported to the adjutant, a cheeky faced flight lieutenant, and he made us feel welcome, but he thought my crew and I had been killed in a crash in the mountains of Sicily. This was surprising news. Obviously our crash landing at Catania had been misreported. Then he greeted our surviving presence with the words, "You'll find plenty of tent accommodation because we've just lost four crews on an attack into Bulgaria!"

He explained that this Halifax bomber squadron we were joining had not long ago flown to Italy after being in action in North Africa. Its role was changing to that of PFF, the Path Finder Force in Italy, 614 Squadron. We crews from Upwood PFF base in England would join with selected crews from North Africa and help to get the new squadron up to strength. More crews were expected to flow through from England. He pointed out that integration would need time and patience, while the North African crews underwent the Pathfinder training we had already experienced.

He smiled and added, "Best of luck, I'm glad you made it. Go and find yourselves some tents and I'll see you later." He returned to his marquee. I surveyed the city of tents, and saw that we would live amongst the olive groves of an Italian farmer. I met Ed enjoying a good joke with himself. He had met the CO. By accident he went into the officer's latrine, and there was the CO.

DAMN IT MAN, YOU DON'T HAVE TO SALUTE IN HERE!

An Australian pilot called Tony Wheeler introduced himself, and offered me a bed in his tent. Tony explained that he had flown on ops from North Africa, but now he and his crew were doing intensive Pathfinder training under the direction of instructors from England. Lunch time had come so he and I walked to the eating place in a large marquee.

We arrived as the BBC midday news from London hushed the men grouped around their tables. My crew had a seat for me and as I sat I noticed the relaxed and casual way the meal was getting going. I liked that. The news included encouraging reports on the battle for Monte Cassino but that fighting on the battle front to the north of us was very intense. As the news ceased, we began our meal. Spam (compressed ham), powdered egg, powdered potato had one redeeming feature, broccoli. A sweetened rice dish followed; not a very appetising meal, but filling.

After lunch, Tony took me out to explore the squadron. The RAF and the US shared the one base, and I saw British Halifaxes standing high amidst American four engine Liberators and Fortresses with single engine Thunderbolt and Mustang fighters among the aircraft parked across the airfield.

The area crawled with the movement of bulldozers, graders, rollers and trucks amongst the many aircraft. The natural Italian soil was full of fine dust, so the pressure was on to build runways, parking bays and taxiways to help protect aircraft from the destructive, dusty conditions. The situation looked chaotic with activity.

Tony and I returned to our tent and before long, Bob Lewis came, "Tom, I've found some soccer players amongst the flyers. They want me to play in a match against a neighbouring squadron team. Is that alright with you?" "Sure thing Bob, that's OK, but remember we are here to fly. I want you fit, without broken bones." "Aye," said Bob.

614 SQUADRON

With the change to become 614 (PFF) Squadron, all the crews concentrated on a Pathfinder training programme. Navigation trips around southern Italy helped to familiarise our crew with Italian conditions and we had more time to perfect our Pathfinder methods and strategy.

Sports and relaxation became a priority in our non flying times. Tony and I made a quoits court between the olive trees and arranged dusty, energetic team games with our crews. I discovered another Australian pilot, Jerry Atwell, and often made myself comfortable on the floor of his tent with his crew spread-eagled around chatting. At 27, Jerry delighted us with nostalgic tales of Australia and his love for the girl in the steel town of Port Kembla in New south Wales.

Action came. 614 Squadron took to the skies in its first attack in its new Pathfinder role. We were briefed for an attack on Hungary. Take off came in early evening and Jerry's Halifax took off just ahead of our own. A slight ruffle of the air came from his slipstream as we followed him into the sky and other Halifaxes followed. We climbed for height and headed towards Hungary.

Beyond a normal apprehension in my stomach, I worried about the huge weather front across the route ahead. Intense lightning flashes issued from the bowels of one hell of a weather front over Yugoslav mountains. I said to myself, "There's going to be heavy icing to contend with in that storm. Oh for a bit more power to get over the thing!" But I knew with our load of fuel, bombs, flares and target indicators, our heavily laden Halifax had no hope of climbing high enough.

Clouds thickened, vicious air currents tossed our plane like a bouncing ball. Our wings flexed upwards and then downwards. Ice formed in layers over the plane's outstretched wings.

We had been flying for over an hour in conditions that I did not like one bit. Shorty's voice came through on my headphones, "Skipper, I think we've got a recall to base." A recall seemed most unusual with so many planes in the air heading out to attack an enemy target.

Shorty came on again, "The signal is very distorted, I can just make out the message. Hang on, I'll check it again." I waited. Shorty spoke again, "It's a rough signal skipper, but it seems like a recall, the static is so heavy that it's difficult to confirm it. Do you think the enemy may be trying to trick us? I could try to verify the call if you want me to." To break radio silence meant a serious breach in security for the bomber force. "Sure Shorty, verify the call please." Again I waited, and worried, for our heavily laden plane was being tossed quite dangerously.

Shorty called, "Radio distortion is worse skipper, but base radio verified our call, they want us to return to base!" "Thanks Shorty." I was mystified yet relieved at the opportunity to alter course away from the storm.

Lifting the bumping and juddering wings of the Halifax into a turn, I told the crew of our recall, and we had to jettison our bomb load. Landing safely would be impossible with such a load. I opened the big bomb bay doors and Ed let the load go into the sea. Hoppy gave me the new course to steer, and I noted relief in his voice. We had all been handling a lot of tension.

Landing on the lighted runway, I let the Halifax come to the end of its run, turned off on to the perimeter taxi way and parked our plane on the dusty parking bay. Fine dust filled the air. Crew members shut down the various parts of the aircraft facilities for which they were responsible, and we made our way out into the open air. On chatting to the ground crew sergeant, we learnt that all the other aircraft were down except one, Jerry Atwell.

A transport vehicle arrived but I continued to wait for Jerry. We gazed across the aerodrome to where the lights of the runway twinkled and hoped that in the distance we may catch sight of red and green wing tip lights of Jerry's plane. "Where are you Jerry?" The night sky remained clouded and silent. Finally we could delay no longer. The transport returned us to the mess tent, where stewards waited to give us our coveted eggs and bacon breakfast.

The boys were full of praise, commending Shorty on deciphering the signals amidst the terrible radio conditions. Shorty had difficulty as usual accepting acclaim. "I should have acted on that recall signal the first time," he said, "I should not have asked them to verify it." He continued to rebuke himself until I had enough of his self effacement. "We were much further into the storm than other aircraft Shorty, you did well to get the signal." "Thanks Tommy."

Jerry's plane did not return. No trace of it was ever found. The bodies of he and his crew rested in some unmarked grave, somewhere. There were no farewells, only a cold hard sky offering silent reminder, "This is war!"

VERY PERSONAL

Our second air operation soon came. We flew northwards to attack a build up of supplies of German armaments. Our target was the railway marshalling yards of the city of Parma, a compact city of 130,000 people in northern Italy. We flew through the darkness with Ed guiding me into the target on his H2S radar. We came in over the large railway facility, and dropped the first lighted flares that hung in the sky on parachutes. Other lighted flares followed, and the city became clearly visible for our second wave Pathfinder aircraft. Their target indicators put a pool of red light across the railway yards. Following bomber aircraft rocked the railway yards with high explosives. The tactics of the Pathfinders had caught the defenders napping, and we made our attack before the defences awoke to what we were doing. At first it seemed easy, but then the guns opened up and centred on my plane. It felt like the enemy having a vendetta against me as a person. Anger arose within me. The war had become very very personal.

GENOA

Our third attack took us to Genoa on the west coast of northern Italy. The Genoa wharves were laden with war materials destined for the battle front.

We came in from the south at 17,000 feet with the time twenty six minutes past midnight. Ahead of us we saw Pathfinder flares lighting up Genoa like day. We could see where Mount Elbe fell steeply from the north towards Genoa, and wharves built into precipitous hillsides stretched out around the bay. German gun batteries poised on the high ground above the wharves were waiting. When their venom spat at us, heavy explosions reverberated through our Halifax. Then the gunners found our range. My stomach tightened with the shock of each exploding shell. Minutes ticked by. Nearer and nearer the target we flew.

Ed Riley, lying flat on his face in the nose of our plane, guided me towards the wharves. "Left left" he called, then "R..i..g..h..t, steady, steady, steady," An age passed as Ed held me with the words, "steady, steady," then at last came, "Bombs gone!" For the next one and a half minutes I continued to keep the Halifax steady, waiting for our camera to take a photograph of the target.

The camera flash went off, but so did some very close explosions from the shell fire that had continued to batter us right over the target. The Halifax lifted. Shell pieces hit one of our motors and other fragments of shrapnel hit cables leading to our electronic equipment. Bob's voice sounded anxious, "Skipper we've got trouble with our port outer motor. I think we'll have to shut it down!" We certainly did have trouble. The motor's instruments went wild. "Here we go engineer," I called as I shut off the motor and feathered the propeller to stop it rotating. The journey home would be on three motors, and I hoped they remained undamaged.

Turning the Halifax away from the harbour, I had some planning to do. We had three and a half hours flying ahead of us. Some high mountains lay across our path, and the weather was deteriorating.

"The H2S has gone on the blink" called Ed. "OK Ed" I responded, "Do what you can to try and restore it. I think we'll need it with this weather closing in like it is." "There's just no power coming to it at all. It's had it!" said Ed disgustedly, little realising that the guns of Genoa had done their work. Our homeward route lay southward from Genoa and I nursed the Halifax along as we flew into intensifying clouds and lowering temperatures. After a long one and a half hours, Hoppy gave change of course eastward to cross the Marchiagarno Mountains.

ICE ON THE WINGS

We now flew through extremely bumpy air. Our wings flipflapped from the effect of the updraughts and downdraughts Then came the icing. It began as a white coating on our wings. Later, banging noises on the fuselage indicated ice being flung off heavily iced propeller blades. Ominous juddering followed. It began at the front of the plane and built up along the aircraft body as the ice overloaded the propellers and shuddered the whole aircraft. Ice was flung off the propellers and then the build up recommenced.

"Engineer" I called, "Use your Aldis lamp. Check the wings for how much the ice has built up!" Movement came from behind me as Bob grasped his Aldis signalling lamp and pointed the beam along the length of the wings. Ice formed very quickly once the air temperature and cloud formation was right. "There's a layer of white ice over our wings and more right along our leading edge," Bob called. "OK, thanks," I responded conscious of the ice now becoming dangerous.

To get out of the icing, we needed to change our height. I could not get the ice laden Halifax to climb higher on three motors and I could not take the plane lower because of the mountains. We had to maintain our present altitude and hope that we would keep flying.

Would there be some sort of warning before the wings received too much ice and I started to lose control of the plane? The question focused my mind on emergency action as the heavy juddering increased. A giant drummer seemed to be playing his sticks along the whole length of the fuselage. Was this my final warning? My stomach twisted into a knot. On and on the fierce drumming went, starting at the nose then working towards the tail.

FROZEN OXYGEN MASK

I tried to work out the best time to warn the crew to prepare to bale out. I had visions of them landing in the mountains, where Italian gangs would not have mercy on them.

"Bob, count the thumps per minute of the ice coming off the propeller blades and let me know if the ice is increasing?" I requested. "OK skipper," said Bob.

"There's the same number of ice pieces coming off the propellers as before" called Bob. "Are you sure?" I asked hopefully. "Yes, I've been timing them. It's a steady count" replied Bob. "I've checked the ice forming on the wings too. It doesn't seem to be increasing."

My hopes rose. "Let me know if you detect change." "I'll do that Skipper" called Bob. "How're you going Smithy?" I called to our rear gunner isolated at the back end of our plane, "Bloody cold," replied Smithy. "There's ice forming around my face and oxygen mask." I tried to encourage Smithy, "We'll get down into warmer air once we cross these mountains." "OK" he grunted.

Time ticked by, but still the icing conditions continued unmercifully. "Ice is increasing!" called Bob. "OK" I replied with a sinking feeling inside me. I advanced the power further on our three already straining motors. Our speed did not increase as it should have. Our ice load had become critical, accompanied by unbelievable vibration.

WE MUST DESCEND

I called to Hoppy and Ed, "I'll have to start descending quickly to get out of this ice." "We should be clearing the mountains any time now Skipper," replied Hoppy. I could see the light from Bob's Aldis lamp worriedly skimming across the top of our wings highlighting the deadness of our motor, now whitened by ice, and the deathly white creeping back from the leading edges of our wings. I pushed the nose of our Halifax downward for more speed and hoped there were no mountains in the way. It was speed now, to keep the wings flying, or else ....!

We lost height rapidly. Down, down down we went. "Clouds are thinning out," called Ed. Our air speed increased slowly. The juddering lessened. We were flying into air where the ice began to thaw. Motors that had been running so roughly through the effect of ice on the propellers, picked up their smooth song again. I believed we had come through.

My hands still grasped the control column; fingers were locked in a tight grip. I flexed my hands, massaging my fingers to unwind them, then tried to balance the pain with my ecstatic feelings about our survival. After being in icing conditions for over an hour, I had not thought we would make it.

Hoppy's voice came through, "Here's our new course to steer, one three eight degrees." "One three eight it is," I replied in measured voice and feeling casual now with the dangerous situation resolved. My flight deck seemed invaded by an atmosphere of peace and security, all so unexpected after such feelings of hazard amidst the mountains.

Bob shuffled behind me locking away his Aldis lamp and then began writing his log to record motor and fuel details. He wanted to know what to write about damage to the port outer motor. Ed went aft to open up his H2S and found cables cut and the equipment damaged by shrapnel. He recorded the details so that radar technicians could begin repairs.

At four o'clock in the morning, I heard other aircraft calling for landing instructions. I joined in, informing base that we were damaged. When the control tower officer heard that we were damaged and on three motors he called, "Do you want priority landing? I repeat, do you want priority landing?" I called back, "No priority, we are going OK." Our Halifax continued to fly nicely and I felt so proud of her the way she had brought us through. The nearer we came to base, the clearer became the weather. It all seemed so ordinary now, an anticlimax after what we had been through.

With still ten minutes to base, I felt comforted seeing runway lights shimmering in the distance, and called for final landing instructions. I lowered the wheels and then the flaps. Bob Lewis shone his Aldis lamp on tyres and the edges of the flaps to check for damage, but all seemed in order.

Our wheels at last rumbled onto the runway, and I let the Halifax run until we were at an out of the way spot, where I shut off the motors. It would have been hazardous to risk taxiing the plane further as there could have been further unknown damage. I called for the control tower officer to arrange transport and then joined the crew as, one by one, they gathered their equipment and slowly made their way out of the aircraft.

Bob and I took the Aldis lamp and made our way around the plane looking at the flak damage. The Halifax seemed like some great creature that had brought us through an experience of much hazard. Quietly I said, "Thankyou." The transport came and we left our plane faintly silhouetted against an early morning sky.

DEBRIEFING

We walked into the debriefing marquee. Loud comments came from other crews, "Here are the types that didn't want a priority landing!" Debriefing had an atmosphere all of its own, with a quiet hum of voices from crews standing or sitting at tables where intelligence officers wrote details of the attack.

The CO, there to get details of our raid for himself, said, "You had a tough trip then Scotty." I told him of our difficulties over Genoa but that I saw the Pathfinder TIs accurately placed on the target. Hoppy spoke up about our flying through icing and that it had been a tough flight for all the fellows. The CO listened. I appreciated his quiet presence, for when daylight came, he and his deputy officers would be busy again in finalising their planning for 614's next raid. He had chosen to shorten his sleep hours and meet us at this early hour.

One by one the crews completed their interview, and moved off to enjoy the special early morning breakfast reserved for returning crews. I thanked the fellows for tremendous teamwork and headed for my tent. Sunrise showed the encampment beginning to stir. A new day had begun.

Tentmate, Tony Wheeler, mumbled a few words as I came in, then he dozed off again. I undressed, and tried to settle into a cold bed. The noise and drama of the night's raid caused me to relive the terrifying flight. The firmness and security of my bed seemed an impossible dream. The insecurity of the night was my reality. I tossed and turned sleeplessly. When I sat up, it was midday. A wash and shave in a basin of cold water refreshed me, and I dressed in time for lunch.

THE EVER USEFULL FIVE GALLON OIL DRUM

LILY DESERTUS

Ed, Shorty, Bob and Smithy met me as I entered the dining marquee. Ed's eager face shone, "Have you seen our target photo from last night?" I enjoyed the enthusiasm shining out from Ed's twinkling eyes, and guessed that our photo had pleased him. "What's it like Ed?" "Spot on!" said Ed, "Our target markers were spot on and the photo even shows the flashes of some of the guns that were blasting away at us when we were hit." He looked intense now as the other fellows gathered around awaiting my response.

I pictured Ed last night crouching there in the transparent nose of the Halifax and guiding us over the target. "That's terrific," I replied, feeling so proud of them all. "What's our plane look like? How's the damage?" Bob replied, "It doesn't look too bad. They hit that motor alright and there are holes in the H2S. But Tommy you were lucky. Shorty found a shell fragment wedged into the floor right by your seat."

Just then the sound of the BBC news from London rose above the hum of voices across the marquee. Smithy led the way to a vacant table. The BBC newsreader included an account of bomber squadrons from Italy successfully attacking shipping facilities at Genoa. It all sounded so remote and unfeeling; different from the experiences of the crews involved; far removed from our reality of establishing a brand new Pathfinder squadron. After lunch, Ed and I made our way to the airfield.

Already the repairers had dug out pieces of shrapnel. Lofty, the corporal held up one piece; black and shiny, it looked angry and vicious. "Do you want it?" he called. "No Lofty, you can have it." We clambered up the ladder frames around the Halifax and examined the damaged motor that had been iced up and useless. The bomb bay had been damaged, also Ed's H2S, and there was the hole by my seat. Shorty was already the proud owner of that shell fragment. Something in the bomb bay had slowed its deadly passage towards me and damage would take some days to repair.

Ed and I walked on the rough path past other Halifaxes where mechanics laboured. A screaming whistling sound echoed in our ears, then came a "thump" as something hit the ground near us. We walked several paces to the spot and found an empty cartridge shell from an American B17 Flying Fortress overhead. Perhaps a gunner had been clearing his guns. I ruefully surveyed the sky, "We survived last night Ed, but I wonder how long we'll survive here with the Americans raining down their expended cartridges?" "They make it bloody dangerous." he replied.

From now on our attacks concentrated on the oil targets of Europe, particularly in Hungary and Rumania. These attacks were meant to reduce the flow of oil for Germany's war machines, her submarines at sea, her planes in the air and her fast Tiger tanks on the land. The flights were long, more than seven hours, requiring careful navigation, much patience and great alertness. The air space through which we flew was patrolled by enemy fighter aircraft.

KARLOVA

South of the Ploesti and Bucharest oilfields in Rumania, lay the air base of Karlova. Squadrons of highly trained Bulgarian pilots flew German Messerschmitt and Focke Wulfe fighter planes from the Karlova airfield and they were causing grievous losses amongst our RAF and U.S. bombers.

Allied intelligence reported, "Fighter aircraft are regrouping at Karlova. An attack at night in mid June would be most likely to catch the aircraft on the ground."

At ten pm we became airborne and flew eastwards towards Rumania. At two turning points, we dropped flares to assist the navigators of following aircraft. But the further east we flew, the more difficult became Hoppy's own navigation. Flying in cloud, we relied on Ed's H2S radar and Shorty's ability to tune into radio beacons as a check to navigation. The H2S radar gave Ed nothing that he could identify on his charts, and cloud obscured the stars so that we could not take star shots. Shorty tuned in to several distant radio transmitters but the transmissions gave unreliable radio direction.

In preparing for this trip, Ed had marked some small towns on his chart as radar checks. We thought they would show on the H2S screen, but he could not locate them amidst the confusing blur on his screen. We passed over Yugoslavia and Hungary and came into Rumania itself. Karlova lay near the southern border of Rumania and Bulgaria.

The clouds became patchy and Ed left the radar to make his way into the transparent nose of the Halifax. He strained his searching eyes into the darkness, trying to locate points in the faint light on the ground. But no reliable check eventuated, nothing by which he could assist Hoppy to check his navigation. We flew on with me studying my map in the dim light, and keeping an eye out for enemy aircraft.

Ed returned to his radar and called, "I've got a blip here that is quite constant, but I can't identify it." A study of our maps showed that the area of the blip was mountainous. "What villages do you have marked on your map Ed?" I called. "The only ones I can see on the map would be hidden in the valleys" he replied.

A jubilant Ed shouted "Bloody hell, I've found something. Ye gods, it's a blooming mountain." Ed's H2S radar had picked up radar reflections from a mountain peak. Ed checked and rechecked and then called Hoppy, "I can give you a distance and a direction to a mountain peak, are you ready?"

I heard Hoppy breathing heavily as he shuffled his chart and navigation equipment, then his voice came through. "Yes I'm ready." "The time is .... NOW!" called Ed and gave Hoppy the distance and direction to the peak of the mountain. This enabled the vital check that Hoppy needed. He worked on his maps and then called me. "Skipper, I've got a new direction and time of arrival over Karlova." He gave me the new course to steer. "Good on you fellas!" I breathed.

My turning on to a new heading meant lifting those huge black Halifax wings against the night sky, then settling them down again as we came out of the turn while all the time scanning the night skies for possible enemy attack. The blackness of night enveloped us as we flew on through enemy airspace to Karlova. Only the small dancing flames from the exhaust stubs of our four motors gave light in the darkness.

BOMB DOORS OPEN

"Skipper, ten minutes to target" came Hoppy's terse call. An excited Ed, "I'm picking up something on the H2S in the direction of the target." The H2S screen had given Ed response signals from the air base at Karlova, exciting news, something we had not dared to expect. An air base could be a difficult target to find even in daylight. Having in mind that this air base had a sting, I called to Smithy, Bob and Shorty, "Keep your eyes skinned for fighters."

"Bomb doors open" called Ed. We began our final run in to the Karlova complex. "Bomb doors open!" I called and air roared through the huge gaping bomb bay. Ed's eyes were on his H2S radar blip of what was most likely our target, and he guided me. "Keep steady," he said sharply as he began counting out the seconds before dropping. "Bombs gone!" I heard the clicks of our heavy bomb like flare containers dropping away from their bomb hooks, and continued to hold the Halifax steady, counting the seconds till the flares opened on their parachutes. Would the enemy air base be below us?

The flares ignited and hung suspended in the sky on parachutes at 12,000 feet above the ground. "Ye gods!" shouted Ed, "We're dead centre over the main runway." With a jubilant Ed in the nose of the Halifax, I flew on awaiting our photo flash to explode near the ground. The attack on Karlova had begun, and I circled wide around the base, awaiting back up Pathfinders coming in to consolidate the attack. But adverse winds and difficulties in navigation had scattered the squadron, so the minutes ticked by and no back up appeared. One by one our flares died. Our vital illumination over Karlova was dissipating.

"Prepare to do another run Ed!" I called, heading the Halifax towards the dying flares. But our run was not necessary. The sky lit up anew as bursting flares were added to our own dying away. Back up Pathfinders had arrived.

Cascading red and green TIs followed. Another Pathfinder had made his run. Ed said he could see the parked German aircraft on the ground as cascading TIs marked the centre of air base administration. More flares came, then another set of cascading TIs fell among the parked aircraft. Vicious blasts hit against our Halifax as the bombers flew in and their explosives fell among fighter planes on the ground.

Ed had a grandstand position in the transparent nose of the Halifax and he called, "Those cascading TIs of reds and greens, have to be seen to be believed." A spectacular fireworks show indeed, it could have been dramatic entertainment except that people were dying in the inferno that erupted below. Hell was breaking loose on the ground at the Karlova air complex at one in the morning.

HOME AND THE GARGARNO

We returned across Hungary, Yugoslavia and the Adriatic sea. An early morning sun shone on the 4,000 foot high Gargarno Peninsula. Ed was in raptures about the view, "Can you see it Tommy?" he called. I could see it alright, but just then I felt more interested in what lay beyond the mountain, our air base and a waiting bed.

I flew the Halifax along the edge of the Gargarno Mountain and then slid gently into the distant circuit area for a landing on the new black bitumen runway of our base. How smooth and quiet it was after the rattling steel that had made up the runway previously.

The sun had risen by the time I arrived at my tent. It took a long time for sleep to come but when it did, I began to dream. I dreamed that I walked in the front gate that led to our house in Perth, but no one was there. The emptiness troubled me and I woke with a start. My gaze met the brightness of full daylight, and I was wet with sweat from Italian summer.

Arising, I sloshed my face in water in the hand basin, then gazed out to the Gargarno mountain. The cloud covered view of the mountain turned my mind to the events of the previous night's attack on Karlova. I shaved and dressed then ambled across to the mess for lunch.

At lunch, I learnt that the General of the U.S. Air Force had received photos following our raid on Karlova. Very enthusiastic about the results, he had phoned through his commendation for our part in the destruction of the air base. The US air force as well as the RAF had lost a lot of valuable crews to the guns of enemy aircraft flying from Karlova.

The Americans found it difficult to understand how RAF Pathfinders could fly long distances at night and locate such difficult targets. American navigators often had difficulty locating their target during daylight attacks. As for the attack on Karlova, an ingenious radar operator called Ed Riley had made the difference there, between success and failure — a radar fix from a nicely placed mountain peak, a most unusual feat.

LETTER FROM HOME

With lunch over, I went to the mail rack and found a letter from my mother. I loved getting these; she was a consistent writer, giving news of the family and people I knew at home.

Placing a chair out in a shady spot under an olive tree near my tent, I sat with a view across agricultural land. Beyond the tilled earth were rocky levels of the Gargarno mountain. I greatly appreciated the rural beauty, but those slopes looked sinister and depressing this day.

With a pad on my knee and a pen in hand in readiness to reply, I read mother's letter. It took time to absorb. The words were in mother's usual style of news, but I came in touch with unusual anguish as she shared her heart.

She had been meeting regularly in Perth with the parents and wives of the pilots with whom I had trained and journeyed to England. One by one, my friends had been shot down over Europe; others had been killed in aircraft crashes in England. Lindsay Fairclough had gone, Jim Mudie too, also Johnny Richards who had flown me through the tops of the gum trees at Geraldton. Arthur Berryman had been killed also George Ives, Kev McKnight, John Love, Max Hubbard and Bill Mitchell who had married before leaving Australia; all fellows with whom I had lived, laughed and relaxed around coffee tables and in the pubs. The devastating news had come to the families in Perth until mother could take the sorrow no more.

"Tom, I can't go to those parent gatherings any more. It's just too much, I feel the heartbreak of it all, it sweeps over me and I can't take any more." For a long time I just sat there shaded under the tree, looking out towards the Gargarno. I felt numb from mother's news. Another deadly swathe had been cut through the ranks of the Forty Club from Western Australia.

The weight of what she wrote bore in upon me, for even more recently, others of my friends had gone missing in action, and I knew that my own survival could not go on indefinitely. I sensed she shared her anguish about her own son. When was his name coming up on the list of those missing believed killed in action? I had my own grieving about the loss of my friends and now, as I took up my pen, I also tuned in to hers.

In the midst of writing I looked out across to the Gargarno and became overwhelmed by my sombre feelings. I thought about it, then realised I looked at the Gargarno mountain as representing my fear of continually flying out to attack the enemy. Much flying yet lay ahead of me beyond that mountain. What really were my chances of survival? I shook off the shadowy thoughts, turned over the page, and began anew.

The words now flowed out to mother. I knew she would be glad to hear I had become a commissioned officer and so had Tony my tent mate. I told her how much I enjoyed the ordinary things of day by day life in Italy; a visit to the markets in the town of Foggia, the produce, the chatter and the enjoyment I felt at learning to live amongst the Italian people. I pictured my mother longing to hear about the flying, but security demanded that I be as brief as possible. I added briefly, "I'm still plugging away at my job. Hoppy, Ed, Bob, Shorty and Smithy are all with me still and I appreciate them increasingly as time goes on. They are a great team."

I decided that the hollow feeling I had about my dream of home, had put me in touch with my mother's painful experiences amongst the families who lost their loved ones. I had not previously been aware of the heartache and hard work which had become her lot.

Satisfied that I had written enough, I walked across to the Officers Mess to post the letter. The notice board called my attention to an important lecture I had forgotten about. It was quite a mysterious announcement really, all crews were to report at four o'clock to the marquee set aside for briefing.

I looked around the mess. Other officers lounged in chairs drinking cups of tea. I saw Tony Wheeler. "What's the briefing about Tony?" "Buggered if I know Tommy, but I did see some big fat guy with Bill Tarling." We headed across to the big marquee and found a convenient seat.

THE MAN FROM BUCHENWALD

Most aircrew were already seated when we entered, and the Intelligence Officer rose to introduce the visitor; "We have with us this afternoon, John, and that is all I can tell you about his name. He has come to us from HQ with high recommendations as a Jewish escapee from Germany. Let's welcome him as we listen to what he has to say." A hush fell upon the assembled flyers and a tall heavily built man arose to speak.

"I am a German Jew, an escapee from a concentration camp in Germany," he began in heavy guttural English, "I am here to describe to you, just what it means for a Jew to be in a concentration camp in Germany today." The Jewish speaker described his arrest and imprisonment in a large compound at Buchenwald, central Germany, and outlined the sad plight of thousands of Jews herded to this prison. The prisoners had committed no other crime than being Jewish born. Hundreds were dying weekly from maltreatment, hunger and disease. Then the speaker described something of his escape to Switzerland. The gripping account had us sitting on the edge of our seats.

Answering a question about other concentration camps beyond Buchenwald, the speaker admitted that he had heard whispers of the existence of other concentration camps; one he knew of was Dachau near Munich in southern Germany. He believed the brutality of the Dachau camp to be worse, if possible, than at Buchenwald. He had come on this lecture tour to encourage and further motivate efforts to end the war and gain release to his people now facing extermination in Germany.

He sat wiping sweat that had accumulated on his forehead. Group Captain Laird, our CO, closed off by saying, "There is official documentation now available to us, that proves the existence of these concentration camps in Germany. All that our speaker has outlined for us today about the treatment and death of these prisoners is a further factor which must fill us with need for urgency in finishing this war." The C.O. thanked the Jewish speaker and then dismissed us, leaving us to put together the significance of what we had heard from the lips of the man from Buchenwald.

I looked across to the Gargarno standing dark and sombre beneath its canopy of clouds. My view of the mountain matched the dark feelings gripping me after hearing our Jewish visitor's words.

OPS ARE ON !

Next morning the names of our crew were listed on the notice board Ops list. Ops were on again. Bob Lewis read the list and came to me blowing his nose and saying, "I've got a head cold Tommy but I'm sure I'll be OK to fly tonight. Och man, I don't want to miss out on flying with you all; you know that don't you!" Yes I did know and further I knew it wise for Bob to arrange for a replacement when high altitude flying could do damage to his inner ear.

But Bob did not intend to miss out on flying with us. Our bonding together meant he had decided our crew could not do without him. He would fly with us, head cold or no head cold. I felt secure in having Bob close at hand in the Halifax. Such a laconic fellow, not excitable, he took his flight engineer role seriously, and had flown with a cold before, so I agreed to him flying with us.

The crews collected for briefing and we saw our target; the large railway facilities in Munich, a city populated by over one million people. This raid would be a penetration into German air space and industries. It involved our being one of eight Pathfinder aircraft marking a target in a sprawled out area of Munich with its massive defences. I highly valued Bob's willingness to fly with us into this concentration of German firepower. Our attack with less than a hundred planes would have no hope of overcoming defences as was the case when the RAF sent seven hundred planes to attack from Britain. This was going to be a tough assignment for us.

Late afternoon that warm June day, we climbed into our Halifax, then word came through that an RAF photographic Mosquito aircraft had detected heavy cloud over Munich. Our take off had to be delayed so that we could arrive over Munich when cloud had moved away. We lay on the grass beneath the shadow of the outspread wings of our Halifax and waited.

Talk arose about news that had filtered through of an Allied invasion of France. The news stirred us, but amidst our own preparations for this attack on Munich, we could not get excited.

Group Captain Laird came around in his RAF staff car and said, "Well Scotty, are you all set for tonight?" "We're as set as we'll ever be sir," I replied and then I asked, "Do you know how long this delay will be?" The CO thought for a moment, then said in his quiet voice, "Not for long now, we are just hoping this cloud will clear over the target so that you can get in there. Have a good trip Scotty." He grunted something more, but too indistinct for me to hear. He climbed into his vehicle and drove away and it was then that I realised what his last muffled words had been, "and a safe return." I liked that. The fellows gathered around me anxiously wanting to know what he had said.

NORTHWARDS TO MUNICH
We flew off into the evening, and headed over the sea towards northern Italy, Austria, and Germany. We had route markers to drop for following aircraft to check their turning points, and our accuracy was critical. I listened to Hoppy and Ed working together, checking and cross checking to make sure we were on track and on time.

Hoppy's navigation also relied on radio information from Shorty. Shorty called up, "I've got a radio fix for you Hoppy. Do you want it?" "Let's have it" Hoppy replied. "I've identified Vienna, on bearing 097, ... time ... NOW!" said Shorty. "Greenwich Mean Time is twenty two thirty six" Hoppy replied, then added, "Thanks Shorty!" Hoppy plotted the radio fix and realised he had to reduce his wind speed calculations for our flight over Austria. Shorty turned to the task of dropping "window", bundles of aluminium foil that jammed enemy radar. Later, Ed said, "Hoppy, I've identified a town on the German Border." They conversed about the location, then Ed passed on the map reference. "Thanks Ed!" said Hoppy as he plotted the details and then worked out our aircraft's position. He called me, "Skipper, I've got a change of course for you," "OK Navigator, I'm ready," "It's three five zero .... NOW!" called Hoppy.

HEAVEN BEFORE HELL
I turned the Halifax to the heading over the alps on that moonlit night, and I startled Hoppy with the words, "Hoppy, look at this!" I wanted him to look up from his concentration and view snow capped alpine mountains, now visible out over the port side wing. With our wing dipping low, we had a grandstand view of snow covered magnificence.

There was a long silence as I continued in the turn. "Who could believe there's a bloody war on!" said Hoppy in delight. His expressed feelings needed no response. I was contrasting this moment of incredible beauty with the chaos of war into which we were heading. Gentle moonlight glinted on our wings and tinged the alpine scene with magical resplendence. But Hoppy's words highlighted the tranquil beauty below us, as an experience of heaven before we flew into hell. In the next hour we expected to fly amongst vast defences of the Munich and Augsburg belt of searchlights, guns and fighter aircraft.

Soon, clouds covered the land. Ed perceived a good radar picture of a large lake just ahead; the Wurm See, our turning point, south west of Munich. Because of its distinctive shape, he identified the southern tip of the lake, and gave Hoppy an accurate turning point for his chart. We flew in over the lake and I altered course so that we could fly straight towards the northern tip that led in to Munich. With every moment we drew closer to the big city.

Then, it all came alive. Despite heavy cloud layers, powerful searchlights probed the skies seeking to pin point our Halifaxes. Four of the 614 Squadron planes had gone in ahead of us and we saw their bright illumination flares hanging in the sky and lighting up the heavy cloud layers covering our target.

Gunfire lined up on us as we flew in behind the glaring light of the flares. On and on we went. Our work tonight would be placing target markers on the actual railway complex itself. But the clouds were too deep and dense for us to see the huge railway yards. We decided to mark the sky above the yards. For this purpose we carried red and green sky markers.

"Bomb doors open!" called Ed as he and I went through our target routine. "Bomb doors open!" I responded as a rushing sound of wind in the bomb bay lifted the Halifax. Ed used electric switches to select his red and green sky markers and called to me, "Bombs selected; steady, steady, steady,"

It seemed an age in which I flew our plane straight and level and just when I thought that Ed did not intend to drop our bombs, I heard his voice, "Bombs gone!" We flew on across the breadth of Munich. The green and red sky markers sent flickering colours across the clouds and we felt the impact of exploding bombs beneath us as the stream of ninety bombers followed us in to do their work. Bomb aimers were dropping their loads so as to fall through the sky markers. We were four miles high, yet we could still feel the explosions on the ground. The Munich railway facilities had become vulnerable, despite the clouds.

As far as my eye could see, enemy defensive activity filled the sky over Munich, and towards the north where Augsburg lay. Searchlights, exploding shells with their wicked flashes of hot steel, and then the sight of cannon fire from enemy fighter aircraft, all lit the sky.

We headed out of the fury of the defences. I pictured somewhere to the north of us, the age old home of my mother's family and the town where her forebears had settled in fifteen hundred AD, after migrating from Hungary. Then on the north east of Munich lay Dachau, the concentration camp where Jewish captives were being introduced to hell on earth. "I hope those Jews will at least be encouraged by the sound of our motors overhead," I thought to myself.

"There's a plane on fire about a mile behind us," called Smithy from his cold position in the gun turret at the rear of the Halifax. I imagined the German air force working out our track eastward from Munich and trying to pick off the bombers one by one. "Keep your eyes alert for fighters!" I called as I saw the searchlight beams now vertical, indicating the path our force was taking.

HEADCOLD IN THE HEAVENS

On nearing our base, I started to descend. Just then Bob's problem of a severe head cold, showed itself. The eustachian tubes from his ears must have been completely blocked. The lower we descended, the more pain he felt. He was totally unable to clear his ear canals.

Screaming with pain, he yelled, "I can't take any more, I can't take any more!" His condition needed urgent help. I peered over my shoulder and saw Bob bowed over in agony, and holding his head in his hands. I called Ed and Shorty to come up from the lower part of the aircraft and assist. They stood around Bob, massaging around his ears, neck and throat. Their presence must have eased Bob's anxiety, for his cries lessened. I took the Halifax lower towards our base, then Bob screamed in greater distress than ever.

I called to the crew, "Listen fellows, Bob is in a bad way, I'm going to climb back up to fifteen thousand feet and restart our descent." I pushed the throttles forward. The Halifax, now much lighter without a load of high explosives and with most of our fuel used, rose rapidly. I looked down and saw the lighted runway of our home base so tantalisingly close, and growing smaller as we rose higher. My crewmen were tired and would have had their eyes on the runway lights, but they hid their disappointment.

We reached nearly two and a half miles high, then levelled out and I reduced power to the motors so that we could start to descend gently for Bob's sake. I called the control tower, and explained the situation. The control came back, Doc Francis would stand by and await our landing. Shorty and Ed continued to massage around Bob's throat and neck, helping him to find relief for his air pressured ears. At each thousand foot mark, I checked to see if Bob could take our continued descent. At last, after a further half hour of flying, I circled the airfield, and went in for a landing. The ambulance met us and Bob disappeared groaning, and still holding his head.

The morning after the raid, I awoke just before lunch and joined Tony Wheeler at the meal table. We sat hushed as the BBC radio from London gave news of the attack on Germany by Lancasters and Halifaxes from Britain and by our aircraft from Italy. The announcer's voice from London contrasted with the tumultuous feelings we had in the planes which carried the battle into the heart of German war industries. After lunch I talked with Doc Francis. He had temporarily grounded Bob until his cold cleared, but I was relieved he had found no permanent damage to his ears.

We completed our next three attacks without Bob. He had to await the doctor's clearance to fly with us again, and he fretted at being left behind while his crew went into action. Our flying for these attacks took us to oil facilities in Hungary, then into northern Italy. By that time we were tired, feeling ready for a break. A leave pass enabled us to be off the base for four wonderful days of freedom.

AT THE FOOT OF THE GARGARNO
With a leave pass in our pockets, my crew and I decided to join Irish pilot friend Paddy Fleckney and his crew, and head to the town of Rodi. Situated on the northern side of the Gargarno Peninsula, we had to drive for several hours over winding, bumpy mountain roads. At last we

came to where the steep rocky cliffs of the Gargarno give way to sandy beach, and there was Rodi.

In the centre of town was an office marked, "Town Major", repeated in Italian, "Maggiore". Hoppy and I made ourselves known to the Town Major, a British army officer. He was a happy individual, thrilled to meet someone who could speak English. He explained that the tide of battle had passed through Rodi, leaving many empty houses under the control of the British army. He allocated us a villa that belonged to a rich Italian family, who had long since fled to the north with the German army.

The villa had many rooms but all bare of furniture. The helpful Town Major showed us mattresses, table and chairs. No one seemed to own anything in this town. We used the furniture and I imagined that at some date in the future, returning owners would argue and try to sort things out. Large empty rooms echoed eerily to our presence. Were the echoes Italian voices from the past; laughing voices, angry voices, voices that combined in low monotone?

We had a find! In a large building beside the white walled villa, there was a white painted paddle boat with seating for two people. Excited over our find, we struggled to carry the paddle boat, and headed for the beach. The two crews discussed at length how to get the heavy boat over the sea wall and then launch it into the water. Eventually it slid over the wall, and became the focus of seaward adventure. Further and further into the Adriatic, we paddled it, two at a time.

By the end of several days, the boat's dried out timbers became waterlogged, and Hoppy and Smithy had to swim for it, dragging the sagging boat as it wallowed in the gentle waves behind them. We returned it reluctantly to the home of its distant owner.

At night time we sat around on our mattresses in a huge room with high ceilings. A big fireplace soon had a fire glowing in it and around this we reminisced about our lives. Many of our friends had gone missing when their planes had crashed in distant places, so almost inevitably the subject of death came up. The Grim Reaper was the personification of all that death brought to our minds. "What is death all about, what happens after death?" we asked ourselves as we talked about fiery death in planes hit by enemy gunfire. We concluded that after death, nothing remained.

Our finite minds could not conjure up eternity, life seemed too short; "There's just nothing after death," we decided, but in my heart I hoped we were wrong. "Surely there must be something more to live for than that!"

UNDER THE SHADOW OF THE GARGARNO

Hoppy and I enjoyed the freedom of long walks together. Laughing at some of our blunders while flying, we relaxed and shared hopes and dreams. On the slopes of the Gargarno, Hoppy called my attention to a plant he had found growing amongst the trees. "It's a holly!" he said excitedly. I considered the prickly bush for a while, but remained unimpressed. Hoppy tried to encourage my approval and exclaimed, "You know, a holly, the trimming that we use on our Christmas trees." I recalled some of the red berry things around Christmas cakes in Australia. People had called it holly. "So that's what a holly looks like?" I said exhibiting my Australian ignorance. Enthralled with his Italian holly, Hoppy explained, "We've got these growing around our house at home. They grow much bigger there."

We walked on, enjoying our ocean view from the hillside, then made our return towards the tall white villa at Rodi. A shy lad with a donkey came along the road and we stopped to talk. At first the lad seemed scared; it was not difficult to understand why. Not long ago, the Italians and British were at war with each other. Now that Italy had capitulated and joined the allies against Germany, it still seemed the Italian population was suspicious of us as enemy occupying their country. However, the lad began to respond as we used our limited Italian to communicate with him. He seemed suddenly quite thrilled to be meeting "Pilota aeroplano" and he offered us a ride on his donkey.

The donkey seemed so small, Hoppy and I so big, yet it had no trouble in carrying us one at a time. "Moneta, moneta," the boy exclaimed rubbing his fingers together. In the midst of Italian wartime poverty, everything needed to be turned into money. We paid the boy some money and he went on his way, chatting loudly and excitedly to us as he went. The next time we met, he had his donkey loaded with produce as high as the animal itself.

BACK TO WORK

We returned to base refreshed, and met up with friends again. We knew we were home when they told us that during the latest op, Norm Dear and his crew had gone missing. Ops would be on again that night.

Next morning Bob Lewis, Shorty, Smithy and I air tested our Halifax. We flew low down near the water of Manefredonia Bay, and had to pull up to avoid some of the large cumbersome Italian fishing boats with their huge ungainly sails. Smithy, needed to test his guns from the tail gun turret.

When all was clear of fishing boats ahead I called, "OK Shorty, drop the smoke flares. Smithy it is over to you to test your guns as soon as you see the smoke on the surface of the sea." Shorty dropped a smoke flare down the chute into the sea and Smithy blazed away with the four guns mounted in his cramped turret. This was good stuff for him. He needed to vent deep tensions that remained built up in him and he seemed to be doing just that as the whole aircraft vibrated with the chatter of his guns. I returned and flew over the smoke flares again to allow Smithy to repeat his practise, and enjoyed hearing him shout his glee as his accuracy improved.

I brought the Halifax in a low run over Rodi, our beach side holiday resort and then up over the Gargarno. Coming down on to the grasslands of the Foggia plain, we sped across the wide expanse of farmland. Birdlike feelings made me forget time. Roads and farmhouses swept by us. Then making a wide turn I returned to our airfield at Amandola.

When our motors stopped, the rear door opened and the ground crew sergeant called, "Ops are on boys and I think you're on the list." "OK Sarge," I responded, at the same time conscious of a sinking feeling in the pit of my stomach. Then I added, "You've got this plane in good nick for tonight," but to myself I mused, "I wonder where we'll go?"

Our names surely were up on the notice board to fly on operations that night. The target turned out to be the industrial city of Milan in the north of Italy.

The afternoon went very quickly. Briefing for the attack was at four thirty, our evening meal was at five thirty, transport to our aircraft was at six fifteen and take off was due at seven fifteen.

However, at seven o'clock, our Flight Commander, Ed Lockwood came around in his jeep and called us to delay takeoff for an hour. An accident had occurred on the runway of another squadron and their aircraft were unable to take off until the runway had been cleared. It was essential that the Pathfinder squadron wait for the nine bomber squadrons so that we could all attack in full strength.

Aircraft and crews at different bases across the Foggia plain, now went into a delay phase. Motors were shut off, crew members in takeoff positions extricated themselves and made their way out of their aircraft and on to the grass at the edge of the aircraft taxiway.

I sat on a patch of grass underneath the outstretched wing of our Halifax. Others took up different positions of sitting or lying nearby. I looked over the Halifax and read its number, JN978. Some painter in the safety of a factory in far away England had assiduously painted the letters. Tonight we would take those letters and fly them to Milan. I tried to picture that painter, perhaps one of the girls I had met on an English dance floor. I had received an exciting Valentine card from her, "I am weak and willing, to be your Valentine," she wrote referring to our loves together .

The one hour delay extended to an hour and a half. I detested delay. It added tension, and in the heat of summer I had already sweated profusely walking encumbered by flying gear up into my pilot's position, then out again. I had worn extra flying gear to offset the cold of high altitudes. I cursed the sweaty clothes, and planned how I would cope with an uncomfortable flight ahead.

OFF TO MILAN

At last the call came to start engines. The activity gave me glad relief. Ed and I started the engines and I rolled the wheels of our Halifax towards the edge of the runway. Darkness had partly descended, and the runway lights stretched in parallel lines towards the faraway distance.

We were sixth in line for takeoff. With Ed helping me to keep those throttles to the full power, we gathered momentum. The end of the runway lights raced towards us and the arms of the waiting night, gathered us slowly upwards. The exhaust flames of our motors flared out into the darkness. Smooth air came at a thousand feet, and Ed relinquished his place beside me, moving forward to his position near the navigator. Bob Lewis shuffled his gear as he settled into his position just to the rear of me.

After an hour we flew into storm clouds. One moment I felt the thud of upward air currents, then the awful thump of the down movement bending our aircraft into submissive descent. Shorty had a fright as a lightening flash shorted out his radio.

In the midst of the turbulence Ed tried to make sense of the reception on his H2S radar. He called, "Skipper, can you see any mountains around here?" "No Ed," I responded, knowing full well that we were well out over the Adriatic sea and the mountains of either Italy or Yugoslavia were fifty miles away. "We're in clouds. Can't you feel them? We're moving into cumulo-nimbus and I want to get out before it gets nasty!" Ed had a revelation. "Aaah,.... ye gods, that's what I'm picking up on the radar then. Just a minute and I'll give you a course to steer to go around the worst of it."

I heard Ed and Hoppy conferring, then Hoppy came on the line, "Skipper, alter course thirty degrees to starboard ... now!" "OK

Navigator, here we go!" Ed had made a most amazing discovery; the H2S could detect heavy cloud formations. This exciting discovery meant that we could steer around the worst part of storm that lay in our path. Ed had added something new to his repertoire of discoveries about the H2S radar.

The storm clouds made me think about the troops fighting on the ground not far away from us in this terrible weather. They were trying to break the German defensive line along the Arno River. American, British, Polish, Canadian, Indian and New Zealand troops formed a rough line that stretched across the whole of the Italian Peninsula. The Allies had captured Sienna and were at the gates of Pisa, Florence and Assissi, ancient cities battered by Allied gunfire in an attempt to dislodge German regiments determined to hold their ground.

To the west of us I caught sight of light flashes on the ground; gun flashes. One of our planes must have strayed too near to German defences. Flashes lit the sky as shell bursts sought out the aircraft.

We flew on northwards and then turned westwards towards Milan. Our target was the large railway marshalling area and our role was to mark out the area with our coloured TIs. We flew in as a canopy of Pathfinder sky flares lit up the industrial area of the big city. The long tense run to the target stretched out endlessly as I tried to keep our Halifax unswerving amidst the gunfire from the ground. Ed picked out the target and our dramatically colourful pyrotechnics cascaded out of the sky to form a ring of colour across the railway area.

At last came Ed's terse words, "Camera flash gone!" At last I had freedom to take avoiding action amidst lights, flashes and exploding gunfire. It was difficult to make sense of all the action and our first need; get clear of it all. Switching Hoppy off the intercom so that he could concentrate on getting us home, made me marvel at his ability to shut himself into his navigation when so much action and danger went on around him. Having navigated us to Milan, he now had to make sure his navigation took us home. Ed, lying in the transparent nose of the Halifax, was now free to observe the progress of our attack.

I SAW HIM

The finger of approaching catastrophe pointed at us as Smithy shouted, "Enemy aircraft attacking from ten o'clock!" The moment that Smithy first spoke, my foot tightened on that right rudder pedal and I had our Halifax ready to wheel into an avoidance manoeuvre. "He's coming in, enemy aircraft attacking, get ready to corkscrew starboard, hold it, he's coming in, hold steady, ... corkscrew starboard ... GO!"

I gave the right rudder pedal a powerful thrust with my foot, at the same time I pulled up the port side wing until it pointed to the sky and the nose of our plane pointed towards the earth of northern Italy. It was the action that Smithy and I had worked out together. Smithy, with his guns trained on the German fighter, was in an excellent position to destroy our attacker.

Pulling the aircraft around into the next part of the corkscrew manoeuvre, I heard gunfire from Smithy's turret, and waited for his clear command. "Oooh, damn!" he called, "Missed the bastard!"

"I saw him, it was an ME109!" called Bob Lewis in his position amidships. I butted in, "Keep your eyes peeled, others will be around." Smithy's careful patter had been very calculated and I appreciated the accuracy of the way he handled the attack; glad that he had judged the time for our turn out of the attacker's pathway.

My eyes focused on the intercom button. I cursed as I recalled switching Hoppy and Ed off the intercom. "What's going on?" Hoppy asked anxiously as I switched him back into our system. "We've just had an ME109 attack navigator. He missed us and we are keeping an eye out in case he comes back in!" I pictured Hoppy and Ed looking at wild gyrations across the sky being registered on their instruments. Our rolling dive and then steep climb were very uncomfortable for those not ready for them.

VOICE FROM THE STARS

Heading away from Milan, our eyes searched for enemy attackers. Below us lay a hostile continent, its very air space belonged to enemy. Unseen operators watched our every movement on their radar screens, and I felt very vulnerable to their gaze. I thought about the reason of my being there in such an exposed situation. I was there because Europeans dwelt within the bounds of a war that caused pain and suffering to innocent people and I longed for it to end.

Looking above, I saw the stars shining in perfect order as we flew. Faint moonlight touched on distant clouds. My roving eyes continued to seek out an enemy that might be lurking.

The search for fighters took my gaze once more amongst the stars and I became absorbed by my view of such perfection. The symmetry was all the more wondrous because we could use the stars as a check upon our navigation. I had a question, "How is it that there is such order in the stars, yet such chaos on the continent beneath me?"

I decided that there was some strange determination in people on earth, whereby we were bent on destroying each other. As if looking for the survival of my own being amidst present destruction, I searched for answers amongst the stars and their friendly light shone back on me.

Then I became entranced by the vastness, the excellence, the clear purity, the perfection and orderly distribution of the stars. It seemed the whole assembly of majesty within my focus drew together all the elements of my riveted attention and a voice spoke, saying, "Some power out there made all this!"

I felt absolutely overwhelmed by the words. The idea of something causing the heavens to happen was a new thought. I had never really considered the cause of all that I saw. Some power out there must be Some Power alright, some great and mighty power.

Then my attention reverted to scanning the sky for fighters and I groaned for answers to the question in my mind, "Why can some power out there make such beauty and order, yet stay remote from the destruction and chaos on earth?" I struggled for answers but no answer came; just the memory of that voice from the stars, "Some power out there made all this." The words registered.

One of our motors began to lose power and operated roughly. Its vibrations went through the aircraft. I lessened power to the motor, and checked and adjusted the controls. Bob and I conferred on the problem, but the motor remained losing power. We flew home on three motors.

After six and a half hours in the air it was still partly dark when we landed. I wrote a request for Jock to sort out the problem with our motor, then boarded the transport to the debriefing marquee.

Tony remained asleep while I crawled into bed. In several hours, he would be up and around, beginning his day. I lay on my bed thinking of the German fighter attack on us over Milan and then my mind went to the stars. For a long time I cogitated, feeling overwhelmed afresh by what happened to me under the canopy of stars. "Did a voice speak?

Was it really a voice?"   I did not know.

DINING OUT

Next evening, Shorty and I had a date with an Italian family in the nearby town of Foggia. We had first met the Italian husband and wife in the Foggia main street and conversed with them. They were keen for us to visit them "a l'ora di mangiare," at the hour of eating.

Walking through the streets and into back alleys we saw tethered donkeys, their droppings, accumulated rubbish and children playing. The home of our hosts was in the Via Vittoria, the oldest part of town, opening off the street and up a flight of stairs. The room we were ushered into had bare plastered walls and stone flooring, furnished with a solid bare topped table and forms as seats. A teenage son and younger daughter eyed us off as we came in.

Shorty had developed a reasonable conversation in the Italian language. I, though a keen learner, could not speak as fluently as he. However, we overcame our language limitations and enjoyed a jovial evening. Sour red wine began the evening meal, as mama and daughter brought such food as the family had to share. Mama had prepared "mozzarella in carozza". Mozzarella cheese was made from the milk of buffalo cows. She fried the cheese in batter and with bread. A salad dish with olive oil followed, then olives and nuts. Papa made sure we had copious glasses of sour red wine, "Molto buono vino," he kept repeating. I had to adjust to its inordinate sourness and longed for some of the Spumanti and Vino wines we had in our mess on the base. However, the sour wine somehow fitted the meal and gave us an added sense of being Italian. Papa and mama had endured much during the German occupation of Foggia and they shared their meal with us as a way of saying, "benvenuto Australiani - welcome."

We loved the warmth of the evening with the family but went out into the night aware that the back streets could harbour inordinate attack in dark corners.

NOTHING WRONG WITH YOUR AIRCRAFT

At ten o'clock in the morning, two days later, I stood before the Deputy CO of 614 Squadron. I could not believe my ears. Wing Commander Haywood looked hard at me, "We can find nothing wrong with your aircraft. I must conclude that you have faked an early return from an operation." My mind boggled with the events of the previous night and I was aghast at the Wingco's declaration.

We had been briefed to attack oil facilities at Budapest, the capital of Hungary. Budapest had large oil storage facilities supplied by huge river barges that were powered along the Danube River from Rumania. One by one, my crew had climbed into the aircraft and settled for our normal take off procedure.

As our Halifax needed repairs after a previous op, we flew a spare plane. The take off run began. From my darkened cockpit, with Ed beside me, I saw the runway lights flash by. It registered with me that I had no airspeed on the airspeed indicator, but we were going too fast to stop the run. The runway lights disappeared and we rose into the night. My eyes focussed on the plane's instruments for flying in the dark. "Ed," I called, "We've got no flying instruments."

Ed peered into the dim fluorescent instrument panels and searched for some sign of activity that would indicate they were functioning. Nothing moved. The dark night enveloped us. I desperately needed even a dim horizon to help me. I had no idea of what speed we were doing, or whether we were climbing or diving. My ears, eyes and hands tuned together to try flying by the feel of the aircraft. I pushed the plane to a shallow dive and then a slight climb, lessening the power to the motors to see how my ear tuned to a slower air speed, then reasserting full takeoff power. All the time I searched the darkness for a dim horizon whereby I may judge the position of the aircraft as we flew, but heavy overcast cloud shut us in to blackness.

The next step involved retracting the flaps and reducing power to the motors. "Well Ed," I said, "Here goes, I am reducing the flaps now." I experienced the usual sinking feeling and then Ed slowly reduced power to the motors. I waited, encouraged we had overcome the first hurdle.

Red and green lights of other aircraft flashed by as bomber squadrons rose into the night sky from airfields around the Foggia plain. The hazard of trying to evade aircraft, while at the same time judging the flying position of our own plane became too much. "Ed," I called, "I'm having to cancel our operation to Budapest tonight. It's far too dangerous to continue!"

Ed came on anxiously, "Do you want to jettison our bomb load?" "I sure do Ed. Get down to the nose and start arranging for a jettison will you. I'll head out to sea. Hoppy!" I called. Back came Hoppy's modulated tones, "You are going to jettison Tommy?" "Yes," I replied, "We need to cancel our op. Can you give me a course to steer and a timing for us to be all clear to jettison. I can't fly this plane to Budapest, we will need to return to base."

Quick as a flash, Hoppy came back, "Steer 081 and I'll time our run to let you know when it's clear to jettison." "Thanks."

At the end of Hoppy's timed run, and with the wind whistling through our open bomb bay, Ed dropped our bombs and TIs into the Sea. I closed the bomb doors with a sigh of relief, free now to give thought to our landing. I practised lowering and raising the wing flaps, and judged the feel of the plane for landing. My senses tuned in to the changing airspeeds as I flew towards our base, and my eyes made out a vague horizon in the western sky.

By going well out to the south of our runway I let the control tower know that we were coming in, minus our flying instruments. My ear tuned to the sound of the air flowing over us so that I did not lose control, and I began a long gentle landing approach,

After what seemed an age, we came through the entrance lights to the runway. I took the Halifax lower and lower until the feel of our tyres meeting the runway surface seemed too good to be true. Feelings of a tremendous accomplishment gripped me. I had not really thought it possible to land this big aircraft without the use of its essential flying instruments. Rolling along the runway at the end of our landing run, I had another rise of tremendous exultation. I wanted to shout and dance.

At last the Halifax was parked, Climbing out into the open air, I felt uneasy. I had never before returned early from an op, with all the other crews still heading out to the target. I made out a report so that the instrument fitters would know the emergency we had experienced, and the repairs they needed to do, then headed off with my crew.

Next day I stood before Dagwood, our pet name for the Deputy CO. The big man, generally good fun in the mess, was now an angry commander. "What have you got to say for yourself?" My exhilaration over the triumph of our landing dissipated beneath the tone of his voice. I could not believe the censure this man dealt me. "I can't understand why no problem was found with the instruments on our aircraft!" I replied. Dagwood looked at me, and said severely, "I'll have your plane checked again!"

The hapless instrument fitters just about tore that Halifax apart and then they found the problem. An Italian grasshopper had crawled into the works and totally locked the instruments off from their essential supply of air. How simple the problem, but how devastating to the instrumentation of the Halifax

APOLOGY

"Scotty, we've found out the trouble with your aircraft from the other night!" It was Dagwood. He added, "Sorry Scotty for blowing off about your early return from the raid into Hungary. You did a good job to get the plane down as you did." "Thanks sir," I replied, "I heard that the problem was a grasshopper in the instruments." "Yes, that's right. But it's not only your grasshopper. We've been having trouble keeping enough planes serviceable with all this damned Italian dust getting into things." "Yes I know, and the ground staff are doing a tremendous job keeping the planes serviced." I had in mind our own ground staff team who worked so hard to keep our plane flying. They loved to receive my "thumbs up" signal of appreciation for a serviceable aircraft.

"Anyway Scotty I hope you have no more trouble with the plane," the Wingco said solicitously. "Well sir," I replied, "it's not our usual aircraft. We had only borrowed it for that particular raid. It's normally flown by Warrant Officer Bill Sparrow, but he and his crew are away on leave."

When Bill Sparrow and his crew returned from leave, they flew the plane attacking the Szony Oil Refinery in Hungary. The defences were intense, and the aircraft was last seen going down over the target.

STAND DOWN

Next day the squadron had a break from ops to help take the pressure off everybody. The social committee planned a party and erected a large marquee near the Halifax parking bays. After the evening meal, ground staff and aircrew met and relaxed together. I appreciated being with our groundcrew because they received so little information about the work we were actually doing. As they talked they told firsthand of their heartaches and their pride in us who did the flying. I had always felt sensitive about making too many requests to unravel difficulties with our plane, for they worked in atrocious, dusty conditions and out in all sorts of weather. So the evening was a rewarding experience of camaraderie between ground crew and the flyers.

Tony and I planned something especially significant. We had been sharing on alternate raids, the Halifax JP279, which went under the large letter K. We had dubbed her Kathleen. We had even found an artist to paint a symbolic Kathleen reclining on the nose of the plane. Tonight we planned to christen her.

A DRINK FOR KATHLEEN

Laden with a tall bottle of Italian champagne, we headed off to Kathleen's parking bay. The dim light of a clouded moon showed the recumbent figure of a provocative Kathleen lying on the proud nose of our plane. We could not reach up to her, but we found an engine fitter's ladder for Tony to climb high, and address our symbol. Tony held high the bottle of champagne, and solemnly announced, "I christen you Kathleen." The champagne bottle bounced against the aircraft, but remained intact. He tried again, but with the same result. He tried a third time and still the bottle did not break. "Your turn Tommy" he called, "perhaps you can do better!" He dismounted the ladder and handed me the bottle.

While watching Tony, I had espied a more solid part of the Halifax than he had chosen. Mounting the ladder, I swung the champagne bottle against my chosen area of the plane and "bang", the bottle broke. "You've done it Tommy!" Glass tinkled and champagne submerged our reclining lady and soaked me. I climbed down from the ladder, and with wet champagne hands grabbed Tony to cheer and share our excitement. From now on Kathleen would have a much more significant place in our lives.

Returning to the party, we warned our ground crew fellows about the broken champagne bottle on the parking bay of Kathleen. They gathered around, and cheered "the bloody Aussies" describing the christening ceremony of the lovely Kathleen.

ITALIAN SUMMER

The hot Italian summer evening grew late. Tony and I planned a swim. Borrowing an RAF vehicle used to transport aircrew, we drove for half an hour to the road block near Manefredonia. The British army guard informed us that it was after midnight and he could see no reason why two Aussie officers would want a swim at that time of night. "Peculiar Australians," his Lancashire voice mumbled as we headed through his guard barrier and drove to the beach.

All was quiet as we lay relaxing in the warm Adriatic at one in the morning. Across the bay, Manefredonia lay with its white buildings faintly reflecting the light from a cloud covered moon. Now and again gently moving ripples became a small wave breaking on the beach. Yearning for surf beaches in Australia, we tried to ride a tiny wave into shore, but it petered out. A walk along the beach made our legs like jelly, and reminded us the hour was late. More than ready to return to base, we flopped into the vehicle and drove to the lone soldier at the guard barrier. Hearing his muffled, "Goodnight," we headed off to join our sleeping mates on the squadron.

11

"I'VE BEEN TO DOC FRANCIS"

At lunch time next day, when Tony knew I was on ops, he came to me with a twinkle in his eye, and said, "Now Tommy see to it that you don't let them dent Kathleen, she's a special lady and we don't want anyone to hurt her!" "OK Wheeler," I retorted with a chuckle, recalling our night adventure with the champagne over Kathleen, "I'll do my best!" Tony added, "Actually I've just done an air test on her and she's good. All the best for your op tonight."

TO THE GERMAN BORDER

Our attack that night would be on Fieberbrunn, near the German - Austrian border. The route took us between Vienna and Wiener Neustadt, two well defended areas of German occupied Europe. We took off without incident and flew northwards. Did a corridor exist in the defences between the two cities? We would soon know.

Part way along between Vienna and Wiener Neustadt, an intense blue searchlight locked onto our aircraft. In a matter of seconds, other searchlights switched on from around Vienna. There must have been forty searchlights filling our plane with intense blinding light. We became the target of heavy gunfire as shells burst amongst the beams of light. I crouched low in my seat so that the glare of the searchlight did not blind me entirely, and I flew by looking upwards to read the instruments arrayed on the pilot's panel.

"Do I pull out of this now, before all the defences really lock on to us?" I asked myself; then decided to hold course for the navigator's sake. The raid depended on Pathfinders maintaining a good steady run into the target. "I'll stay straight and level and hope we can get out of the Vienna area before their guns get us," I decided.

Within seconds, the Weiner Neustadt defences added their gunfire and searchlights to our dilemma. We were like a fly caught in a giant web of exploding shells and light beams in a darkened sky. The gunfire ceased, an ominous sign that fighter aircraft were in the vicinity and due to attack. The rear gunner called, "Skipper there's a single engine plane coming at us through the searchlights, an ME109 I think, and there's another, I'd say its a Junkers 88, twin engined."

GET WEAVING

Smithy continued his urgent call, " You'll have to get weaving Skipper, NOW!" The Junkers 88 twin engined fighters were especially geared up as night fighters so I dived the Halifax through eight thousand feet and then pulled the nose nearly vertically upwards. Gaining height so rapidly, our speed fell off quickly. With heavy pressure on the rudder pedals, I took our plane from a steep climb into a steep dive again, using a manoeuvre called a "stall turn", trying to fox the searchlights and escape the fighters.

My tactic did not fox the searchlights one bit. They hung on while I sweated and used all my strength to get that heavily loaded Halifax out of the lights and away from the fighters. I repeated the stall turn. Thoughts clicked through my mind, "It's worked before, so why not now?" We had beaten searchlights over other targets, why not now? The crews on the searchlights were good, too good. I felt desperate.

Group Captain Don Bennett at Upwood, had warned us, "When sixty searchlights lock on to your plane, it will be impossible for you to escape being shot out of the sky. So the secret is, do not let sixty searchlights lock on to you! Do you get that?" I certainly did. His words echoed in my ears. I had an awful pain in my stomach as I realised that I was now proving only too well the truth of his words.

An idea, a ruse, came into my mind; Shorty! Shorty had been operating at the rear of the Halifax, dispersing window, a code name for strips of aluminium foil, which he sent down a chute in bundles to confuse enemy radar. "Shorty," I called. "Yes Skipper." "Empty all your boxes of window in a heap on the floor of the plane. Open the rear door, keep it open and when I give the word, heave it all out the door in one big heap. Have you got that?" "Yes Skipper!" called Shorty. I had no time to explain my plan in detail.

The rear part of a rolling, diving, climbing plane was a tough, awkward place to be. Oxygen masks were essential at this height and

Shorty would be holding on as he got to work opening the boxes of window, then he had to lock open the rear door of the Halifax. Through it, he would gaze down on Vienna, and I did not want him falling out.

"Ready Skipper!" came Shorty's Aussie drawl. I was amazed at how quickly he had worked. I pushed the nose of the Halifax down until the air screamed past us and every part of the plane strained under the added speed of our rush towards the earth. Pulling back the control column, I put the aircraft into an almost vertical climb. She responded beautifully despite being heavily loaded. With our speed falling off as we climbed, I called "Hold it Shorty ... get ready ...."

Forcing the Halifax into a vertical position, I made as if to turn left at the top of the climb, a feinting move that I hoped would trick the searchlights and the fighters coming in. Then I shouted to Shorty, "Go!". The huge pile of aluminium strips would have exploded into the air, giving the enemy searchlight operators the impression that they still held our plane. I had to keep ahead of those searchlight operators, keep them guessing, so instead of continuing to turn left at the top of the climb, I reversed the Halifax out of the left turn and into a right hand turn that had us diving towards the earth. The searchlights stayed on the exploding mass of foil long enough for us to escape out into the darkness of the night.

From the view of the operators on the ground, it would have appeared that our Halifax had exploded. Perhaps the gunners cheered as they saw it. "That was tremendous Shorty," I called exultantly, "We foxed the lights, but Smithy, keep an eye out for those fighters.

Just then our plane shuddered and there was a thump. We had flown through the slipstream of someone just ahead of us. Ed yelled, "Bloody hell!" My nerves were on edge and I had quite a fright at coming so near to another aircraft, but I had too much on my hands to enquire how close we came. We had covered a lot of distance in our gyrations across the sky, and I needed to settle on to our course so that Ed and Hoppy could get on with their work of guiding us to the target.

KATHLEEN, LADY OF THE NIGHT

The night wore on, the moon rose in full brightness, and night became like day. We ran Kathleen in over the target. One enemy fighter passed us, glistening in the moonlight, then a second swept past. It was proving to be a tough night, and we felt thankful to get out of the area and settle down for a quieter flight home.

Clambering into our transport vehicle at Amandola, Ed wanted to talk about the hot reception over Vienna. "I was in the nose, when the searchlights got us, every corner inside the plane seemed to light up. Then the guns got a line on us, and I couldn't see how they would miss us. Did you feel the mighty thump, and we passed through the slipstream of that other plane?" "I sure did." said Smithy, "What was it?" Ed exclaimed, "The tail of a bloody Halifax whipped across our path. I could have reached out and touched the gunner, he was so close."

They could all talk now with the emergency over and Shorty asked, "Say Ed, how do you think the rear gunner of that plane felt, looking into your face, up there in the heavens. Perhaps he thought you were an angel come to get him?" "Me? A bloody angel!" exclaimed Ed, "You must be joking, but he was that close I could have reached out and touched him."

I commended Shorty on his prompt action in ejecting the huge pile of aluminium foil over Vienna. He laughed and said, "I didn't do much Tommy." "But how did you hold on in all that bucking of the plane?" I asked. "Well" he said pensively, "It wasn't easy, because I had to keep unplugging my oxygen supply, but I found a spar on the side of the plane and I hung on to that. I looked out into those searchlights through the open rear door and all I could see were glaring lights and then all of a sudden I saw just sky and I held on for dear life."

At debriefing we learnt another pilot had seen us caught by the cone of searchlights, and had tried to sneak his plane through underneath us while the Germans were busy with us. His rear gunner still looked white as a sheet after gazing so closely into Ed's face when our plane swept past him in the near collision.

We counted our losses. Once again it had been a costly attack. Maurie Harrison and his crew were missing. Other crews reported a number of aircraft going down under the guns of German fighters. Maurie's crew and our crew were friends; we had been together at Marston Moor and had trained together in PFF at Upwood. I went across to my tent thinking about them and walked around for some time, waiting, hoping for their return, keyed up listening for the sound of Merlin motors in the sky. Increasing light of early morning turned into day, but still no sound came from the missing Halifax. The empty sky seemed uncaring about my feelings.

PHOTO ALBUM

I had an agreement with Maurie's radio operator, to protect each other's photos in the case of one of us going missing. Like me, he loved photography. I had a heavy feeling as I lay on my bed thinking, "Now is the moment we talked about. He's not coming back, I'd better do something about his album." I arose and went to his tent. His two albums and his camera were just where he said they would be, for sending to his mother. Tomorrow I would know more about what had happened to him. I lay on my bed and tried to sleep. I must have slept soundly, for when I sat up the day was well advanced. I checked on my friend's tent but found it empty. The RAF Police had taken charge of all his goods. I learned that a German night fighter had destroyed Maurie's Halifax near Klagenfurt, south east of Vienna.

OIL TARGETS

For months we flew seemingly endless trips to the oil targets at Bucharest and Ploesti, near the Black Sea in Rumania. Others were in Hungary and northern Italy. Ed Riley, in irrepressible fashion, produced a sketch labelled, "very experienced Pathfinder crew!"

On and on through the hot summer months of June, July and August 1944, the attacks on oil targets continued. Germany needed the flow of oil for her machines of war, particularly her submarines. England had been brought to her knees by the consistent sinking of ships from all over the world bringing food and war materials to supply her. The bomber attacks on oil supplies, besides weakening Germany in her war effort, were crucial to the survival of the British people themselves.

OUR OWN SURVIVAL

The wearing effect of gunfire and our continually being shot at, took its toll of us emotionally. The squadron was losing crew after crew from fighter attacks and from ground gunfire and it made us wonder just how long we could last on these trips. I could see the emotional cost mounting. We flew together, but talk on the ground became difficult.

One night, over the Bucharest oil refineries, heavy concentrated gunfire came up at us. Claude Caldwell Wearne's plane went down nearby us. His starboard wing was hit and in no time the plane was a mass of flames as it exploded. He was a pilot from Sydney, and we missed his many pranks on the squadron. Tall, London born, Walter Carrington and his crew went down and then others followed including Bob Langton and his Canadian and British crew. Canadian Bruce Prange came back with all his crew gone except his wounded bomb aimer and the plane in tatters. The rest of the crew had parachuted out when the situation seemed hopeless. Another of our crews came back with their brand new Halifax riddled by cannon fire from a German Focke Wulf fighter.

HOW ARE YOU ?

Long hours of flying were hard on us all but particularly wearing on Hoppy. Navigation on these trips proved difficult. There were long parts of the flight where few navigation checks could be done even when Ed used his H2S Radar so well. We often flew over Yugoslavia, Hungary and Rumania and much of those countries lacked big towns and lakes that could be easily identified on the H2S, so most of the navigation was done by just plain hard work; a star shot, Shorty's radio direction finder, a river reflected in the moonlight, or just plain dead reckoning. In the midst of all this, Hoppy began to feel that his mind did not handle the navigation problems clearly. He had been very quiet and uncommunicative for a long time and I knew that he had become very tired. I worried about him.

As a commissioned officer, I had the role from time to time as Duty Officer checking the Sergeant's mess where Hoppy dined. At the lunch time meal, there was Hoppy, eating slowly as was his usual quiet way, but his lined face concerned me. "How are you Hoppy?" I asked. "Oh I'm going OK," he replied in his non committal way. He just did not look OK and I longed to break into his feelings and know how he really was.

Next morning I came out of the Intelligence Section where our target photographs were interpreted by expert staff. I met Hoppy. He looked even more strained and pale than when I had last seen him. There we were, two deeply feeling flyers, needing to communicate; both hesitant to start. "I'll not be flying with you any more Tommy" he said slowly. I had been dreading this moment, trying to avoid it. "Is that so Hoppy?" I replied anxiously, "What makes you say that?" He said quietly, "I've been to see Doc Francis and he has put me off ops." I tried to grasp the significance of Hoppy's words. "For how long?" I queried. "It's for good," said Hoppy, "He has grounded me." I had not expected such finality and my heart sank in dismay.

We stood facing each other shaded by the branches of an olive tree. The grey dust underfoot still remained hot, and the heat made me aware of the oppressiveness of these moments, "I'm going to lose Hoppy!" I tried to dispel my rising tide of shock, disappointment and anger. It seemed important to me that Hoppy had gone to the doctor without first telling me about the effect of his tiredness on him. He did not have to tell me of course, it was just how closeness worked with me. I valued so very highly our oneness as pilot and navigator.

I recalled my own anxieties over the way Hoppy had been showing signs of distress. I longed to reach out to this man; he meant so much to me, but I could not find words amidst my own sense of loss.

"Tommy, I've thought of someone who could replace me." Hoppy's voice broke into my unhappy thoughts. I tried to overcome my feeling of emptiness, "Who?" "You could think of asking Bill Scott to fly with you. He's looking for a crew and could fill my place." I gasped, "But what are you going to do? Are you taking on some other sort of flying?"

The world of flying was my life and I tended to only think in those terms. "I'm finished with flying," retorted Hoppy. A look of utmost relief came over him. He had told me his momentous decision and I represented something from which he had to move away. There seemed nothing left for me to say. I put my hand upon him, "I'm going to miss you Hoppy!" We parted. I stumbled away needing to cope with the anguish within me, and not noticing the heat of the burning Italian dust.

At the Officer's Mess, officers relaxed in comfy lounge chairs, reading mail or magazines, or doing crossword puzzles. I saw Reg Facey there. Last night Reg had parachuted out of his Halifax after it collided with another near our base. The pilot regained control of the plane but Reg had already parachuted out. I thought, "Perhaps Reg will talk about last night and take my mind off what's going on inside me about Hoppy."

But Reg, still shocked and sore, did not want to talk about his near disaster. He had walked in by himself, across ploughed fields for three miles in darkness, without any boots on his feet. They had fallen off when his parachute jerked open.

Now nursing his tender feet, Reg opened up a magazine, turned to a crossword puzzle and began working on it. Disconsolate, I went over to the notice board. The Ops list had just been put up and my crew was listed to fly. Hoppy's name had been scratched out and I saw that the name inserted was our deputy navigation leader. I liked him, although we had not flown together before, but Hoppy's name scratched out was the last thing I needed at that moment.

Thoughts about Hoppy no longer flying with us reminded me of my crew. I had neglected them as I tried to sort myself out. Wandering over to Ed's tent, I explained to him about Hoppy. He was quiet for a few moments then said he had known Hoppy was going to the doctor. His laughing eyes clouded as he affirmed how he had enjoyed being teamed together with Hoppy and would find it hard to adjust to working with someone else. Other members of our crew drifted in. Shorty became quite outspoken, "We can never expect to replace a fellow like Hoppy can we Tommy. No one could be as good?" Bob Lewis wanted to know what we intended to do next and I was able to announce our temporary replacement.

As for Smithy, the lines of his finely chiselled face told their own story of strain. He remained quiet. I tried to push away my anxiety about him, for I sensed he was drifting further and further away from communication about himself, and I longed for him to say something, but no expression came.

Hoppy chose to become an air traffic controller. He came to me one day looking very cheerful and wanting to say farewell as he went off to his training course. He looked so much less strained, and I commented on it as I said farewell News of him came through to me from time to time. When he completed the Air Traffic Controllers course he received a commission as an RAF officer. He sent me a photo of himself dressed in his officer's uniform and peaked cap. I could not help comparing the photo to the British sergeant I had first met when we began flying together.

NEW NAVIGATOR

For such an interdependent crew as ours, the loss of Hoppy had been like losing our right arm, a replacement would not be easy to find. The navigation officer, sensitive to my feelings about Hoppy, wanted to talk about a replacement. I warmed to this ex speedway driver and went to see him. "Come in Tommy, sit down," he said. I sat on his hard chair with its legs that dug into the dirt floor of the marquee he used as his office.

"Tommy, what about taking Bill Scott? He has been on the squadron now for some time since his own crew was transferred. He is available." "That's interesting," I replied, "Hoppy mentioned Bill as a possible replacement, but in the air, will I understand his lilting geordie words? Already I have a Geordie, a Lancashire man, one from the Midlands and a Scottish brogue. That's my problem!" "He's a good navigator!" added the Nav officer.

I had first rubbed shoulders with Bill on our rough rugby football field. Square jawed, broad shouldered, and with solid frame, I knew it could be good to have Bill in action with us, but I continued to worry about the difficulties I had in following his dialect.

But the Nav officer still believed Bill would be the best replacement for Hoppy. He looked squarely at me awaiting my reply. I said, "Well, I know that he's a good navigator, but I'd like to keep open with you about how he settles into our crew. If I think it's not going too well, I'll let you know. How would that be?" "That's fine with me Tommy," replied the Nav leader, "In the meantime, I'll let Bill know our decision." ""Thanks," I replied, stepping out of the marquee and walking into the biting heat of full sun on this airless Italian summer day.

Walking between the olive trees towards the mess, I met up with Tony Wheeler, who said brightly, "Tommy, I've got a few fellows together for a trip to the beach for a swim. How about coming?" "Are you dinkum Tony? That sounds spot on, too right I'll come. Which vehicle are we going in?"

TO THE BEACH

The beach lay at Manefredonia, at the foot of the ominous Gargarno Peninsula. Our group of English, Aussie and Canadian flying men arrived there and the first person I noticed was Bill Scott. I sat with him and told him of my talk with the Nav leader. "Yes," said Bill, "He's been talking to me about joining up with you and I'm looking forward to it. I've been waiting around the squadron since my own crew were transferred, and I'm bloody sick of it. I'll be glad to get going again."

His voice made him sound almost gruff, but a voice that could also be enticingly friendly, inviting response. This, I liked and hoped that I would be able to decipher Bill's words when we engaged in quick chatter amidst the noise of flying.

He told me about his work at home in a Tyneside power house prior to joining the RAF. "My father was a Geordie!" I said, and seeing Bill's amazement, I added, "Yes, but he went to Australia in 1903, quite a long time ago eh!"

He was quiet for a while and then went on, "It's bad luck about Hoppy being grounded." "Yes it is, but then you've had your disappointments too." I replied thinking of Bill losing his crew.

I appreciated his sensitivity about Hoppy and how dinkum he was in being willing to face ops again. Making a run for the waters of the Adriatic, I called, "Come on Billy, let's have a swim."

The warmed summer waters of the Adriatic did not stimulate and refresh as cooler waters would have done, but we floated lazily and Bill shared about his life in the RAF. He said, "I actually enlisted as a pilot and did 10 hours flying Tiger Moths in South Yorkshire in January 1942 amidst snow flurries and ice covered pools."

Bill continued, "In April, 1942 I went to California and began flying more powerful planes, but I never went solo. Perhaps I could have made it if I'd had a different instructor. I felt angry with him for the way he treated me and I felt glad when I heard later that he had been dismissed."

"Next step found me as a trainee navigator at Edmonton in Canada in summer heat, ninety degrees, and in winter minus ten degrees. Ooh it was cold, and those bloody planes needed their undercarriage raised by turning a handle 198 turns."

"Later, as a crew in Whitley bombers, my pilot managed to get one into a spin at ten thousand feet, and I thought curtains had come to us for sure, as the altimeter seemed to unwind so rapidly. However, he pulled out of the spin at about fifteen hundred feet so I'm alive to talk about it.

Bill was silent for a while, then said, "Do you ever think of after the war? I do, I'd love to go back and complete my powerhouse engineering certificate one day." I noticed his strong emphasis about his going back one day.

I explained that I found it difficult to consider what the world would be like when peace came. If given the opportunity to be a civil engineer, I would grasp it, but for now I lived a day at a time. A future did not belong to me just yet. "Anyway, I'm looking forward to having you join us," I said as I recalled my talk with the Nav leader. Bill replied, "I'm looking forward to it too. How did your op go last night?"

FRANCE

"We went into France. It took Ed and the navigator a while to settle in together, but we had a tremendous trip. Seven and a half hours of flying out over the Italian mountains, past Rome, Sardinia, Corsica, Marseilles and southern France to Valence in the Rhone Valley. We attacked in conjunction with the allied invasion of Southern France. What a dramatic moment that was, when Ed's radar picked up the images of over a thousand ships moving in to make their dawn attack on the French coast.

Then we flew on up the Rhone valley to our target, and our TIs went down right on time. I'd say we caught the German air force on the ground, and the whole raid became a spectacular success." I finished explaining about our attack and Bill was lost in thought for a while. "I'm really looking forward to getting going with you Tommy!" I was feeling less apprehensive now about my language difficulties with Bill.

With arms and legs moving gently in the salty Adriatic, my flesh responded to the relaxing motion. Tony called for our return to the squadron, "Time to go Tommy!" It seemed all too soon. Thoughts about last night's attack made me feel very tired, and I just wanted to remain losing myself in the pleasant movement of my body in the water.

The squadron would be out again that night and my duties included that of marshalling pilot, helping to assemble the Halifaxes near the end of the runway ready for take off. However, when I had fulfilled those duties, I was free. I could look forward to a rest night from flying, relaxing over some Spumanti wine, then visit my boys and welcome Bill Scott into our team.

12

STARS OVER THE OILFIELDS

With our rest day completed, I went to the notice board and read the Ops List. My crew was there with Bill Scott as our navigator. Strongly aware of tension sweeping over me, I knew that each one of my crew would go through similar strain. It came as soon as we knew our names were on the Ops List, and continued until about dawn next morning when we would be able to tuck ourselves into bed after the night's operations.

Bill and I met as we walked in opposite directions across open ground between the tents and marquees. "Briefing time is four pm Billy." "So it's on ch Tommy! I've been spending time with Ed, talking over how we'll work together," Bill replied. "So you're sorting out procedure already. I'm glad about that. You two geordies will get on fine, I'm sure, and you'll certainly be speaking the same language. See you at briefing Bill." "Right, I'll catch up with you then Tommy!"

Briefing, a high security exercise, was held in a large marquee, conspicuous to all in our tented town. Guards checked those attending so that only operations personnel received the sensitive briefing information.

About a hundred men, gunners, wireless operators, flight engineers, navigators, bomb aimers and pilots assembled in the marquee. It was a tense time waiting for what our target might be, but men broke the tension with jokes and wisecracks, or sat quietly talking. Bill sat in the chair usually occupied by Hoppy. He seemed excited, and my crew were more animated than usual at a briefing.

"Attention!" boomed the voice of our tough South African Wing Commander. The assembled flyers stood to attention as Group Captain Laird, our CO, walked in with the navigation officer. They had arrived from Group Headquarters with final details of our target. The CO took the stand, "Sit down men", he said gently. Chairs banged together noisily.

A breathless hush settled as the CO turned to a large wall map now being uncovered for all to see. We gazed intently, searching out the heavy lines to identify our route. Ed, quick off the mark, whispered, "Bloody hell, it's Bucharest again."

Speaking slowly in his cultured English voice, the CO said, "Tonight you will be attacking the Prahova Oil Refinery at Bucharest. You are to go in and destroy oil supplies urgently needed by the enemy to maintain his war effort." After further preamble he called his staff officers.

The navigation officer rehearsed details for our navigation. We would be dropping route markers for the following squadrons of bomber aircraft needing navigation points on the long arduous flight that now lay ahead. Take off time, 9.00 pm, time on target for the bombers, zero hour at 1.00 am next morning. First Pathfinders were to go in at zero hour minus fifteen minutes so that our target indicators marked the target by the time the bombers started coming in at zero hour.

The officer for intelligence detailed fighter aircraft defences along the Dalmatian coast, the Danube River and around Bucharest itself. We would also face gun emplacement defences plus searchlights.

The bombing and weapons officer listed bomb loads and armaments. The engineering officer emphasised the limits on our fuel supplies, encouraging pilots to nurse the engines for the arduous eight hour flight, so that we could have fuel in reserve for any delays in landing back at base. He did not want aircraft ditching into the Adriatic through lack of fuel.

Our blonde headed expert in radar and electronics, spelt out what we could expect from our electronic aids: our radar pictures expected over the target; the "Gee" equipment's signals that would peter out long before we reached Bucharest.

"Hmmmm the weather! Well fellows, anything can happen tonight and it probably will!" In these familiar words, the "Met" man outlined weather patterns he expected us to experience along the way. Weather patterns over Europe depended on observations from high flying Mosquito aircraft bringing back vital weather data, and were very tricky for him to map out accurately for us.

The officer for communications and signals, gave codes for the night, and details of radio frequencies for radio operators. Our flight commanders gave times for our meal, and what flying rations we could pick up. "Transport vehicles will pick you up at 1950 hours.

Any questions?" boomed the South African Wingco. No one spoke. Most of the crews had been into Rumania before. "Atten—tion!" boomed the voice again. We all stood as the CO and his officers departed. With note books in hand, crews remained to jot down information from the map. Eventually, meal time came, and with it, sporadic conversations as each man coped with his thoughts about the flight ahead.

Ground crews welcomed us as we dismounted from our vehicle. Our Halifaxes sat waiting near the end of the runway like huge birds with wings outstretched. The summer sun still shone, reflecting its heat off the wide runway stretching into the distance. Bill dressed in warm flying clothes for upper air coldness, puffed with exertion as he carried all his navigation gear to the rear door of the Halifax and disappeared inside. Others followed. I checked the exterior instruments and fittings around the Halifax and then did my long walk up into the pilot's seat. I called each crew member and then called Bill, "Are you OK navigator?" "All set skipper" came Bill's voice, reassuring and clear.

Ed stood at my side as engines roared, and "Kathleen" picked up speed along the runway. A wind had sprung up across the runway and Kathleen's tendency to swing to port on take off seemed much stronger than usual. Racing past runway pointers, we sped on towards the far boundary, left the earth behind, and had a view of our tent city settling down for the night. At one thousand feet, Ed went forward to his nose position, followed by Bill and Shorty who had been waiting aft in their take off positions.

A BAD START

With our port wing well down in a turn, I took "Kathleen" in a wide circle so as to bring us back over the centre of the air base, starting point for Bill to navigate us to Bucharest. Several thousand feet below us the runway seemed to explode. A sheet of flame spread out across the ground. It dawned on me that a loaded Halifax had come to grief with petrol and bombs blowing up.

Straightening up out of the turn, I called to Bill, "Start navigation .....NOW!" "OK Skipper" Bill called back. Smithy from the rear turret called, "Oh no! There's a plane crashed on take off!" "OK Smithy," I replied, realising that he had to see it. "That cross wind is a bit strong down there and someone didn't make their take off." I wanted to cut down talk about it as much as possible and save the crew from undue tension.

Thus our first flight with Bill Scott as navigator, had begun. We climbed towards eastern darkness, and the crashed Halifax glowed like a beacon on the runway behind us. He would be one less Pathfinder to back up our target marking when we reached Bucharest in four hours time.

Crossing the Adriatic Sea, we came to the coast of Yugoslavia with its high mountain ranges. An enemy fighter came out of nowhere and crossed over in front of our nose, apparently without seeing us. "Rear gunner, keep your eyes peeled, that fellow doesn't appear to have seen us but he may come back again!" "OK Skipper" Smithy's worried voice came back from his lonely position sixty five feet away from me in the tail of the Halifax.

Deeper into enemy occupied Europe, we flew. As we came to the area of the Danube River, streaks of gunfire just to the north, alerted us to an enemy fighter attacking one of our planes. My eyes followed the curving ball of flame plummeting to earth. It all looked so unreal, slow motion finality to a plane and her crew, now a glow on the ground. I called to Smithy, "Watch out for enemy fighters coming up from below rear gunner." Our plane would be more visible to an enemy below us. "OK Skipper" came the retort from the distant gunner.

Cloud formations thickened. Pillars of cloud rose majestically above us as rising masses of air thrust them into upper heights. "Navigator" I called, "There are seven or eight tenths of cumulus cloud formation around us. I hope it clears a bit before the target." "OK skipper, we're crossing the Danube now, would you steer 282 degrees for Gui Gui our turning point for the run in to the target." "282 degrees it is" I called to Bill as I turned the Halifax on to the new course.

GUI GUI

I pictured the mighty Danube river eighteen thousand feet below us.

With its headwaters in the Swiss alps, it flowed nearly two thousand miles until it emptied into the Black Sea to the east. On its waters, river traffic plied to and fro in a continual stream. Many of the barges contained oil for Germany, carried from the wells of Rumania.

We headed for our turning point at Gui Gui, pronounced Joo Joo, a well defended industrial town, on a bend in the Danube. We had to fly over Gui Gui as an accurate turning point for a direct radar run in to the target at Bucharest.

From Gui Gui, the Danube ran north east towards the Black Sea, that huge Russian Lake, over 300 miles across, where holiday makers of Europe once flocked for summer vacations. Now in wartime, the area mounted heavy batteries of guns and searchlights, defending the oil facilities of Ploesti and Bucharest. I thought of the importance of Rumanian oil to the German submarines that sent allied ships to the bottom. I hoped that tonight we would cut off oil to at least a few of those subs.

BOOMPH, Boomph boomph! Heavy explosions around us indicated German and Rumanian gun batteries below at Gui Gui. Clouds billowed above and the flashes of exploding shells gave ugly fiery glints amongst the beauty of towering cloud masses. An explosion under our tail must have given Smithy a big fright for he yelled into his microphone, "Bloody close skipper, bloody close .... can't you get out of here?"

Before I could answer, Bill's voice came through, "Steer 010 degrees skipper!" "010 degrees it is navigator" I called back and then to Smithy I said, "We're turning north out of this stuff rear gunner, I'm turning now." Just then another set of eight explosions rocked along our port side scaring me into realising that those gunners determined to prevent our escape.

I turned to port, heading right through the smoke of the exploding shells. An acrid smell of the explosions came into the plane "Have you gone bloody mad?" Smithy spoke worriedly as he saw the smoke of exploding shells go past him. "Calm down Smithy" I called back, "That ack ack has already finished exploding there and shells don't explode in the same spot twice!" I hoped that what I said was true, because I sensed that the gunners below us had our every move on their radar. Even our turning to fly northward seemed to be expected by them. Their shells followed us as we headed north to Bucharest.

I appreciated Bill's calm, "Alter course" amidst the cracking explosions of the ack ack. It had been a good time to choose to turn across the line of exploding shells, but Smithy's shake-up by the gunfire worried me. In his position, alone in the tail, he had an unenviable job, with time on his hands, watching, scanning the darkness for an approaching enemy. I just hoped he would hold together as we approached our target, for enemy guns would be even hotter there.

"We're heading into the clear now rear gunner," I called, wanting to assure him that all was well as the flight proceeded. "Keep your eyes skinned for fighters!" "Right skipper" came back Smithy's voice, tremulous now after the explosions and showing his strain.

BUCHAREST AHEAD

Bill and Ed concentrated on a final assessment of correct wind speed and direction for feeding into the bombsight, preparing for our attack. Ed called, "The radar shows Bucharest forty miles ahead. I'll go into the nose now!" Ed left the screen of his radar set and moved into position lying in the nose of the Halifax. Gazing down into Rumania, his eyes tried to pierce through the darkness below. Finding that impossible he concentrated on setting up his bomb sight in readiness for guiding me the last few minutes into the target.

Flying above Bucharest defences, in cloud, the wings of our Halifax bumped and flexed under the strain of heavy updraughts and downdraughts of air. At any moment, we expected to see sky flares ahead, lighting up Bucharest as the leading 614 Squadron Pathfinders went in.

Glare filled my eyes. It was a German master beam searchlight. We had no warning, flick, we were caught. Other searchlights came on us. Ed in the nose, tried to shield his eyes, and Smithy in his turret, said he could not see a thing. I crouched down in my cockpit, keeping my eyes glued on to the flying instruments and away from the intense light as I put our Halifax into a dive. Then the gunfire started, so much more accurately and intense than at Gui Gui. Our wings and nose took the brunt of the onslaught.

Still in a steep dive, we broke through cloud and I gazed down into a hell of gunfire and exploding shells. A curtain of exploding steel was slowly engulfing us. I pulled the plane back up into a climb gaining thousands of feet in quick time. As I levelled off back at 18,000 feet, Smithy's voice called, "Dive starboard, dive starboard." His call and my response saved us from collision with a plane crossing over our tail, "Good on you Smithy." We had avoided collision, we were free of searchlights and gunfire but we had ruined our run in to the target. "Damn it!"

I saw guns and searchlights engaging other aircraft coming through the storm clouds on their individual attacks, then I saw the Pathfinder sky flares hanging on their parachutes. Ed saw them too. How long they had been there we did not know, for we had been blinded by the searchlights. I planned our next run, dismayed that Bucharest defences found us so early on our first try. But our relief was only momentary. The cone of searchlights locked on to us once more and the guns located their bursting shells around us.

Ed had a fright as wind came in through his section of the Halifax damaged by shell fire. Thankfully he had not been hurt. He tried desperately to get some glimpse of the landmarks below that would enable him to guide us over the Prahova Oil Refinery, but clouds hid the refinery from his view.

Even in cloud, the radar controlled searchlights continued to hold us. Searchlights and gunfire worked together, determined to hunt us down. Still the target remained hidden.

We had lost height in the last manoeuvre so I pointed the nose of the Halifax upward, reaching for the upper air for which our bombing windspeed had been calculated. But even as we climbed for height, the searchlights, and then the guns focused on us once more. We felt their anger being poured out furiously. I levelled out at bombing height and grimly held the plane on course waiting for Ed to give some direction towards the refinery somewhere below us. I recognised Ed's exasperated voice, "Bugger it! I can't see a thing."

THE SKY FLARES

Amidst Ed's exasperation, we were horrified to see the lead Pathfinders' sky flares slowly and majestically dying away. The attack had not gone at all well. I guided the plane towards the dying lights but again the searchlights fixed on us, blinding us all by their intense glare. By the time I broke free of them, the sky flares had disappeared. All our flare illumination of the target area had ceased.

One enterprising Pathfinder must have seen something, for a green TI glittered as a shower and fell towards the ground. I dived down through cloud to gain some view of the target indicators but Ed could not identify just where they had fallen. I continued in the dive to get away from the gunfire and the searchlights and headed for a dark part of the sky. Turning our plane in a circle with the big port side wing silhouetted against the clouds, someone shouted, "You are not going in again skipper?" I could sense a pleading in his voice.

CONFERENCE IN THE SKY

"Have you got any suggestions navigator or bomb aimer?" I called. Silence reigned for a while, then Ed spoke, "It's bloody impossible. Just for a moment I saw the canal and railway to the west of the refinery, but then I lost them again and beyond that I could not identify a thing." I felt the tenseness in Ed's voice as he spoke, then Bill added, "with the illuminating flares gone, I vote we give it a miss!" Then a voice piped in, "Me too!" Smithy in his lonely position in the tail must have had a buffeting as I had thrown the Halifax around amidst the attack.

As these men spoke I sensed the rawness of all our nerves. The crew waited on me to make a decision. I hated leaving our job unfinished. An alternative run at low level had to be ruled out because the target markers could explode in the plane if we tried to drop them at low level. They were not set for low level. "OK" I said, "we'll not be making a drop tonight. What's the course to steer for home navigator?" Bill gave a deep sigh and said, "Course to steer is 281 degrees." I set the ring of the compass to 281 and turned the nose of our battered Halifax westwards. We checked for gunfire damage to our motors. Fortunately they sang strongly and fuel supplies held.

A sense of gloom descended on me as we set off on the long flight home. "If only those flares had lasted a bit longer!" I sighed. Eventually we flew into calm air, and I pictured the British men and women who built our planes and gave us the explosives and shipped our fuel supplies. It pained me to think of the effort to put on the attack and now our failure in the vital moments of battle. We had never been beaten by the defences before. I vowed I would never let them beat me again.

THAT VOICE AGAIN

In trying to handle my deep gloom, my eyes went to the stars. I responded to their glow quite unconsciously. The rush of air and roar of motors faded. I had the sensation of being suspended in space. The stars represented to me an imposing presence and I was comforted by them. At what stage I became aware of experiencing an inward balm, I did not know. All I knew was that once again, a presence had spoken to me. Did the stars really have a voice? It was a fascinating question, but I had to put it aside in my need to get our aircraft back to Italy.

We finally arrived back at Amandola air base, and the debriefing officer sat to record our account of the attack. Ed gave his report like a tactician, detailing the defences around Bucharest with an accuracy that surprised me especially as we had twisted and turned across the Rumanian capital, and had hardly seen the ground. Determined to make the most of the information he had gleaned this night, Ed realised that there would be the next attack for which the squadron needed to prepare. Bill's account remained cheerful and positive in a way that impressed me. He had maintained calm throughout the pressure of our attempts to press home the attack and I recognised his value in our team. We experienced the loss of a key Pathfinder team when our Canadian deputy flight commander and his crew did not return.

The CO was there to listen as we spelt out the details of our trip, and I watched the tanned skin of his handsome unlined face. A big man with broad shoulders, he carried heavy responsibilities but his expression gave no hint of blaming us for the failure of our night's work. Bucharest and Ploesti remained tough targets and tomorrow, he and his officers would sift through crew reports to try and establish a better strategy for our next attempt to cut off German oil supplies.

Daylight had come by the time I went to my tent. I gazed intently into the sky, longing to hear the sound of Merlin motors, hoping our missing Canadian would return. One lone star remained visible. It took my thoughts to a voice, a presence, amongst the stars over Rumania. I wondered if I would survive long enough to understand what that voice was trying to say.

THE ANGUISH OF SMITHY

Smithy did one more attack with us after Prahova, then he could take no more. His pale sensitive face showed his inner agony. He went off for an appointment with Doc Francis and was gone for quite some time. When he returned he came to me, "I'll not be flying with you anymore skipper," he said, showing me the doctor's certificate exempting him from flying. Despite Smithy's difficulties during our last attack on Bucharest, I had a rise of sadness at the thought of losing him.

A courageous sensitive man, I would miss him. He and I had worked hard together to harmonise his gun firing procedures and my flying, in readiness for fighter attacks. "So the time has come for you to leave us Smithy," I said sombrely, "Do you know what you will be doing?" "No, I haven't a clue," he said sadly.

When I heard that he had been transferred to other duties out of 614 Squadron, I wished we could have given him some big award for his bravery in the twenty five long flights he had accomplished with us in attacking enemy targets. But Smithy's courage and dedication went with him when he disappeared from the squadron overnight, and a sergeant gunner became Smithy's replacement in our crew.

FRENCH PARTISANS.

Night attacks on the enemy continued as our new crew members settled in. Southern France became our target once more as we backed up the Allied invasion from the south. The defences plagued our way, especially around Marseilles. We assisted French Partisans to rise up behind the German front line, by attacking German facilities at Valence in the Rhone valley.

The flight was a very long eight hours, and daylight had come before we returned to Italy. Other members of the crew had moved around the plane, and used the toilet facilities, but I had not moved far from my flight deck. After landing, I went out for a most painful but joyful response to a call of nature. "Hurry up Scotty," my crew called as they waited for me to board the transport to debriefing. But hurry, I could not.

The inimitable Ed sketched his impressions of our weary crew.

BOMBAIMER! STOP ADMIRING THE SUNRISE AND WAKE THE B----Y NAVIGATOR UP, WE MUST BE NEARLY HOME NOW.

At debriefing the CO asked, "How did it go Scotty?" I outlined for him our flight via Corsica to the Rhone valley. The CO then sprang a surprise. He had a matter he wanted to discuss, and made an appointment for me to see him next day.

SOMETHING IN THE WIND

I awoke to gnawing hunger pangs that alerted me to the nearness of lunchtime. Summer heat bathed me in perspiration. Having washed in the small basin, I dressed, and made my way towards the Officers Mess. After lunch, I awaited my appointment with the CO. "Something is in the wind," I thought to myself, for he normally worked through his flight commanders.

Some time later Bill Scott met me, "What's going on Tommy? I heard that the CO wanted to see you." The news that the CO had given me, had stunned me. "Well Billy," I responded, "We are temporarily off ops." Bill looked at me in disbelief, "Whatever for?"

I thought of Bill having settled in with us as a crew, and here we were standing down from participating in further raids. The earnest look on Bill's face moved me. "Well Billy," I said, "We are standing down so that we can begin flying Liberators!" Bill's look of incredulity matched my own feelings very well.

PREGNANT DUCK

We had watched the US Air Force move their bulky Liberators around the airfield. Low to the ground it seemed to waddle, so we called it the "pregnant duck." Several Liberators with RAF markings had appeared unannounced on our air base, and I had wondered about those planes, never for a moment dreaming that I would have to fly them.

The Liberator, the American B24, had four engines, a long 108 foot wingspan, and a deep bulky fuselage. Its engines required less maintenance than the Merlin engines on the Halifax. That meant more valuable hours in the air. Dusty conditions in Italy had been hard on the Halifax, hence the RAF decision to change the aircraft.

The CO had explained, "The U.S. Air Force is making specially equipped Liberators available to us for use as RAF Pathfinder aircraft flying at night over Europe. You will be the first to convert on to the new planes Scotty." Dumbfounded, I had no ready answer for him, only a cry, "Sir is there no alternative?" I faced the thought of leaving our proven Halifax with disbelief. The makers of the Halifax produced new models continually and we had been looking forward to flying the more improved and powerful aircraft. "I'm sorry Scotty. We must make the change and your crew has been chosen. You can feel honoured." "Well sir, I suppose we will just have to give it a go," I replied, feeling despondent at the change.

Bill Scott listened as I outlined my conversation with the CO and I concluded, "So that's it Billy. What's more, I would like you and the rest of the boys to come to Africa with me tomorrow as passengers in a Liberator. We've got to pick up a new Halifax and bring it back to the Squadron." "I'll be in that", said Bill, "I could do with a trip to Africa". "Good", I responded, "we will be flying down to Maison Blanche, the airport at Algiers." "I know it well," said Bill, "We landed there on our flight out from Britain."

Our first flight in a Liberator took us out over the Mediterranean Sea to North Africa. As we flew in towards Algiers, the city glistened like a pearl, white and shining on the edge of the bay. I felt entranced by its Islamic people. Moslem dress dotted the city streets, and the sound of Moslem chant came from numerous mosques dotted around the city area. The very French Algiers had an extensive night life taking my mind back to the Panama Canal and the wild experiences my friends and

I had there.

Food available on the streets tempted us. However, being sensitive to the possibility of tummy wogs, we ate RAF meals at the Maison Blanche airport, and limited ourselves to coffee in the cafes. Thinking of our menu on the squadron, we bought vegetables and cases of wine, and loaded them into our aircraft.

Entering the plane for the trip back to Italy, Shorty proudly flicked through a wad of Algerian francs, handling them with a fond touch. He had been selling flints for cigarette lighters and had a healthy trade amongst Moslem vendors on the streets. I chuckled at the thought of Shorty accomplishing no mean feat, outsmarting the street vendors. On our return to Italy, his tent returned to "business as usual". His young lady in London had sent him lighter flints, and Shorty was able to do a roaring trade with them amongst other things, from his tent on the base.

MAKE A NOTE ADJ., THEY MAY AT LEAST TAKE THE SIGN DOWN WHILST I AM MAKING MY INSPECTION.

The Halifax we had flown from Algiers, JP322, was the fastest and most delightful I had had the privilege to fly. On landing back at base, I had handed over the speedy plane, and faced our change to Liberators with sadness. A little later I saw Halifax JP322 as a battered wreck after a German fighter with cannon fire raked it from one end to the other during an attack on Ploesti oil fields. How it could have flown back to base in that condition I could only guess.

TONY'S AWARD

In the process of readying myself for dinner, I looked up to see Tony Wheeler come into the tent showing great excitement. He blurted out "Tommy, I've been awarded the DFC, what do you make of that?" "Tony, that's terrific news. Good on you, cobber!" He and his crew had flown many times against well defended targets and had continued their attacks in the face of stiff opposition, especially the Ploesti oil fields.

I would miss Tony. We had been Aussie cobbers together in the same tent for months on end, and had been alternate pilots on "Kathleen" our baptised Halifax. He had sad news about our plane. Damaged again on the last raid, she now sat awaiting repairs, and needed a thorough overhaul. She had served us well.

As Tony and I went into the mess for drinks and the evening meal, the CO came in to congratulate him on his D.F.C. The mess rang with further acclamation for his well earned award. He had now been posted to Egypt to become an instructor on Liberators, training new crews including some who would come to 614 Pathfinder Squadron.

Our last evening together ended at the Manefredonia Beach, very late at night. Manfredonia town, across the waters of the bay, hid in wartime darkness. The fleet of tall masted fishing boats anchored in the bay, gave no sound or movement. Our feet splashed gently in the lapping waters of the Adriatic. We had much to reminisce over as we sloshed the warm water, and walked along the wide sands of the long sweeping Manfredonia Bay. Refreshed, and facing the parting of our ways we headed back to Amandola.

THE LIBERATOR

A Canadian Flight Lieutenant introduced me to flying Liberators. I sat in it and began to get the feel of flying a totally different kind of aircraft. The pilot's seat felt like a lounge chair and the plane did not stand high off the ground like the Halifax. The Liberator had a nose wheel, which meant I had to land in an unfamiliar nose down attitude. But the list of differences did not stop there.

Bill Scott's navigation cabin, behind the pilot's flight deck, was like a plush office. Ed Riley had his radar office next door to Bill so that they could work closely together, while Shorty's radio room was at the rear of the aircraft. We decided that Liberator offered us far more comfort and interesting flying than we had thought possible.

After landing one day, Bill announced, "I've got to admit it, the Lib is a good kite, come and look at my office!" I followed him into his navigation office and gasped, "Whatever are those for?" "Those," said Bill proudly, "are where I hang up my pencils and rubbers and rulers so that I can find them." During flight, Bill had discovered that his navigation equipment fell from the table. In devising a solution, he had provided hooks on which he could hang the various items. His office looked like a butchers shop with tools of trade hanging within easy reach around the wall. "Well I must say you're a genius Billy!" I exclaimed. Bill's broad features glowed.

However, not all aspects of the Liberator were as easy to accommodate. Ed became gloomy about his radar office being too far from the bomb aimer's forward position in the nose. Much to his disgust, he had to hand that over to a new bomb aimer. To add to his dismay, he also had to hand over his enjoyed position of being my assistant at takeoff time. Bob, our flight engineer, did it. He occupied the comfortable second pilot's seat and carried out his duties from there. But on the positive side, Ed gained a vastly superior radar, called H2X and in time he began to value it.

For me, the change to Liberators involved much trepidation about its history of being quick to catch fire when hit by flak. But I settled in and began to appreciate the aircraft. The motors were a special source of gladness. They had excellent supercharged power for use in the upper atmosphere, whereas the Halifax motors had lacked such power at height. I looked forward to taking advantage of that power over enemy targets.

TO WAR IN A LIBERATOR

"Can I come with you tonight Scotty?" The questioner, one of our Wing Commanders, looked at me seriously. "What's on?" I asked blithely. "You're on ops tonight, didn't you know?" responded my superior as his eyes searched my face. "I know now sir," I responded, my heart skipping a beat. It had been some weeks since we had flown

"Kathleen" on our last op into action. "So we really are back on ops?" I queried. Deep down within me, I recognised my familiar dread at the thought of flying into action.

"Yes Scotty, you are on ops tonight, don't you think you are ready?" asked the Wingco. "As ready as I will ever be sir. The Liberator really is a good aircraft, and we've had some excellent training runs. It's great having the navigator and radar man so close at hand."

"So, can I come with you tonight?" repeated my superior. "Well if you are game sir, I'm glad to have you along." I responded. He added, "Perhaps I'll pick up a few hints about the Liberator on the way." With that we engaged in discussion about the Liberator. As a seasoned operational pilot, he had flown many aircraft, but not a Liberator. He came as second pilot.

THE BRENNER PASS

Our target in northern Italy included a railway complex that handled war material coming out of Germany. If we could destroy the supply handling facilities at Bronzola in the Brenner Pass, we would deprive the enemy of an important flow of armaments to the front line.

With the Wingco by my side, I coached him in operating the Liberator. Taxiing towards the runway, I felt strange watching the Halifaxes, like great birds, taking to the air and my own plane of vastly different type, being the last to go.

Finally, I received the green signal: my turn to move our aircraft out to the take off point. I appreciated the smooth power of the four motors as the Wingco and I opened up the throttles, and the aircraft gathered speed. The long run took us towards the far boundary of the airfield, with me continuing to describe what the Wingco needed to do to assist as co-pilot. The wings grasped the evening air and lifted us high. The vague outline of the Gargarno stood outlined against the Adriatic sea disappearing into the dimness beyond. I felt comfortable as Bill's voice gave me the course to steer, and I set the plane to fly northwards out over the sea.

Gun flashes on the Italian mainland identified for us the battle front where a ground attack was in progress. The Wingco and I surveyed the gunfire and talked sympathetically of troops bogged down and feeling the battle's fierceness, as battle hardened German soldiers tried to hold their ground against slow Allied progress.

Once clear of the battle front, we turned west, crossed the coast of northern Italy, and headed towards Lake Gardo. From there we turned north again towards the Brenner Pass in the Alps.

UMPH ..umph ...umph. Shells exploded just off our starboard wing, and the explosions crept nearer as I tried to maintain course. When shrapnel from the exploding shells sounded like rain falling on us, I pulled the Liberator around in a tight turn, calling to Bill that I had to get out of the range of the guns. The gunners would have had their radar operators tracking us, and waiting for us to get lined up in their sights. I cursed our misfortune for we had tried to fly through a corridor between the defences.

Bill added a few more lines to his navigation chart as my sudden turn westward took us away from the worst of the gunfire. By the time I had flown for three minutes at right angles to our original course, Bill had readjusted his navigation to give me a new course to steer for our target.

We flew in over Bolzano and I felt a sense of mystery in attacking an unseen target that was situated in the darkness of a deep valley between alpine mountains. Our role in conjunction with three 614 squadron Halifaxes, provided sky flares to illuminate the target area. We made two separate runs, dropping sky flares to give illumination coverage over Bolzano and its surrounding mountains. The mystery of darkness gave way to illuminated railway sheds, lines of railway trucks, row upon row of railway lines, showing the organised flow of materials to German front line troops.

Six Pathfinder Halifaxes went in to drop their red and yellow target indicators, and the target area became bathed in cascading colour. Then the bombers flew in to do their work and we looked down on a very accurate and a highly successful raid. The railway yards at Bolzano would cease to function and its flow of armaments to the German front line would be held up for some time.

After five and a half hours in the air, we landed and sat conferring about the route and our flying over heavy defences. The Wingco had helped to plan for safe entry into Bronzola, and confessed to his shock when so many heavy gun batteries had opened up on us. Next morning, repairs began on the shell holes in the wing of our new Liberator.

AN INTRIGUING INVITATION

Later that day I stood outside the Officers Mess talking to one of the navigators. "Why don't you come Scotty?" he asked. He had invited me to a meeting arranged at a neighbouring air base. The weekly meeting, a venue for discussion, centred around the meaning of existence and the question of life after death. As the navigator talked, I felt very interested. I had questions about existence, so I decided to go with him. I was on duty that afternoon, and I asked, "Is it on next week?" "It's on each Thursday afternoon Scotty, I could meet you next week and we could go together. How would that be?" "Ok, it's a date," I responded, intrigued at the invitation.

My crew and I had engaged in many searching discussions about meaning and life after death, but we were so limited, and had no answers. Perhaps I would find an answer at next week's meeting.

When next week came, the navigator's plane had failed to return from a raid. I had not discovered the venue for the meeting, or any answers to my questions.

FAREWELL KATHLEEN

In the midst of these events, the Wingco came to me one morning and said, "Scotty, we want you to go down to Algiers and pick up a new Liberator. When could you be ready to go?" "Algiers, what an exciting thought," I mused. "Well sir, I'm not on ops tonight, we could go this afternoon." I replied. "OK, I'll make the necessary arrangements. You can fly down in "Kathleen", she's due for overhaul there," the Wing Commander replied. He sensed my thrill at the opportunity to fly "Kathleen" again, and said, "I knew you'd be pleased.".

After lunch, I gathered my crew, and settled into battle scarred "Kathleen" displaying her symbols of forty six attacks on distant targets. After two and a half hours flying, we circled the glistening white Algiers, and landed.

We left the plane sitting there on that foreign tarmac at the Maison Blanche airport. She looked so proud but so alone. I recalled Tony Wheeler standing on the tall ladder, swinging a bottle of champagne, trying his best to baptise "Kathleen" in Italian bubbly wine. When it finally did happen, we had laughed at the thought of sending her forth christened. Now at Maison Blanche, I stood looking at the worn and faded painting of the scantily clad girl on the front of the plane. Her fine seductive lines had taken us into battles all over Europe. "Farewell!" I said quietly, feeling it a most inadequate salute to an aircraft that had meant so much to me. I turned and followed my crew into the waiting RAF transport vehicle.

SOMETHING NEW

Algiers gave us the opportunity to stock up again on fresh vegetables and wines for the squadron mess. We had crates of them loaded into the brand new Liberator. I read the number, KG945, then looked across to the maintenance yard and saw "Kathleen" parked in position ready for the mechanics to swarm over her. I wondered what would be her future and ours?

KG945 rose comfortably over the city and then headed for Italy. When I saw her next, she had the letter "A" painted on her side and a shooting star with the name Altair, painted on her buxom front. She was named after one of the stars we used in navigation, and I gasped at such unimaginative decoration. Then I learnt that Altair had become our aircraft. I missed the boldness of "Kathleen" displaying her femininity so charmingly on our Halifax. "Whoever thought up this conglomeration?" I asked the ground crew sergeant. "The Wingco told me it was the CO's idea sir," he said sensing my disgust. I never did get used to the unglamorous shooting star on Altair. My love for the stars was only for the real ones.

ALTAIR

We took Altair on an air test to become reacquainted in her new paint. In the back of the Liberator sat Sam, our ground staff mechanic who came along to see how his plane flew. A rapid climb took us high above the clouds, where we checked all the plane's functions. The two gunners tested out their patter, talking me through evasive action against simulated German fighters. How well the big plane stood on her wing tip in tight turns. I might not like her name but I liked her ability to turn for quick evasive action.

Losing height, I flew low across the Foggia plains, over picturesque expanses of water at the foot of the Gargarno. Then, I climbed the plane up over mountains that led to the beach resort of Rodi. There was no sign of life at the big house in which we had holidayed with Hoppy. From Rodi, we circled low over the sea for the gunners to test out their guns. We carried bigger guns than the Halifax and the chatter of their firing, shook the whole aircraft.

For one last adventure I flew along the runway of an American airfield with the Flying Fortress B17s parked in bays well off the runway. Two officers stood gazing down on us from their tower. I felt good giving the Americans an Aussie visitor in their own B24. Out over the fields again, across the Manefredonia road, then a wide sweeping turn took us in towards our runway at Amandola.

Shorty warned me as we landed, "Sam's looking very pale Tommy!" I parked Altair and climbed out of my seat. Sam sat looking ashen but he used his Scottish brogue to good effect, "I'd have got a bloody boat if I'd known you were going to fly so low over the water." He struggled unsteadily to his feet and mumbled, "Can't even bloody walk properly!" I kidded him along a bit and said, "Come on Sam, surely you enjoyed a bit of fresh air over the ocean." "No I did not," he said determinedly, "I'll stick to my bloody work on the ground from now on." Jock cared about our crew but maintained outward gruffness.

TO WAR IN ALTAIR

Our first battle operation in Altair, took us to a target north of Vienna. A full moon rose over the horizon, an open invitation for the German air force to attack and attack they did. They played havoc with our stream of bombers and one of our Halifaxes arched through the sky with flames marking its pathway to the ground. At debriefing, we learnt that another of our key Pathfinders, Ian Bruce was missing. His loss meant that our crew was the only one of the six crews from Marston Moor and Upwood to remain flying. We missed their reliable friendship. Our crews had always been there together, sitting at briefings and sharing one another's problems.

ATHENS

December came, and with it, continual demands for crews to be operating. Then we received a call to fly urgently to Athens. Group Captain Jarman, the strategic planner for operations of the whole RAF group in Italy, wanted to go to Athens where warfare had broken out.

He needed to see conditions for himself, and the planning required for his strategic bomber force.

In 1944, Athens, that most historic of cities, had celebrated the retreat of the German army and had embraced the British deliverers in great excitement. The British had installed a royalist government and this had stirred the ire of the communist party. Civil war had broken out between the royalists and the communists. The British army had tried to step in and maintain order, but the Greek E.L.A.S. communists had them pinned down and short of ammunition. My flight with Group Captain Jarman would help to ferry urgently needed ammunition to the British Army.

We flew from Amandola in Altair loaded with boxes of ammunition. The one and a half hour flight took us via the Ionian Sea, the Gulf of Corinth and the Saronic gulf to the Kalamaki Airport at Athens. Being winter, rain squalls swept in on us as we flew. Nevertheless I was entranced by the rugged mountain coastline and the historic Greek islands. At the entrance to the gulf of Corinth, I flew below rain clouds and headed for an island.

Then I saw it. An exciting but fearsome slab of rock standing like a mighty monument reaching up through the clouds. I turned the wings of the Liberator almost vertical to avoid it. Then, with my heart pounding at my ribs like a hammer, I settled the plane down, saying to the Group Captain, "That didn't show on the map!"

The Gulf of Corinth ended and we flew over the Corinthian Canal, now entirely devoid of ships; a sunken ship lay like a cast off toy blocking the channel. The canal ended, and the waters of the Saronic Gulf opened out before us; we were nearly at Athens. To the left, lay the harbour of Piraeus with the ancient Athens behind it. To the right, we saw the aerodrome of Kalamaki, our unloading point; but what were those puffs of smoke on the airfield? Clouds of dust showed artillery in action. Communist E.L.A.S. forces must have been firing from the hills and exploding their shells on the airfield.

When RAF Spitfire fighters appeared making diving attacks on the gun emplacements, the firing ceased. I headed Altair for the runway as words of entreaty flowed through me, "Come on Spitties, keep those guns silent just a bit longer. That's it, make those gunners keep their heads down!" Altair sank lower until finally her wheels touched and she rolled over the damaged runway. Keeping the plane moving, we roared along a taxiway that led to a central point surrounded by soldiers.

Group Captain Jarman went out to talk to the Army CO, while Bob Lewis rushed out to organise the unloading. British troops swarmed over Altair. The men, their bare shoulders wet with sweat even in the cold air, grasped urgently needed boxes of ammunition. A major came in, "Keep your motors running and be ready to move out, those guns can begin firing at any moment!" His words confirmed my own thoughts exactly. After what seemed an age, the Group Captain returned, and Bob poked his head in and said, "All done". He closed Altair's big wrap around doors and I roared the motors as we moved along the taxiway to the take off point.

As soon as our wheels lifted off Kalamaki runway, I turned Altair towards the blue waters of the gulf and gazed towards stark white buildings. The Athens of history brooded over Piraeus Harbour, while, above the city, Mount Lycerbettus frowned over all. This was my historic and exciting moment; Athens, a name in history, had become for me a place of my own history.

The Group Captain shared that he was not pleased to be risking the strategic bombing force in such an enterprise. An interesting commander, he had a way of getting alongside me in sharing problems. This unostentatious person carried his rank with dignity and made me feel that my conversations were of high value to him.

On return to Amandola, the clouds lowered. I had the joy of flying over 614 squadron tent city at very low level.

Group Captain Jarman expressed his appreciation of conversations during our trip, and I farewelled him into his waiting RAF car, conscious that a bond had developed between us. However, I might not have been so friendly if I had known his plans for us on Christmas Day, just three days away.

That evening in the Officers Mess, the CO came to me, "Scotty did you have to make your return from Athens so low?" His eyes searched my face.

CHRISTMAS PARCEL NOT DELIVERED
Awakening to Christmas morning, 1944, I saw Italy covered by undulating snow. Row after row of tents made up the enclave that

housed 614 Pathfinder Squadron personnel amongst olive trees on the air base at Amandola. The layer of white completely camouflaged everything.

With a duffle coat warming me against the biting cold, I walked toward the tents where my seven crew members stirred. Under one arm, I carried a Christmas food parcel received from Australia and I mused on the excitement of my boys when they saw the parcel.

"Scottie!" I turned to see the rugged up figure of the adjutant calling me across the snow. "Scottie, ops are on, your crew is needed at briefing straight away!" I groaned, gritting my teeth in exasperation, "Surely we can have Christmas without war." Glumly I acknowledged the call and moved on to the tent where Ed responded to my voice, "Coom in mun!" I stepped into the tent's cosy interior and for a moment, his warm welcome lifted my spirits. Repeating the adjutant's message, I received his Geordie response, "What a bloody bind!" He echoed my rumbling groan adequately.

Three hastily assembled crews sat for the Christmas morning briefing. It was grim news. We three crews were to fly our heavy bombers to the mountains of southern Germany and make an assault on Adolf Hitler's secret bunker at Berchtesgarten. Security information revealed Hitler was likely to travel from Berlin and be at Berchtesgarten in time to receive the Christmas parcel we were risking our lives to give him.

The first part of the route had to be flown at low level to help hide our presence from enemy radar. With snow storms sweeping across Europe, the plan involved very risky flying. I said to Ed, "At least the storms will help to hide us from enemy guns." He only grunted. He realised, only too well, the hazards we faced in flying amongst the cloud covered Austrian and Bavarian Alps to seek out Berchtesgarten. Apprehension gripped us both as we faced the extreme unhealthiness of the assignment.

We came out of our briefing wordlessly and went to breakfast. Later, changing into flying gear, we had nothing much to say to each other. Our minds filled with tremendous questions as we considered our attack. Its absolute boldness was about the only thing in its favour. Carrying our parachutes, thermos flasks and navigation material, we clambered aboard an RAF transport vehicle taking us to our aircraft.

A slow journey through the snow brought us to the airfield where a scene of furious activity met our eyes. RAF men with brooms seemed to be everywhere, clearing away ice and snow, sweeping the runway, the taxiway, and clambering over three of our planes to brush the broad flying surfaces.

When we reached our aircraft, my crew slowly clambered aboard. I walked around our plane, examining the wings, tail and fuselage before making the climb that led to the flight deck. When I started the four motors, the throbbing song of their power helped to settle me and to feel more accepting of the task ahead. We had an important job to do and I was determined to complete it.

I finished the long cockpit check of the big plane, at the same time keeping an eye out for the green light signalling us to taxi out for take off. Looking again to the control tower, I wondered at the continued delay of the awaited signal. Then something made my stomach muscles tighten and a cry of utter disbelief flowed out of me, "Oh no!" "Bloody hell!" said Ed.

Rolling down upon us, enveloping everything in its path, an intense black cloud soon enfolded our plane, rocking and juddering it and blocking out my windscreen with snow. Time swirled by as I sat waiting, watching the circling hand of the ticking clock; the only movement amongst the forest of aircraft instruments. Eventually the storm passed, and I could open my storm window to gaze out on a scene of complete whiteness. Nothing moved out there except our whirling propellers sounding out their song. The swept surfaces of our aircraft and the runway again lay under snow. Sweeping would have to begin all over again.

A sign of life appeared as a snow covered jeep drove towards us. It stopped in front of our plane; the driver stood up, raised his arms and I recognised the operations Wing Commander giving us the signal to switch off our motors. I cut the power. The ensuing silence was very peaceful and I sat for a moment to enjoy it. Then, making my way on the long journey out into the open, the ground crew Sergeant met me. "Ops are cancelled sir," he said in Scottish brogue. "Are you sure sarge?" I asked. "The Wingco says so sir," he replied. "Happy Christmas," I said with a rueful smile, thinking of all the hard work we had put in, and all of which would have to be repeated next time. I called along the aircraft, "Ops are cancelled fellas, happy Christmas!" Ed collected his gear and muttered, "A bloody silly idea anyway!"

The secret allied informant in Germany had learnt of Hitler's changed plans for Christmas. He would stay in Berlin. The Fuhrer's Christmas parcel would need to be delivered somewhere, sometime later. "Come on blokes," I said as we exited the plane and our flying boots crunched on the snow, "Let's go and enjoy our Aussie Christmas parcel."

MAFIA, ETNA AND THE EXPEDITOR

With the attack on Berchtesgarten aborted, my crew and I could spend Christmas night in Foggia. Our Adjutant had taken days to search through the war damaged streets, to find a venue for our squadron to celebrate Christmas. He had found a hall, a large one sufficient to seat everybody. The delighted owner had said joyfully, "Si, possible, si possible!" They had struck a deal and preparations for Christmas went ahead.

Arriving amongst the decorations on Christmas evening, we were stunned. For a moment, I thought the reds and greens of Christmas a bit too close to the reds and greens of our cascading target markers, and had to readjust my thoughts. But the results of the messing committee's hard work had given us long tables adorned with Italian holly and bare walls transformed by art work and entwined colour.

Adornment included a special by the Intelligence Section. The staff had produced a photographic enlargement that overlooked us from high on the wall. The squadron crest had an eagle holding a target indicator bomb that looked real enough to drop on us.

Row by row we took our places at the long tables. The cooks had saved up appetising delights for a long time and fresh food had come from Algiers. Watery English beer and Italian wines abounded. I favoured the Spumante champagnes for the evening.

The meaning of Christmas was expressed by the Chaplain. His words for some reason frustrated me, and I made myself unpopular by flicking peanuts across the hall. Bruce Prange, one of the Canadian pilots objected, "I've had enough of that Scotty!" He reminded me that some of the officers wanted to listen to the chaplain even if I did not. However, I had listened but I had not understood.

Navigator Len Palmer responded to the need of a squadron song about Pathfinders at war. With his ready chuckle and good tenor voice he sang his own composition.

"We're going to lay down lighted signposts from way up there in the sky, this way to the target they all read ......

On and on he went, giving vivid word pictures of Pathfinders going to distant targets in the darkness. Cheers and claps evidenced his immediate success, with numerous requests for copies of his song. His rendition made me freshly appreciative of this buoyant officer willing to share himself with others on the squadron.

BOXING DAY 1944

Next day, Boxing day, my fellows had planned to use the evening to celebrate our deliverance from our crash on Boxing Day 1943 at Leeds in Yorkshire. However, our names appeared on the ops list to fly, and the celebration had to wait.

That night, Pathfinders headed up a bombing force attacking an important German target in northern Italy. A large railway bridge over the Tagliamento River, in use day and night, carried truck loads of supplies for German forces. The destruction of this bridge would help to lessen the flow of armaments down through Austria and to the war front.

From the air, a bridge, even a big one like the Tagliamento, was a difficult target, especially when guns were set up round about it to save it at all costs. The big guns were waiting there for us as we flew in.

Ed had trained in a new bomb aimer called Budd. On this trip, he needed coaching to keep his eye on the bomb sight and to leave the German opposition to us. Nearer and nearer we went with Budd verbalising the run in, "Right, steady, right right, steady, hold it there, hold it, steady, ... bombs gone!"

Taking Altair in a tight turn, we gained a grandstand view of Budd's efforts. Ed gazed out of his radar office window and shouted that the red and yellow target indicators landed across the bridge. It thrilled me to see these results of Ed's training. We could hope now that following bombers would destroy the bridge.

On landing back in Italy, the CO met us at the debriefing marquee. "You're looking done in Scotty." "Yes sir, I'm feeling quite tired." "You'll be interested to know I signed a two week's leave pass for you and your crew today. Can you have a good break away from the squadron?" "I sure hope so sir," I responded, determined to take him at his word.

When I awoke next morning, an excited Budd awaited me, "the Tagliamento bridge has been breached Tommy, German rail traffic has ceased to cross it." The exciting news had been confirmed by photographs from a high flying Mosquito aircraft. Budd exuded enthusiasm. My crew could now take their leave passes and rest easy.

HOLIDAY TO REMEMBER

Two weeks lay before us; how strange it felt to be free from flying. Shorty and I, both now with the rank of Flying Officer, rode in a US Army truck across the Italian mountains. We arrived in Naples at sunset, and alighted near the piazza where a dramatic scene was about to unfold. Arrayed in front of their national flags, British, American and Italian army officers with detachments of soldiers filled the whole square. The strong notes of a bugle sounded, and the flags moved slowly down from the mastheads. The pageant signalled this part of Europe free of German domination. The Allies had taken over. I felt envious of the Army, able to be so in touch with a local population. We never saw things like this in the air war.

A Marchesa, an interesting lady of noble birth, gave us hospitality. Welcoming us to her beautifully furnished home, she explained that German army officers had billeted with her during German occupation of Italy, and she had protected her home against them damaging it. Now she wanted us to protect it also. Shorty and I chuckled at her effective way of setting her limits.

Our first evening passed with us enjoying her quaint use of English. She had many anecdotes about her German officers, and she was quite unabashed in sharing how she had become quite fond of some of them. We discussed with her about our plan to journey southward along the west coast of Italy to Sicily. In no time she had us surveying an irregular wartime schedule of the Italian railways.

Two mornings later, at Naples station, we boarded a train travelling to Reggio on the southern tip of the "toe" of Italy. The train stopped frequently and we heard the words, "Pane, pane, pane ....(bread bread bread). Young Italian ex soldiers earned money by selling. No longer earning wages after the collapse of the Italian army, their poverty distressed us. An ex soldier in our compartment had sold his tunic for food and money to make this journey. Shorty and I discussed together how best to help him, as he shivered in the mountain cold. Shorty reached into his satchel, and handed a warm singlet to the soldier. He received it with profuse ,"graciesimo, graciesimo," and hastily climbed into it. The singlet hung loosely over the small bony chest, but he displayed it for all in the compartment to see. We had won a friend, while others nodded, "molto buono, Australiani!"

The further south we went, the more were the wayside stops, and the more we sensed mystery amongst the people. Mountainous southern Italy was home to differing dialects. The women were especially distinctive with their richly embroidered aprons. On their laps, they nursed large bundles. I was curious to know the contents, but I never found out.

We passed breathtaking views of sea and mountain ranges, and then Reggio was only an hour away. From there we would need to cross the straits to Sicily. The young soldier offered us easy access to Sicily on a boat operated by a friend. He insisted we accept his offer and so we left the train at the next stop.

He helped carry our gear down a steep timbered hillside, and the train disappeared from view. We came on the margin of the Straits of Messina, and I saw two boats around which men were gathered. I surveyed them and had a premonition of danger. Admonishing myself for getting caught in an affair like this, I recalled being warned of this Mafia country and its grasp after money.

The price of the boat trip was high; too high, but we had no chance now of turning back. We paid our money with quiet apprehension, and the leader pointed us to places amongst goods packed into the high sided boat. The second boat, similarly loaded, set off from shore.

Off we went, six rowers pulling at their oars and moving the heavy boat out into the Straits of Messina. Part way across the Straits, a voice shouted, "Polizi!" A police boat had been sighted. The boat owner called to Shorty and I, "Giu, giu, giu... down, down, down." Shorty and I crouched low, hiding ourselves amongst the stuff in the boat.

Rowers strained, muscles bulged and water flapped against the sides of the boat. I felt sure they had done this before; they seemed to be enjoying the challenge of a chase. I gazed upwards from the bottom of the boat, feeling excited at being in this race across the Straits. My heart beat wildly.

Arriving at a little cove, we became hidden by overhanging branches. The police had not yet appeared, so I awaited their arrival and pondered what my own status would be before them. No sound or sight of watercraft disturbed the quiet of a gathering evening mist. "Has the second boat been caught?" I mused, then wondered, "Perhaps there is some collusion between police and rowers, some means whereby police receive payoff if they do not pursue." Certainly the rowers were not about to enlighten me.

Once on shore, local men met us. I recognised Sicilians speaking their own form of Italian. "Molto dollaro americano ..." were some words I recognised as the rowers talked about the value of their mysterious cargo. Shorty and I were ushered along a pathway amidst conversing men, almost as though they no longer knew us or saw us.

Coming in amongst housing, they left us at a shop with the words, "il autobus una momento, una momento." (A bus will come in a minute) We crowded into the shop, where everyone talked or shouted. A young man came, "Molto freddo, molto freddo!" (very cold very cold). His minimal clothing established his identity as another ex soldier. Sharing our solicitations about the cold, but feeling anxious about the non arrival of the bus, we asked, "Per favore amico, que ora e il autobus?" "Stasera, stasera!" (tonight, tonight)

We tried to get the young soldier's ideas about accommodation in Messina overnight. He held up his hands and shrugged his shoulders, "Bomba, bomba, molto molto," indicating scarce accommodation amidst the wreckage of war. An hour passed, then two hours. Our anxiety mounted. The area had an ominous name, Lido de la Mortella (beach of the dead). Its name did nothing to lessen our thoughts about our bones being left to bleach there.

"Il autobus," the magic words for which we had waited. The bus came, rusted and war ravaged it may have been, but to us it was salvation. The shop owner ushered us aboard with words to the driver, "Marina, Englisi." We were going to the Royal Navy HQ in Messina. Obviously our rascal Mafia friends had taken care to get us handed over to the Navy.

THE ROYAL NAVY

A long bus ride saw us set down at the gates of the British Naval Station in war ravaged Messina. The guard handed us over to a naval Commander who checked our credentials with carefully controlled suspicion about our unusual arrival. We were dirty and exhausted, our uniforms crumpled; we spoke English with the Australian accent, and we had arrived late at the HQ in a noisy, smelly, broken down rust bucket of a bus driven by a Sicilian.

Eventually, a Lieutenant Commander hosted us, and arranged a steward to bring in a meal. I relaxed over the meal, and enjoyed a few drinks afterwards, but conversation remained cool. I decided that the Lieutenant Commander had been allocated the task of keeping an eye on us, and determining who we were.

We gathered that the reason for such care was that the Navy ran clandestine boat operations into the waters of German occupied Yugoslavia. Trained British officers took in armaments to assist weary Yugoslav partisans defeat German forces.

Early next morning we were awoken and breakfasted. On parade with naval personnel for the raising of the White Ensign, we then boarded a navy vehicle going along the coast of Sicily to Catania. The driver seemed to have had orders not to say much to us, so Shorty and I made the most of sitting back to enjoy the magnificence of the north Sicilian coastline. Our view of the Mount Etna volcano, our holiday destination inland from the coast, had us breathless with anticipation, remembering our previous stay.

The earlier crash of our Halifax at Catania had given us some friends. What good friends they proved to be. An RAF car with quite a voluble driver would take us the forty mile journey to Mount Etna. Upwards from Catania we went, past orchards, orange groves, and stands of bananas and figs. A little higher, we came to vineyard country. This changed to forests of chestnut, birch and pine, and higher still, bare lava, void of life and desolate. Finally, amongst the upper snows around the volcano, there was the Albergo Etna, a resort offering us a restful holiday with skiing facilities. It was the stuff of which our dreams had been made. Given a key to our rooms, we flopped on our beds with thoughts of ten days relaxation for tired bodies and exhausted minds.

Next day we were introduced to delightful servings of hot food, real meat, lamb and beef, and real vegetables, broccoli, pumpkin marrow and onions. Such food we could not imagine in our austere mess in Italy. The local foods refreshed our palates and did much to restore us.

Snow continued to fall day after day and we heard that a cold snap had whitened the whole of Europe. The weather was ideal for our skiing adventures down through the valleys where branches of mountain pines bowed under a weight of snow.

Mount Etna rose to 10,700 feet and was the highest active volcano in Europe. Just over a year before, the Albergo Etna resort had been in German hands. Field Marshall Kesselring had planned much of the defence of Sicily from this point.

HOW DO WE RETURN TO ITALY?

Our two weeks passed in fulfilling pursuit of mastering the art of skiing. Now, with Mount Etna deep in snow and no traffic in or out, Shorty and I pondered the question: "How do we return to the squadron?" We would ski out. The resort manager spoke dubiously about the idea, and tried to prevail on us to change our minds. But we were determined, and at last he offered us the skis and food for our journey.

Skiing away from the resort went well for a time. Direction and landmarks fell into place nicely, but clouds descended, enshrouding us in mist. We saw a shepherd lad, and decided he must know his own area, so we kept pace with him on a parallel course. When the mist thickened, we asked him to tell us the way to the Autostrada (the main road). He gazed at us with a look of horror, then broke down and howled. The lad had thought we knew the way to go, and he was following us.

Fortunately we had a compass, and made the most of going in the general direction of a village which lay lower down the mountain. Later, the Sicilian lad recognised some land marks and departed.

All day we skied, going lower down the mountain. Towards nightfall, signs of habitation led us to a village. It was an exciting moment. We had reached our goal, and a place to rest for the night. Snow ploughs had worked to clear the road from Catania as far as this village, and the first bus was due to leave next morning.

We arose in time to board the bus to Catania. With a friendly driver, we were able to explain about our journey. He drove right into the Catania airport, and deposited us at airport administration, where we hoped to get a flight to Italy. Thanking him Sicilian style, we gathered our satchels and entered an office used by ferry flight pilots.

Our entrance gained instant recognition and a warm welcome from a Flight Lieutenant, one of the ferry pilots I knew. "No planes are going up to Italy Tom. There have been no flights in or out of Catania for over a week. The cold snap has closed down the airfields," he said emphatically. I looked out over the Catania runway and saw a hopeful sign, machinery at work clearing away snow. Feeling desperate, I replied, "But we've got to get back to our squadron. I see the runway being cleared, isn't there something flying up to Italy?"

WHAT'S AN EXPEDITOR?

He thought for a moment, then said, "We've got an Expeditor that has to go up that way. Would you take that?" "What's an Expeditor?" I countered. "Come and see for yourself!" he replied.

Shorty and I followed him out into the snow and came to an aircraft parking bay. "Voila the Expeditor, fast twin engined passenger plane produced by the Beechcraft Company in the USA," said the Flight Lieutenant opening the door of the plane and showing us over its works. Then he said casually, "Tom, why don't you take it for a few circuits? Here, I'll start the motors for you."

The plane had been sitting out in the weather and its motors proved obstinate. After much difficulty, he started one, then asked me to start the other. "There you are, it's easy," he said happily. "Here are the flying details, speeds, petrol consumption, it's about all you'll need. I'll fix it up with the control tower that you are doing some circuits. Is there anything else?" he queried, oozing confidence in me, far beyond my own.

After the big four engined planes I had been flying, the Expeditor had amazingly few switches and knobs, but I needed time to adjust to the unfamiliar layout. Even using the radio to call the control tower took a while to manipulate. Finally ready for take off, I taxied the plane to the runway where newly swept heaps of snow down each side, added to our need for care in flying the new plane.

The take off required only a short run, then we were in the air. "You feel OK Shorty?" I asked. "Yes ..." said Shorty apprehensively, then "How do you think she'll go?" "She's great," I replied with more confidence, but feeling my way in the climb away from the runway. I sensed Shorty worrying that having got the Expeditor into the air I might have difficulty getting down again. However, the plane landed smoothly enough. With each landing, he relaxed a little more, and so did I.

I completed four circuits of the airfield with a landing each time, and began to enjoy flying the fast, manoeuvrable little plane. A much happier Shorty looked across at me, "You've got the feel of handling it now Tommy." "Yes, I reckon so. It's quite sensitive." I looked at the time and worked out that we could do our flight to Italy in daylight, "Come on Shorty, let's go and prepare our flight plan for Italy."

With the Expeditor back in its parking bay, we returned to the ferry flight office and found the flight lieutenant keen for us to get going. "Tom can you take a passenger?" he asked. "Where does he want to go?" I questioned. "Could you put him off at Grottaglie, there's a U.S. air base there?" Just then the passenger appeared, an RAF officer, and we were introduced. I said, "We'll be glad to drop you off at Grottaglie, I'll let the control tower know that we need to land there."

With the Expeditor being refuelled, the ferry boys gave me a map, weather report, and radio frequencies for our flight up to Italy. I submitted a flight plan to the control tower officer and included our landing at Grottaglie. He gave us the necessary clearance.

It was a beautiful day for flying, cold, but with very few clouds; although I did expect more clouds to form up in Italy. Our passenger settled comfortably, belting himself into his seat. A man short of stature, he explained he worked with the Americans in co-ordinating their bombing results with what our squadron and our RAF group were doing.

TO ITALY

Flying off into a clear sky that contrasted with our misty ski descent from Etna, we had a distant view of the mountains of Southern Italy. The sky radiated an intense blue that the Mediterranean reflected in the resplendent colours of turquoise jewels. Shorty explored the new type of radio equipment, while I, enjoying the view, opened the pilot's side window. I had developed the habit of opening my side window after takeoff in the big planes. I loved the feel of the fresh air blowing on my face prior to having to put on my oxygen mask.

But with the Expeditor, that open window created a surge of air rushing from the plane. The air moved so strongly that it took with it, my map and all our carefully annotated data from off my knees and floated it all out into Mediterranean skies. I could not believe my loss, and turned the plane, the more easily to see my papers. There they were, our map and notes floating gracefully to the sea below, and I had to watch them go. "Shorty" I groaned dolefully, "my map has gone!" He seemed totally speechless for all his radio frequencies and other data were on those notes.

Feeling amused at our ludicrous situation, a laugh bubbled within me, "Shorty, I've heard of people up a creek without a paddle, but we are going up to Italy without a map!" He opened his wide mouth into a grimace and asked, "Are you going back?" I shook my head in the negative, and caught sight of our passenger sitting back comfortably, leaving the flying to Shorty and me.

In not having a map to check our navigation, I now needed some radio checks. "Do you think you could get Grottaglie beacon on your radio?" I felt concerned lest the clouds appearing over Italy should close in on us. For the present, I continued to fly the course I had determined while on the ground, and it kept us within sight of the coastline.

The radio had Shorty guessing for a time, and I thought he would never get it working. Then I heard his glee, "I've got Taranto Tommy!" "Good on you!" I exulted. He worked the Taranto radio beacon, a frequency he drew up from memory. The information helped me to gauge our general direction to Grottaglie. I estimated that the wind had come up stronger than forecast. It seemed almost by accident that we arrived over the top of the US air base.

The Expeditor touched down on a runway surrounded by melting snow, making the area a sea of water and mud. Vehicles caught in the quagmire could not move. I made sure we did not move off the taxiways, and parked near the control tower. I took a deep breath, and climbed the stairway up the control tower to report to the Americans. Stepping out of the plane had meant stepping back into Italy

The controllers were engaged in radio contact with a formation of Liberator bombers returning from a raid on Klagenfurt south of Vienna.

I watched them land and then file past us, their motors roaring, and their brakes making ear piercing screeches. I felt a kinship with the American crews, and pictured how they would feel after their first raid in a week of snow across Europe.

The U.S. Captain responded to my need of a map, "Sorry, there are none to spare here. You will have to go down to the navigation room." I looked at the muddy path to a distant building, shook my head, and returned to the plane. Our next stop would be the main aerodrome at Foggia.

WATERLOGGED ITALY

Clouds and rain lay ahead, and I would have to navigate from memory of the terrain. I needed Shorty to get beacon information on his radio. "Tommy, there is a radio beacon; I may be able to tune in to it." Shorty assured me. "OK," I replied as I taxied out. There were alternatives in my mind about flying without a map, but if Shorty could get that beacon on his radio, so much the better.

We became airborne and flew northwards, keeping the high Appenine Mountains to our left. Snow glistened where the sun shone through overshadowing clouds. Large areas of water on the plains showed where snow had melted. Eventually Shorty tuned into a radio beacon and co-ordinated our navigation. I spoke my appreciation, "Good on you, you've DONE it!"

After two hours of flying, I felt excited at the appearance of distant white buildings, Foggia! Farmland and the airport had large areas under water. Southern Italy seemed to be waterlogged. I circled to check out the runway, then landed. Water sprayed off our landing wheels and showered the plane in a wet ending to our very satisfying two weeks away.

Reporting to the control tower officer, I handed him the plane's papers, then asked for transport out to our squadron at Amandola. I hoped there would be someone to ferry that beautiful Expeditor up north to the battlefront, as the Commander of the Allied Army needed it.

Shorty and I sat back in the RAF vehicle bumping along the limestone road to Amandola. I recalled to Shorty our luxuriating in a hot water bath in preparation for the evening meal on Mount Etna. Shortly, the RAF driver would deposit us at our tent city at 614

Squadron and there would be no luxuriating in a hot bath tonight. We would be home.

14

"THERE'S A BOMB AT MY DOOR"

Settling back into tent life at Amandola, we experienced the biting cold of January weather. Ops continued. In the midst of a briefing on an attack on Udine in Northern Italy, a phone call came through for me. I had never been called out of a briefing before, so it must have been a high ranking officer breaking protocol like that.

The CO of main aerodrome at Foggia had discovered that I was the only one in the area who could fly the Expeditor, and had received permission for me to fly it to the battle zone. Army and Air Force communications had run hot to get someone to fly the urgently needed Expeditor to the Commander of the Eighth Army bogged down under pressure from German attacks.

The CO's voice came with urgency, "Can you fly it up there tomorrow Scotland?" I thought of our pending raid that night, swallowed hard and said, "Yes sir, I could be out there by ten tomorrow morning." "Right, we'll have the aircraft ready for you."

I returned to my empty chair at the briefing. Next to me, Bill was full of questions. I whispered to him, "How would you like to go up to the battle front tomorrow?" He looked at me as though I had gone crazy, "We are going up past the battle front TONIGHT!" "Well" I replied, "I have a plane to fly to the battle front tomorrow, and I hoped you would come to navigate." Bill, full of more questions, finally said, "If we get back from this one I'll be in it; makes me think positively about tomorrow anyway." So we agreed. Then tuning our minds to the voices of our briefing officers, we prepared for an attack on a German fighter aircraft complex at Udine.

LIKE A CHRISTMAS TREE

Udine, in northern Italy, was two hours twenty minutes flying from Amandola. We arrived in the area at five minutes past midnight. Our new bomb aimer, Budd, whom Ed continued to train, lay in his position waiting to guide me in over the target, ten minutes away. Ed sat with his eyes gazing at the radar picture of the target area as we flew in. He coached Budd, "OK, the target is thirty five miles away, we are dead on course and you should pick up the aiming point straight ahead."

"There's nothing to see in the darkness yet," said Budd. The minutes ticked by. The sky ahead became marked by angry flashes. Exploding gunfire indicated the first 614 squadron planes had reached the target. Bursting light showed their sky flares hanging in the sky on parachutes, and looking for all the world like a Christmas tree hung with bright candles. The attack on Udine had begun.

The bomb aimer's voice came through excitedly, "I can see where we are. The illumination flares must be right over the top of the target; there's snow everywhere. We've a way to go yet!" Budd began to guide me in, "Left ....." I steered the plane, noting grimly that the guns had begun to get our range. I heard heavy breathing. Someone had switched on their microphone; probably one of the gunners in the tension of the moment. Budd should be the only one now with his microphone on. "Switch off that microphone!" I called. "Left ...," came Budd's voice again, "steady .....!"

"Gunfire close astern!" the top gunner shouted. "Not long now gunner," I called.

I was anxious lest the gunfire put us off our run. "Steady ... steady ...," droned the voice of the bomb aimer. The moments ticked by. "Steady ..., steady ..." "Bombs gone!" We flew on. "Camera flash gone," he called. I turned the plane out of the line of gunfire and circled around to see Budd's green and yellow TIs glowing where they had fallen. They looked good to me. "Can you see them Ed?" I called as I gazed past a faint reflection of light from the ground, outlining the nearly vertical wings of our turning aircraft. "Yes, I see them, bloody good," responded Ed's geordie voice as he looked out the window of his radar cabin.

TO THE BATTLEFRONT

Next day, shivering with the cold and trying to wake up after our attack on Udine, Bill Scott and I drove the twenty miles to the main aerodrome at Foggia. Alighting at the control tower, we met Aussie pilot Peter Raw, who welcomed us to fly the Expeditor. Peter was Officer in Charge of the Communications Flight at Foggia. He planned to fly a small single engine Beechcraft and follow us to Forli.

Peter's eyes played over the lines of the Expeditor standing where I had parked it. He had decided it was ideal for use in his Communications Flight and he plied me with questions about its performance. I sensed his envy, "Too bad we are taking it to the front line eh Peter?"

Bill and I completed our flight plan then submitted it to the control tower officer. Armed with an extra map amidst our other navigation gears, we made our way out to the Expeditor. It had been refuelled but otherwise stood just as I had left it.

I checked over the plane, then took my seat after Bill who sat in the co-pilot seat to do his navigating. The motors started readily. I taxied out on to the runway and our aircraft climbed into the sky with Peter Raw following us in his little Beechcraft biplane.

Wide awake and warmed by the plane's interior heating, I flew as low as possible, hopefully out of sight of straying German fighter aircraft. Bill's face showed his eagerness to enjoy this daylight flight.

The central spine of Italian mountains rose to 9,000 feet. We flew beneath their shadow, slopes covered with snow, and much of it now turning to ice. Parts of the mountain side were vast glistening sheets. At times we flew along the coast where high crashing waves were whipped up by strong winds from the east. Bill shared his enjoyment of nature's wildness, contrasting his hours of darkened flight during our operation to Udine the previous night.

Map reading as we went, Bill pointed out rivers, towns, mountains where the Eighth Army had pushed back the German defenders. We talked about the cold weather and its painful effect on the soldiers slogging their way over Italian mountains and valleys against the German Army. Step by step they had worked their way northwards until now they were in the province of Forli, our present destination.

We came in low over the town of Rimini only recently captured from German forces. Inland from Rimini and 2,000 feet higher, the small separate Monarchy of San Marino boasted two thousand people living in an enclave from Italy's history. I raised the nose of the Expeditor and climbed above Rimini to skirt San Marino and enjoy a glimpse of this ancient town sitting on Mount Titano, surrounded by pinnacled walls and high towers.

FORLI

It felt eerie to fly into Forli province, the battle zone where great armies faced each other. The area was historically famous for its early Roman and Christian history, but we doubted that the troops would appreciate history in their present battle situation. We gazed over surrounding rural peacefulness. All signs of warring armies lay hidden from our eyes.

Bill located the airfield and we circled. It seemed empty apart from a lone flight office. I landed the Expeditor and stopped outside the building. A door opened, and an army major strode towards us. He poked his head in our door and shouted directions above the noise of the motors, "Move out quickly, we want to keep this area clear."

I parked the plane on a piece of ground protected from the wind by a grove of trees. Bill and I climbed out. Now the second time of saying farewell to the Expeditor, I felt a twinge of sadness as I left behind the adventures it had offered me.

A cold wind made me shiver, and I noticed how quiet the battle front seemed. Was it the quietness before an imminent clash of power? The major awaited me, so I went to him and handed over the Expeditor's papers. His abruptness and unwillingness to engage in conversation added to the tension of the battle zone and I felt glad to be moving south again.

Peter Raw had landed and kept the motor of his plane running. He opened the door and welcomed us into its warmed interior. The single motor powered into a loud hum and in a very short run, the sturdy little biplane climbed away.

A FOREST IN THE DARKNESS

Hidden in the minds of planners was the fact that in two nights' time, 614 Squadron would be leading the bomber force into this area in a remarkable attack. 614's job would be to locate a forest in the darkness of night, drop ground markers at three points of a triangle around that forest. The bombers would go in and expose part of the German army concealed with transport and guns, and waiting to pounce on Allied divisions.

But for now, with two hours flying before us, the skies were quiet. Peter opened a box of food, and we enjoyed getting to know a fellow Australian over lunch.

LETTER FROM HELEN

Bill Scott and I returned to Amandola and I went to the officers mess to see if I had received any mail. One letter was there. I took it and sat in a chair amongst officers chatting noisily around me in the hour before dinner.

My sister Helen had written, a delightful letter full of news about herself and others in our family. An interesting comment at the end of Helen's letter caught my eye, "Laurel sends her love." "Whoever is Laurel?" I asked myself aloud?

I decided that Laurel was probably a nurse friend at the Fremantle Hospital where Helen worked. I tried to picture such a cheeky person. My first response discounted anyone who would send such romantic words lightly. On reflection, I decided I would reply in like fashion, "Give her my love." I too could be flippant in the safety of such overseas communication. Having made this decision, I went to my tent, flopped on the bed, and relaxed after the activity of the last 24 hours.

PARTISANS IN YUGOSLAVIA

A call came to us to drop supplies to Partisans fighting the German Army in Yugoslavia. At 5 pm on an overcast evening, we flew under clouds to a tiny clearing on a tree covered hillside in Yugoslavia. Not a person nor a house was in sight; nothing moved on the ground. An aura of mystery hung over the location.

A thin wreath of smoke grew out of the ground, and spiralled into the air. It was our drop point. I flew around the area as my team checked for enemy, but the only movement came from the faint rising smoke.

With our bomb doors open, and feeling very vulnerable, I flew low over the small area of cleared ground and kept myself ready for possible German gunfire. Ed pressed the drop button for his load of containers to leave the plane and Shorty counted them one by one as they clicked out of their hooks in the bomb bay. The containers floated to earth on parachutes: supplies of food, ammunition, boots, uniforms and medicines.

At our lowest point we caught sight of someone, a Partisan perhaps, standing beneath overhanging trees, leaning on a long stick and gazing intently at us as we flew by. We knew that shortly after our drop, other Partisans would come out of the bush and drag the containers into hiding. At the same time they would prepare to ward off attacks by German soldiers who were ever on watch to discover Partisan enclaves.

PARTISANS AGAIN

Amidst our continued nightly attacks on German targets, a further call came for us to drop supplies to the northern part of Yugoslavia. A big battle loomed there between the German Army and Yugoslav partisans, so the whole RAF force of strategic bombers was called in to carry the huge amount of supply containers.

Flying over a snow covered Yugoslavia, I glowed inwardly as the mountainous terrain reflected back satin white beauty. We flew in, searching for snow covered wheat fields, where a large "X" should mark the drop location. Discernible beneath the snow, roads criss-crossed the landscape, with timbered country on the high ground and farmland on the lower slopes. Ah! A wheat field Its vague outline showed beneath heaped up snow and I flew lower so that Ed could identify it.

Aware of German astuteness in laying a trap, everyone in the crew searched the slopes for a hidden enemy. Ed felt sure we had located the right area, with roads and fence lines tallying up to our map references. Yes! There was the "X". The Partisans had not exposed the dark soil beneath their "X", and we nearly missed it.

I took Altair in low and Ed let the load go. With our motors roaring, we climbed from the snow covered wheat field and flew adjacent to a nearby ridge, as other aircraft behind us, came in to make their drop. Ed called, "Look over towards the trees on the ridge, there's a cottage level with us, see in front of the cottage two women standing in the snow." We gazed, for a moment entranced by this sign of habitation. There they were, two heavily clad women with their hands raised. Ed added, "It gives me a bloody good feeling when I see people like that. At least what we're doing seems to be appreciated."

Looking back, we saw the drop zone fairly covered with parachutes and containers. Marshal Tito's Partisans had received abundant supplies of equipment for their coming action against the German army.

COMRADE COLONEL IT READS "CONTENTS OF CONTAINER 200 BOOTS ANKLE RIGHT. STOCKS OF BOOTS ANKLE LEFT AT PRESENT EXHAUSTED. WILL BE DELIVERED WHEN AVAILABLE."

WARM WELCOME TO A NAVAL BASE

Next morning a warmly rugged figure came into the officers mess as I sat reading and sipping a cup of tea, awaiting breakfast. It was Bill Neubeck, an Aussie pilot who had transferred to flying Liberators soon after my crew. Bill and I were chess players together. He said loudly, "Early morning briefing chaps!" "Not before breakfast surely," I grumbled. "Yep, breakfast will have to wait." "What's on today Bill?" "Looks like we're in for a daylight op somewhere Tommy!" replied the handsome Australian.

I liked the open face of Flight Lieutenant Neubeck, friendly, warm and smiling. "Perhaps it will be another one to the Yugoslav partisans. I don't mind those," he said. "Yeah," I replied, "Oh well, I suppose we'll have to get to the briefing." Bill Neubeck went out of the warmth and stepped into the cold of the Italian winter. I followed him, needing to find members of my crew for the briefing.

Our target turned out to be the naval base at Pola on a large peninsula at the northern end of the Adriatic sea. Aerial photographs had revealed large supplies of German guns and ammunition being transported for storage in warehouses on the Pola docks. We would fly northward along the Yugoslav coastline and turn northwest to make our attack on the docks.

A wintery sun shone upon us as we watched Bill Neubeck's Liberator takeoff and climb towards the north. Our plane followed soon afterwards. An hour later, from the flight deck of Altair, we had breathtaking views along the coast of Yugoslavia. The high, rugged Dinarske and Velebit mountains fell steeply to the Adriatic. Patches of rich green forest burst out of the valleys. Villages clung precariously to the rocky slopes, overlooking island after island that dotted the deep waters of the Adriatic. Bill Scott revelled in the easy navigation with Ed's H2X radar producing clear definition of the coastline.

Yugoslavia was still occupied by Germany, so we flew out of range of German defences waiting to pick us off. Sunshine sparkled on the Adriatic and made us feel privileged viewers as we flew serenely above a world at war. "I would like to come back here one day," I called to Bob sitting next to me in the second pilot's seat. Bob, jotting the fuel and engine details of our flight into his log, lifted his head to gaze across to the coastline, "It's no' bad!" came the broad Glasgow reply.

CAVALRY CHARGE ACROSS THE SKY

Pola defences were wide awake as 614 Squadron Liberators flew in. A concentration of gunfire put black clouds of flak bursts hanging in the sky and I realised that Altair was lined up in the sights of the gun batteries below. The bursts came thick and fast, but exploded just ahead of Altair, so close that I wanted to put the brakes on, as if in a car. I dropped our speed back slightly, hoping that the gunners would not detect the change, but they did. The shell bursts came nearer.

I wanted to pull the Liberator around in a turn that would take us out of it, but Altair raced on and the explosions crept ever nearer. "Hang on Skipper," came the bomb aimer's voice, "I can see the target. l e ft, ... l e f t, ... left, left, ... steady ... hold it there ..." I steered the Liberator and watched as the exploding shells made their tell tale black clouds. Out of the corner of my eye, I caught sight of the other Pathfinder Liberators arrayed across the sky as if in a cavalry charge. We flew together into the shellfire.

UGLY GLOW

Then the guns found their mark. A Liberator near us gave off an ugly glow of bright flame and black smoke. In seconds, billowing flames engulfed the wings and then the whole craft. The plane slowed and lost height, split into two parts, pieces coming away as fierce hungry flames trailed into a long falling arc behind her. Parachutes came out, how many, it was difficult to tell; the sky seemed filled with smoke, flames, aircraft and two or three parachutes falling in amongst the chaos.

"Hold steady .... hold steady ..." came the voice of Budd our bomb aimer, "That's good ... hold it there ..." I still missed having Ed in this bomb aimer role, but Ed was adept now at taking us into the target on radar, and needed to back up the visual sighting of Budd. Our bomb doors rumbled open and we flew on into the fury over the naval base at Pola, fiercely alive now with gunfire and exploding shells across the whole canopy of sky. Budd called, "Steady ... steady ... Bombs gone!" Our TIs fell towards the docks. At some thousands of feet below us, they exploded into green and scarlet rain. The aiming point would soon be a glow of green and red, marked out for the bombers following us in.

"At last" I thought, realising how sick in the stomach I really felt as I watched the other Pathfinder Liberator, its flaming pieces arching out of the sky. "Skipper, course to steer one eight one," called Bill Scott. "One eight one it is" I replied as I lifted the big wings of the Liberator into a turn towards the south and out of the black pock marked sky over Pola.

LOOK AT THIS

"Oh skipper look at this!" called the rear gunner, "We've got it, we've got it, there's a pillar of smoke shooting thousands of feet into the air. You ought to see it!" He continued to describe his view of the destruction of the ammunition warehouses at Pola.

Once more I raised the wings of the Liberator into a turn and called, "OK, here we go in a turn so that you can all have a look." And look they did, each of the crew gasping in amazement at the black smoke that poured out of the docks at Pola and billowed up twenty thousand feet. The German ammunition stores had received direct hits and exploded. "A wizard prang," said the rear gunner as half an hour later he could still report the black smoke of Pola appearing on the horizon.

Sunlight of early afternoon continued until we reached the Gargarno peninsula. Cumulus clouds gathered in splendour over the rocky mountain. I thought about the anguish of the crew in that exploding Liberator, those who would never see the Gargarno again.

At debriefing, Bill Neubeck and his crew were missing. We waited for news of him, but it was months before the Red Cross filtered the news that the bodies of Bill and his bomb aimer were discovered in the wreckage at Pola. The rest of the crew landed by parachute, were rounded up by German forces and imprisoned in Germany. We missed the Neubeck smile and warmth on the squadron. I looked at the idle chess board and was reminded of our unfinished competition.

After an air test in Altair during the following week, the US Air Force phoned. They had observed Altair flying low across their base and after voicing their objections they decided they wanted to meet a crew operating one of their planes. Ed and I were invited to share coffee with them in the US Air Force mess.

NEW AUSTRALIANS
Replacement crews continued to be a pressing need on 614. In fairly quick succession, three Australian pilots with their crews, appeared on the squadron. They had all been trained to fly Liberators and had been through the Liberator course in Egypt where Tony Wheeler instructed. One by one they came with me as second pilot in order to get the feel of what it is like to attack a defended target. They all looked so fresh and so Australian, and I enjoyed the contact with these men from down under. As well as news from Australia, they brought news of Tony and his romance with Catherine, serving with the British WAAF in Egypt. I awaited news of wedding bells.

PROMOTIONS

Promotions came to my crew. I enjoyed seeing Ed Riley commissioned and joining Shorty and me in the officers mess. Bill Scott had been promoted to warrant officer and presided over the sergeants mess.

Altair's nose became emblazoned with the painted stars of thirty eight operations over enemy territory. Then one night disaster struck.

On March 4th 1945, we flew a night attack on a build up of German equipment and troop concentrations at a place called Casarsa. Our target marking work required us to make four runs over the target area. On the fourth run, the aircraft shuddered violently and my intercom went dead.

"Heck, what's that?" I shouted to Bob Lewis in the co-pilot seat next to me. I could not call any of the crew and they could not call me. A touch on my right shoulder alerted me to Shorty leaning over me, "Tommy an incendiary bomb has dropped into our plane right by my door." My thoughts spun around in my head, "We've run under one of the bombers as he dropped his load over the target. Blast that fourth run!" Thinking about the judder in the aircraft, I turned to Shorty, "Has the bomb exploded?" "No," replied Shorty, pulling aside his oxygen mask to talk to me. "It's just sitting there." "OK" I replied, "Hopefully it won't explode now. Have you checked for other bombs?" "No!"

I motioned to Bob, "Bob, go with Shorty and assess our damage. Check everything. Get your Aldis lamp and check our wings for holes. Report back as soon as you can." The bomb we had received was designed to explode and set fires going, fires that no amount of water could extinguish. "Amazing that the bloody thing hasn't gone off already!" I muttered to myself. I waited. It seemed like an age while Bob inspected the plane.

Bill Scott passed me a note giving our course to steer for home. The Liberator flew nicely enough, the motors continued smoothly. Bob returned. He and Shorty had found a lot of damage from nine bombs. Some had dropped right through our plane, while others were now being dislodged by crew members at the rear of the aircraft. The damage seemed endless: radio unworkable, hydraulic lines severed, intercom not functioning, and worst of all, holes in the wings and the flaps. The flaps, an extension to the wing of the plane, assisted the pilot to fly the plane at lower speeds in take off and landing. Holes in the wings meant that we could have a fuel leak; we would need to keep a careful check on our fuel supplies.

Momentarily my mind whirled with all the possibilities. Will we be able to lower the undercarriage to land back at base? If we do get the wheels down, will they hold when we touch the runway? Without our flaps I would have to land at high speed and that would put the undercarriage more in jeopardy. The crew would need to be ready in crash positions. Anything could happen.

WILL WE BALE OUT OVER NORTHERN ITALY?

Possibly Altair would not get us back to base. She was badly damaged, and we had another two and a half hours' flying. Most of this would be over the Adriatic Sea. If we crashed into the sea, we had no radio to give our position or to give Amandola base any idea that we were in trouble. My thoughts went to the crew, "I must give each one an opportunity to bale out over northern Italy while they have a chance."

Bob visited each one of the crew members with my message and offered them the chance to jump by parachute before we crossed the enemy coast and headed out into the Adriatic Sea. All decided to stay. Who can tell the thoughts of each of my eight crewmen as we flew across the coast and out over the sea? That coastline represented a last chance of survival if the Liberator did not hold together.

The minutes ticked by and still the plane flew on. I waited for some tell tale jolt that altered the way Altair flew, some indication of the failure of the rear section of the plane. My whole body tensed ready for sudden response. Bob rejoined me on the flight deck. I had another message for him to give to the fellows, "Bob, tell the fellows down the back end of the plane to keep their sky watch going. Enemy planes may still be around. We don't want to let up."

In the meantime, the flight went on, navigation and radar fixes continued and I planned our landing procedure.

I decided that I would take the plane well out from the runway and so make as gradual an approach to landing as was possible. With our faster landing without flaps, I would not know till the last moment if the braking system worked. Thus we needed someone standing by at the rear with parachutes tied on to secure parts of the aircraft; an open parachute after landing would assist in slowing us down.

EMERGENCY LANDING

Amidst the tension of the moments, I decided to allocate the crew their various tasks: Ed Riley, organise helpers to lower the undercarriage wheels. Bob Lewis, shoot out distress flares for the control tower to know we were in trouble, then also assist me in landing the plane. Shorty, organise an alternative braking system, and prepare a team to release parachutes as we land.

We flew in from the north east and saw the friendly Amandola runway lights glimmering in the distance. Bob's first distress flares cast a red glow into the sky, and red shadows waved to and fro across my instruments.

The time had come to test our undercarriage. Ed Riley went to the nose position, lay on his back and used his feet to force the nose wheel to move. Two fellows went to the centre of the plane and began winding a large handle in an attempt to get the heavy wheels to move. But they remained obdurate.

Desperately the men persisted with the lowering procedure and ever so slowly there came a hesitating rumble from the landing wheels. Perhaps some oil still remained in the hydraulic lines and was assisting the straining muscles of the crewmen. Gradually, then more definitely, the undercarriage moved. Bob shone the beam of his Aldis lamp on to the lower side of the wings and shouted, "Wheels going down!" His words came as music to my ears, "But will it lock into place?" I strained my neck around to gaze underneath the wings, hoping by dint of will to get that final important movement. I looked at my array of instruments. Indicator lights showed green, the main wheels had locked down, and the nose wheel locked into place! Human strength and hydraulic motors had worked together. I sighed in relief.

An awful concern for Ed's back came over me. I had seen him struggling with his part of the mechanism lowering the nose wheel, "Damn, I should not have let him!" I said to myself, determining to check up later.

Ten miles south of Amandola, I turned Altair for descent towards the runway; time for the fellows to get into their crash positions. Bob shot off the second set of red flares that rose in a high arc above our aircraft.

Dancing red shadows flickered on the inside of the Liberator as flares signalled our distress. A welcome green signal came from the distant control tower at Amandola, then another. They had seen us.

Approach to the runway brought us lower and lower. Bob Lewis stood by to relay my messages. Shorty at the rear awaited Bob's signal to open the parachutes for slowing us after landing.

We came in over the edge of the airfield, going well above normal landing speed. The beginning of the runway came and still I kept plenty of air flying over our wings. Forcing Altair down on to the bitumen, I heard the anguished squeal of tyres as they reacted to our speeding weight. Shutting off power from the motors, I allowed the plane to settle more and more heavily and then the wheels gave their welcome rumbling sound. The undercarriage was holding, and gave no sign of collapse. Number one hurdle had been accomplished but the runway lights were flashing by at far too great a speed.

Gently pressing the brakes, I tested for braking power. Lights continued to flash by, our speed did not seem to be slowing. Then, imperceptibly for a moment, I felt a retarding force, then more strongly, the brakes began to grip. We had some braking power. I did not dare release that touch on the brakes in three quarters of a mile of runway. One slight release and I could have lost all the remaining brake fluid. We slowed and I did not have to ask Shorty for the emergency parachutes.

The end of the runway came into view before I felt we were slowing down sufficiently. Altair ran to a stop on a piece of rough pavement well off to one side. We had arrived! Drained of energy, I flopped over the pilot's control and then noticed that I had left the motors running. I shut off their fuel supply and switched them off. The Liberator became silent apart from the tinkling noise of heated metal shrinking as it cooled.

After a while, a gentle hum of tired voices accompanied the crew picking up their baggage. A scraping sound meant the exit door was being raised to let us out. I looked out my pilot's window to see fire tenders arraigned around us. This time I did not need them, not like at Catania in Sicily a year before. The 614 Squadron repair park would house Altair from now on, but there had been no fire and for this I was very, very, thankful.

Time passed; I continued to sit, letting my mind adjust to our safe return. A vehicle stopped — our transport! Slowly, I collected my gear and made my way out to breathe in the fresh Italian air. Going out into the darkness to relieve myself, I then walked across the grass to the vehicle and flopped into the unyielding upholstery. All I wanted to do was rest my head and unwind my tensed up muscles.

REPAIRS FOR A VETERAN

Late next morning, I met Ed and we wandered down to see Altair. There she was, already towed into the repair area. The engineering officer saw us coming, "Whatever happened last night?" We shared with him the story of our attack and flight home. "Come and look at how fortunate you are to get back!" he said with a knowing emphasis.

We clambered into Altair and explored through the familiar flight deck and wide fuselage. The sun shone brightly through large holes from the damage of last night, lighting up the inside of the plane. The officer showed us three big structural members in the rear part of the fuselage. One main structural member was severed completely, and two were holding together by a mere fraction of metal. Two further members were cut more than two thirds through. "It's remarkable that you got back," the officer emphasised again. He explained how little strength remained to keep the plane flying.

Shorty's radio office showed damage from a falling bomb. How had he escaped from awful injury? The crew had finally thrown the bomb into the sea. We went outside and saw more damage to the port side wing with holes right through the flaps area. "I see what you mean," I said, conscious that the engineering officer also had been touched by Altair's remarkable return.

Ed and I lingered. We had grown secure in flying through enemy air space in this bulky Liberator with the star Altair painted on her. Not once had she let us down. We voiced our goodbye to the plane whose long wings and broad fuselage, had carried us into action thirty eight times. Tomorrow would see us needing a new plane as our crew went back into ops.

In the weeks ahead, Altair did emerge from the repair park. A ferry crew came from Algiers to fly her south. They took Altair on to the runway. With her familiar roar she made her long run and climbed into the sky. She and her crew were not heard of again. No emergency call came, no indication of trouble. That the aircraft dived into the sea, seemed obvious, but where? What of her crew in those last moments before the plane plunged? No one remained to tell just what had happened. What shocked us was how different it could have been for ourselves as we battled to fly Altair back over the Adriatic, in the early hours of March 5th 1945.

ROME

A weeks' leave seemed like reward indeed, after our adventure with Altair. Ed and I chose to go to Rome, which had celebrated freedom from German occupation six months earlier.

The RAF vehicle took us via Naples and along the Appian Way that stretched northwards. Near Rome, we drove parallel to a massive Roman aqueduct supplying water from the mountains to the timeworn city. The aqueduct had survived over two thousand years since the reign of the Emperor Claudius. Its tall strong legs strode across the countryside for mile after mile. I admired its survival and wondered if any evidence of our work would endure like this Roman monument. So many of my friends had been laid to rest beneath Europe's soil. What would survive of their efforts? Would anything be remembered of them?

Ed and I stayed in a hotel near the ancient wall that had once been Rome's protection. Near the hotel, a towering gateway had once been guarded by Roman soldiers. As we appraised the ancient stones and brickwork, a voice spoke my name, "Hullo Scotland."

STRATEGIC PLANNER

The voice seemed familiar. I looked up. It was Group Captain Jarman, who had flown with us to Greece, several months previously. "Hullo sir, we were just checking out this wall!" We stood chatting for a time, agreeing to meet again later at the hotel.

I was struck by the sensitive face of this lean framed man. The Group Captain's work co-ordinated British and American air attacks of the strategic bombing force. He said that the name of our crew had come before him from time to time and he was glad he could thank us for the job we had been doing. He assured us he had worked hard to get our PFF squadron brought to the attention of the RAF in London, because the war in Italy had often been overlooked by the government and the planners in England. This saddened him, because he felt the whole bomber and Pathfinder force in Italy worthy of greater acknowledgement than it had received from Britain.

We reminded him about his planning the Christmas day attack by Pathfinders on Hitler's lair at Berchtesgaden. That the attack had to be aborted, was one reason why we stood before him alive. "It's not easy to be a Commander," he said in response.

THAT VOICE FROM THE STARS

The Tiber flowed wide and strong through Rome. Ed and I headed across the river at the Castel San Angelo and walked towards Saint Peter's Cathedral which sits in Vatican territory.

People entered the Cathedral at the high mounted statue of the Apostle Peter. Reverence meant kissing the quite worn big toe of the statue. Michelangelo's ornate paintings of heavenly beings adorned the magnificent dome that sat high above the floor. I gazed and gazed, taking in the painter's expenditure of energy to produce such symmetry of human form, and the huge figure of a man pointing his fearsome finger at me.

We saw altars coated with gold, and visited long galleries filled with treasure beneath the cathedral. I tried to compare the Being worshipped here to the one who had communicated with me out beyond the stars whilst flying. My mind had no answer. A question remained.

DID 614 SQUADRON DO THIS?

Moving away from the Vatican, Ed and I walked across the Tiber to the broken monuments of ancient Rome. Triumphal arches and broken columns littered the roadway where the pride of Roman legions had marched in the time of the Caesars. Ed looked at the wreckage of time and said, "I'm sure 614 Squadron was not this far off the target!" "Are you sure Ed?" I asked with a laugh.

We headed for the Colosseum, that ancient theatre raised for the sport of the Caesars, the killing of gladiators and persecution of people. From where Caesar sat, viewing across the huge arena, I could hear again the roar of the vast audience asking him to give them more blood and more death. Across the now broken floor of the arena, I saw the passages beneath and through which lions, gladiators and persecuted people had made entrance to the arena itself.

WELL THEY CANNOT BLAME US FOR THAT DAMAGE, WE HAVE NEVER BEEN THIS FAR OFF TARGET.

A small plaque mounted on a stone nearby caught my eye. It translated, "A memorial erected by the Christians of Rome to the thousands of Christians who perished here by order of the Caesars." I felt deeply moved as I read the words. The plaque had a touch of love about it and I sat, letting memory recall the facts of history. Persecuted people had been thrust into this arena to face wild beasts, others had been sewn into animal skins and caused to expire by heat of the sun, others still had been cut down by gladiators to the enthusiastic cries of a blood lusting Caesar.

"So they were christians," I mused as my eyes returned to the words on the plaque. These courageous dead spoke about the way they valued something else greater than their own lives. I went away with Ed, feeling I had been in the presence of a greater reality than I had ever known.

NOT INDESTRUCTIBLE

We sat by the Tiber river and talked about how much longer we would be together. We had flown in nearly sixty attacks on enemy targets, and were not indestructible. We needed to stop, and that meant the parting of our ways.

I looked at Ed's sensitive face, and observed how fine he appeared as an RAF officer, but it was the stoop in his back that concerned me. He had experienced a lot of pain after our crashes, and his latest act, forcing down the nose wheel of Altair, had added to his problem. I believed that our visit to Rome celebrated our coming towards the end of more than two tremendous years of flying together, and now we talked of what lay ahead for us. Australia had a war on its hands in the Pacific. I expected to be sent back there, while the claims of the RAF would come upon Ed.

MONTE CASSINO

In returning to Amandola, Ed went via Naples while I took another vehicle making a journey through Monte Cassino. This town in the mountains had been a German stronghold, holding Allied armies at bay for two months. The strongest German resistance had been set up in the monastery on top of the mountain, and German resistance only broke when, with the Pope's enforced permission, the huge building was pounded by attacks from bomber aircraft.

The vehicle drove through the Rapido valley to Monte Cassino amidst signs of bitter fighting. Monte Cassino itself seemed to be a town of the dead. As far as my eye could see, there was desolation, shattered wreckage, bullet marked road signs pointing at crazy angles, and now being restored. Crosses marked the graves of the fallen, buried where they had been found. Two British war correspondents lay in a cared for plot surrounded by white painted fencing, beside a shattered building. How great had been the cost of winning Monte Cassino!

NEW LIBERATOR

Next day I joined Ed back at 614 squadron. He took me to see the large letter "A" painted on the side of a new Liberator numbered KG951. It was Altair's replacement.

To air test the bulky aircraft, I took my crew on a flight across the Foggia plains to the Vesuvius volcano. Flying low at first across farmland, we climbed above the zig zag road that led up the mountains to Avellino, then came to the volcano. A year before, Vesuvius had exploded, sending highly destructive clouds of dust into the air. Now she had quieted. I flew around the rim, so that the crew could focus on the signs of activity within the crater. Their excitement was reward indeed.

On our return flight we tested our guns, radar, bomb sight and radio, plus the way the Liberator handled in flight. Bob Lewis checked our speeds against engine power and revolutions, and we were thrilled. This aircraft had more power than we had known in Altair.

By the time we dived from height to fly low over the farmland and return to Amandola, we were ready to face the enemy again.

BUDD

Crew briefing introduced us to our target, a big railway junction called Gemona, in the north of Italy. Our route to Gemona placed us in conflict with heavy weather coming through from the north west.

We had a new trainee bomb aimer allocated to us. Budd, our previous trainee bomb aimer, had graduated from the operational training Ed had given him and would be flying with another crew. After eight attacks on enemy targets, he had learnt much from Ed, and had flown with us on our final flight in Altair. So we would miss such a man who had played his part well in our crew

Soon after take off, clouds surrounded us and icing, thin at first, gradually built up on our wings. The power performance of the new Liberator kept us climbing for height and with Ed guiding me on his radar we avoided the worst of the storm. The plane rose through the danger zone and into air temperatures where icing created no problem.

Hours later, we returned from Gemona to hear news that shocked us. One of our planes had iced up and nearly crashed. Two crewmen were down in the Adriatic. One of them was our man Budd. But with night time darkness, and a raging storm at sea, the search was being delayed till early morning light. What hope had those men of being found, I wondered? I sought out the troubled pilot to find out how it had happened. He unfolded a terrifying experience.

On the way to the target, he had flown into icing conditions. The ice had built up so rapidly that the plane had gone out of control, spinning down towards the Adriatic. Believing the situation had become hopeless, he had given the order for his crew to abandon the aircraft. Budd was the first to take to his parachute, and another member of the crew had followed. Then amazingly, the pilot had found his plane coming out of the spin. He had called on the crew to halt their parachute escape. With two crewmen down in the Adriatic and the remaining crew distressed, he had returned to base.

As early morning shed its light, search aircraft flew over the previous evening's route to Gemona. Ed and I waited around for news of Budd, but with the storm unabated, the search aircraft had to abort their flights. Freezing conditions down on the ocean meant that Budd and his companion could not have lasted long. Ed and I departed for bed with heavy hearts.

It took us days before we could accept that Budd had gone. We kept thinking that he would appear. It seemed such a twist of fate for him to lose his life in the Adriatic sea now, after our last hazardous flight in Altair had saved him with our crew, from such a watery grave. His body was never found.

TWENTY MINUTES LATE

March 9th 1945 came with news of the German Army retreat over the River Po in Northern Italy. The whole army was being transported at night across this river. German ingenuity concealed huge collapsible bridges during daylight, and the allies could not stop the movement across the river at night. Supplies of equipment and munitions kept pouring into the front line to enable the enemy to put up a furious fight and so make their escape. It was known that one of the main supply routes came through Verona, the city of Shakespeare's Romeo and Juliet.

Our crew was detailed with nine others to lead the bomber force in an attack on the big rail junction at Verona. To Verona and back meant a five hour flight lay before us. With all our crew in place, I began starting the motors of KG951. Three motors started readily, but the number four motor refused to activate. Time ticked by. One by one the 614 squadron planes roared away into the night, their exhausts belching the flames of full take off power. Bill voiced my own anxiety that the continued delay gave us little hope of making the target on time.

Our ground crew sergeant worked frantically, removing cowlings from the engine and readjusting the starting mechanism, while I pleaded with our number four motor, like a Juliet pleading with her Romeo, "Oh Romeo, Romeo, wherefore art thou not going Romeo?"

Twenty minutes passed, and still KG951 just sat there with only three motors running. "Baaaaang!" A shattering explosion rocked the plane; at last the motor had blasted into life. Clouds of smoke streamed away from the exhausts into the darkness.

With final checks on all the motors, something like a cheer rose in my throat. I gave my "thumbs up" appreciation to the ground crew Sergeant, and rolled the Liberator along between the lights at the beginning of the runway. With a loud rumbling roar, we commenced our take off run. The end of the runway lights raced towards us and we rose into the night sky; a lone Liberator chased the squadrons that had now flown far to the north.

"Navigator" I called. "Right Skipper?" responded Bill from his navigation office. I continued, "We're twenty minutes late. It's going to be really interesting to see if we can get to the target on time. Let's make the route as direct as possible." "I'll work on that," replied Bill. Then I laid out my plan. "I'll get up to height quickly so that you can work out your upper winds. You let me know what speed we'll need to get there on time. I'm sure this plane can give us an extra good turn of speed." "OK, I'll let you know," responded Bill, bending over his charts.

A GOD WE KNEW LITTLE ABOUT

The fellows joined in the excitement of our race against time. The motors drank in their fuel, our weight lessened, and the Liberator built up speed. The hours ticked by. We had to stay clear of the Allied front line, and so flew towards Venice, where that city's lights blinked off and blackout hid it from us; only Ed's radar revealed its presence. It was time to turn westward. Padua appeared on the radar and then, after another fifteen minutes, Verona. We circled the city and came in from the north west, beginning our run in to the huge railway area as the sky flares of the earlier Pathfinders lit up the sky. The vast area of Verona's railway system lay illuminated below. We were right on time. Then the guns opened up. Their ugly, angry flashes bit at us from out of the night sky. Sweat ran down my body in the tension of our attack.

We were lined up ready to drop our target indicators when the new trainee bomb aimer cursed and declared, "They are stuck, the T.I.s won't drop!" I coached him along and said we would do another run.

He checked his electric circuits and Ed checked the bomb bay. On our second run, the TIs held again and did not drop.

I turned at the end of the run and said, "You must get them away this time." Each time we turned and came in again, the guns were there with their shells exploding all around us. Perhaps I even prayed to a god I knew little about, but hoped fervently would watch over us.

We figured that some moisture in the bomb release system had frozen and prevented release on our previous two runs over the target, but now on our third run, Ed and Shorty banged away at the release mechanism and finally our TIs were gone. As we turned at the end of the third run, I could see the broad acreage of the railway yards at Verona and knew that our boy had made an accurate drop. We headed for home to find that our five hour flight had been accomplished in four and a half hours.

At the debriefing, other crews asked, "How did you make it to the target on time?" Bill, with a twinkle in his eyes, was equal to all the questions, "Oh, we've been up there so many times that we can choose the right type of cloud and it adds forty miles an hour to our speed!" He made the untruth sound very convincing.

I went to bed in the early hours of morning and lay down to sleep. My active mind retraced every detail of our flight to Verona. I noticed that some of my crew had been tired and edgy, and I felt the same. I began to worry about them. Also, I rehearsed my own difficulties in facing the gunfire directed at us as we went in to attack. I shuddered inwardly as every exploding shell brought pain to my being, making my stomach muscles tighten more and more.

A weak autumn sun shone from a clear sky by the time I awoke next morning. I dressed and made my way out of the tent to begin my day. Ed met me, nodded his head and said, "It's a clear photo of the target." "Great, our trainee bomb aimer must be feeling good about that, have you seen him?" "Yes, he's pleased alright, and he's busy just now showing all the doubters that our TIs had actually been placed on the target." Ed's nimble fingers had already produced a sketch from the previous night, and he drew it out to show me.

"ONE MORE DUMMY RUN OVER THE TARGET AND YOU'RE ON YOUR OWN MATE"

I'm going in to check on my mail Ed, has it come in yet?" "Yes, I saw a pile of it come in a short time ago," said Ed. In my mail that day, I received another letter from my sister Helen. Enjoying the sight of an envelope from Australia, I decided that I liked her becoming a more regular correspondent. She wrote about concluding her training at the Fremantle Hospital near Perth so that she could become a nursing sister at a country town called Manjimup.

Great concern came over me when I read that my sister Elsa had joined the RAAF and had been posted to Melbourne. I could not believe that mother would be left alone to fend for herself. But then, somewhat relieved I read that my sister Pat resigned from the Womens Land Army in order to be with mother, but I knew that such a resignation would not be easy for Pat. Once again Helen closed off her letter with the words, "Oh by the way, Laurel sends her love." "That cheeky girl again!" I said to myself as I put the letter away.

SIXTY TWO OPS

The Russian army needed our co-operation now, as her units forced the Germans to retreat through Rumania and Hungary, and then to pull back through Yugoslavia. On March 20th 1945, we were briefed to attack a large railway complex in Yugoslavia. The Germans had been sending supplies through there, trying to reinforce their army against the Russian attacks. Our attack proved to be highly successful and it became the conclusion to our long list of flights over enemy targets. It was my sixty second operational attack and time for Ed, Shorty and me to stop. We had flown to distant targets in Germany, France, Austria, Rumania, Hungary, Yugoslavia, Bulgaria, Greece and Italy. It was enough.

For God's sake don't wake that lot up they finished their sixty second Op last night.

The RAF in London had considered what tally of ops entitled Pathfinders to the permanent award of the coveted guilt eagle Pathfinder badge. For Pathfinders flying from England, the tally was forty five ops. The tally for 614 squadron flying from Italy was set at sixty. Ed, Shorty and I had gone beyond that and were one of the few members of the squadron to complete such a tally of attacks. The harshness of the battle through 1944 meant that many of our crews had been cut down long before attaining the prize we now received. Tony and I had been the only two Aussie pilots so far awarded it in Italy.

Cessation of our operational flying meant that my crew would now disband. In a last act together, we eight fellows enjoyed journeying into Foggia town to be photographed, and to party together. I felt proud of the them all. The crew motto throughout had been, "On time, all the time," and they had all worked together in upholding this motto. Even when engine trouble made us late in take off, we had managed to make up those essential minutes and to be there, on time. Accurate timing was one of the essential ingredients for the squadron's successes.

Our last target photo showed that we had maintained the accuracy for which the strategic planner, Group Captain Jarman, had commended Ed and me when we met him in Rome.

My crew and I now drove over the bumpy road from Amandola to Foggia and discussed our future. Ed, Shorty and I would fly no more ops, but this was not so for the others. Bill Scott had been invited to join a crew who had lost their navigator. Bob Lewis also had been asked to fly five more ops to make up his tally of sixty. Our bomb aimer and two gunners had been appointed to fly with other crews.

The many photographs we had taken over enemy targets were not to be compared to that taken by the photographer in Foggia town. It showed my weary crew grouped together and trying to smile. We reckoned we would not have given the photographer a job in our team. I passed copies of the photograph to each of the fellows and told them how highly I had valued them. We were a successful team only because of the contribution each one had made in our flying together.

PROCEED TO EGYPT

"Scotty, your posting has come through." It was the voice of the Adjutant calling as I entered the Officers Mess. The Australian Air Force wanted Shorty and me to proceed to Egypt, and await a ship that would return us to Australia. Ed had been appointed to the Pathfinder base at Gransden Lodge in England. "Thanks for the info Adj," I said as sadness touched me in facing this final split up in my crew.

Farewells to our squadron mates went on for several evenings, then the CO arranged for his staff car to convey the three of us to Naples for our flight out of Italy. At the airport there, I enquired about getting seats on aircraft flying out. The result was quite exciting. An RAF pilot agreed for Ed to join his bomber crew flying to England via France, and a US pilot made seats available to Shorty and me on a DC3 Dakota going to Egypt. I advised the transit clerk about the arrangements and he promised to call us.

It suddenly felt painful to be parting from Ed. I tried to voice something, but my words were cut short when the call came for Ed to board his aircraft. Parting became a hasty event, and a moment of anguish as Shorty and I watched him limp his way across the airport tarmac. Winds blew from the mountains to flap the jacket that covered his spare frame and disturbed the cap that hid all but the tails of his straight unruly blonde hair. He boarded the plane to England, as a loudspeaker bade Flying Officers Weekes and Scotland to weigh in and be ready to board the flight to Cairo.

15

TWO EGYPTIAN BROOCHES

The Dakota flew out from Naples airport taking Shorty and me on an unhurried flight over southern Italy and a Mediterranean that we knew so well. Then came Malta, Libya, and a desert of sand dunes.

Those endless sands: I found myself not wanting to go any further, longing for the plane to turn around and take me back. The war had not yet finished, and tired as I might be, I was not ready to move away from it.

Still more sand! We continued to drone on, and I pictured Australian soldiers fighting from defeat to victory across these wind blown ridges. Pat, our boarder from home, had soldiered here. He had sent my family some photos of his life amongst these sand dunes; then he had fallen defending the island of Crete.

Flying across Egypt, brought us to El Alamein, that area of north Africa where the German army had come to a halt in 1941. General Rommel had come so close to capturing Cairo and Alexandria, the two main cities of Egypt. One step more, and Germany could have gained oil supplies from the Egyptian and Sinai oil fields. Such oil for her war machine would have changed the course of the war for us all.

Desert conditions continued until at last we flew by the pyramids of Giza near Cairo, and landed. Our vehicle drove through Cairo to Heliopolis, a suburb full of palm trees and verdant growth. Continuing on, we alighted at RAF quarters on the edge of flat empty desert, a depressing place to wait for transport to Australia. Having been so deeply involved with my crew and the challenge of being on operations, I needed time to adjust. The quarters at Heliopolis made me feel like a prisoner, shut in with nothing but my tiredness.

TWO EGYPTIAN BROOCHES

Visits into Cairo brought some change. People, crowds, donkey carts, shouting drivers, cars, blaring horns, Cairo began to stimulate me and then gave adventure as I came to grips with Egyptian lifestyle. Learning to speak a type of Arabic enabled communication with Egyptian people and the shops.

Filigree brooches caught my eye and I purchased two beauties. Priding myself on the purchase of the two brooches, I then purchased a few other gifts for my family. The gifts nestled in my bag protected by clothing and items packed around them.

Meeting people from an affluent part of Cairo, I befriended an Egyptian girl. Her beauty and dark skin gave me my first real closeness to the black races. By then I was posted to a rest centre at Kasfriet on the Suez canal.

TREMENDOUS NEWS

A month passed with still no news of shipping to Australia, but other exciting news did come. The German army in Italy had crumbled right along the battle front. Separated from the drama of this great event, Shorty and I waited eagerly for details.

It appeared that 614 squadron had led the RAF bombers on a night attack on the enemy just behind the front line in northern Italy. The Pathfinders had flown in and placed their TIs to mark out vital points of the German front line for the RAF bombers to drop their explosives. The result had been to totally demoralise German troops. Such close co-operation between the army and a strategic bomber force had not been so successful before nor attempted at such close proximity to the front line. American planes had attacked in daylight the next day. All along the battle front, German soldiers, bewildered by the fury of the onslaught, had surrendered in whole divisions. They had sat down amongst the hills to the north of the river Po and could fight no more.

But in Germany itself, the battle raged on for another two weeks. The Russians fought their way in from the east and joined up with the Allied forces attacking from the west. Allied armies halted impatiently waiting while the Russians captured Berlin. Then Germany surrendered unconditionally. The Russians took control of a large area of Germany and southern Europe. It was a big disappointment to those nations that had fought so long and hard to make Europe free. Down in Egypt we were aghast at the thought of Russia controlling so much territory.

Germany's collapse was exciting news, but it brought me face to face with my own pain in trying to face the future. Somewhere inside me there was a big ache, and nothing I did seemed to assuage it.

MORE GOOD NEWS

Australian aircrew from other RAF units joined us at the rest centre near the Suez Canal. Then came our sailing orders. The Winchester Castle was leaving from Port Said, and would return us to England. I could think of nothing that would enthuse me more. Shorty was ecstatic about seeing Else, his young lady who lived near London.

An exciting train journey adjacent to the Suez Canal, brought us to our waiting ship. Once on board I walked the decks, planning my return to England. War dangers still persisted. The unconditional surrender of Germany had not yet brought the actual surrender of all her forces. Danger still lurked with German submarines in hidden places. Our ship travelled on full alert and at night, a total blackout prevailed.

But shipboard life remained very relaxed. Working in with fellow Aussies, I arranged a boxing tournament in which we all participated. The meals made from fresh foods that we had not seen for a long time, enticed the return of my appetite. After meals, Shorty and I sat watching the Mediterranean waters roll by, and dreamed together about our future. Shorty wanted to build a new house on his parents' farm and make up to them for the hardships they had endured. Daring now to think positively about the future, I shared my ideas about becoming a civil engineer. It needed five years of study, but offered me exciting possibilities for a career.

SUNSET IN THE MEDITERRANEAN

One evening at sunset, I stood alone by the ship's rail. Several hours of daylight yet remained and the passing waters at this spot were of great significance to me. Here, in 1916, my mother's ship had sunk after an attack by German submarines. Here my eldest sister had nearly perished as a babe in mother's arms after the attack. Here also, in early 1944, my crew and I had flown overhead towards Italy and the battle for Europe.

Gazing towards Italy, I saw storm clouds gathering over that northern horizon. So often such storms had been across our flight path on our journey to attack distant targets. My thoughts went to the fighting through which I had survived whilst I had been with 614 squadron, and the friendships I had been privileged to experience.

With the menu card from the evening's dinner table in my hands, I drew out a pen, and as the words tumbled out, wrote my impressions:-

I look out across the sea and I feel every thump of the ship's engines like the echo of a distant heartbeat. With every thump, I experience an increasing separation from that part of me that I left in Italy; the mates, the experiences of laughter, of comradeship, of sincerity, of flak and bombs, of flame and shattered bodies, of fear and cowardice, of sudden bravery.

On the reverse side of the menu I scribbled:-

What memories I leave behind as today's radio news tells of events in Munich, Bucharest, Verona, Ploesti, Plovdiv; all are places that the war has printed indelibly into my life. I leave those places behind, but my memory of the events and the people remain within me.

THE GIB

On May 21st 1945, the Winchester Castle drew into anchorage at the Rock of Gibraltar, affectionately called the "Gib." I gazed at this one thousand four hundred foot high British fortress which Britain had captured from Spain in 1704. The echo of moving vehicles sounded out over the water as army traffic drove in and out of huge defensive caverns the British had carved into the limestone. This powerful fortress enabled Britain to police the narrow entrance to the Mediterranean Sea, eight and a half miles across to Morocco on the north west corner of Africa.

The Winchester Castle, with eight other ships in a convoy, headed for the Atlantic Ocean. Five naval ships shepherded the nine through submarine infested waters.

In the Bay of Biscay the ships rolled and pitched as winds screamed through the rigging. I pitied the small naval ships nosing into the troughs of waves, their propellers stuck high out of the water. It all looked violently uncomfortable for those on board.

Nearing England, the skies continued to storm and the seas to rage. Amidst it all came the sound of aircraft motors. A British four engine Sunderland circled us. "Welcome to England" it seemed to say, and I lifted my heart in anticipation of being back in the land I had grown to love.

After five rough days at sea, the Winchester Castle sailed into the waters of the River Clyde and headed towards Glasgow. This long neck of water gave us close up views of Scottish villages and Clydeside shipyards. Recently a centre for building ships for war, they were already building for peace. I reflected on the word "peace". The word sounded nice, but what did it really mean?

The nearer we drew to Glasgow, the more I thought of the Lewis parents; the shipyards were their life. I had written a letter to them assuring them of Bob's expected return from Italy, and felt proud that in some way I had a part in Bob's survival through the war.

WHIN COTTAGE

My feet touched the firm ground of Scotland and my first thought was to go to the family home, Whin Cottage at Beaconsfield, near London. I could be quiet there. I would phone them from London and see if it would be alright to come. The train sped through the countryside, and I drank in the memories of this land, home to me before going to Italy.

My aunt woke me to a bright sun of early summer, as she pushed back the curtains. "Do you know that you have slept for fourteen hours?" I had arrived at Whin Cottage the previous evening and now rolled over in this most comfortable bed, looked at my aunt and responded, "This bed is beautiful. Do you really want me to get up?" Gazing at me seriously she said, "Tom, you'll need to get up soon, it's nearly lunch time. You and I need to sit down and have a good talk. I don't want us to miss out on that you know." Then as if an afterthought she added, " Can I bring you a cup of tea to help you wake up?" "Great!" I replied, "That'll just touch the spot." Then I rejoined, "I want to know what has been happening to you all since I left for Italy. So you have some talking to do as well as I!"

She went quietly out the door. I luxuriated amidst the sheets and the soft warm eiderdown. The windows of this attic room gave views over the tops of beech trees and added to my enjoyment of pleasant seclusion. Soon my aunt delivered a cup of tea on a tray, and I relaxed amongst the pillows feeling like a king. I had forgotten the delights of a well brewed cup of tea and a soft bed.

Stepping downstairs for lunch, I saw my uncle sitting in his big armchair, with the newspaper before him. A usually reserved man, he now greeted me warmly, enthusiastic about my return to England. He was home on leave from the navy, and being over sixty, he now wanted to retire.

At lunch around the table we conversed about events in England while I had been away. They were agog about daughter Betty walking along the street one day when an enemy plane had flown along the street with its guns firing. Soon afterwards an RAF Spitfire had roared by chasing the enemy and she had felt somewhat restored.

This typical wartime family faced return to peacetime living after nearly six years of conflict in Europe. For me, peace had not yet come. War still raged in the Pacific area. Australians still fought against Japanese; peace in the Pacific remained a distant goal. I finished washing the lunch dishes, then my aunt called me. She sat, gracefully gowned in a long flowing dress, on the lounge by the window. "Come Tom," she said quietly indicating a place beside her, "Tell me what you've been doing."

Over the week I stayed in the home, I dug gardens, planted vegetables, raked the grounds, and enjoyed being in touch with the earth and daily life in the home. But times of extreme weakness and weariness troubled me. In an unexpected moment I became bereft of energy and had to stop. There seemed no answer to the problem; my body seemed to have reached a low point, and I longed for the tiredness to go away.

BOURNEMOUTH

Phone calls to a family at Barton on Sea, near Bournemouth, brought me in touch with the Newmans who had befriended me when I first arrived in England; a lifetime away it seemed. They invited me to spend a week with them at their home aptly named Rest Harrow.

I arrived to find the table set for the evening meal. They gathered around the meal just as I remembered them in days gone by; dad, the two sons and mother. I was especially glad to see eldest son Bill there, home from Medical College. But for me, returning to the house was not easy. The friends who had been here with me previously were now all dead, but I could still hear their voices. Jim Mudie, Lindsay and I had holidayed here, and we had greatly enjoyed golfing days together at the Barton on Sea golf club with another Aussie flyer, Alec Saint Smith, who had also perished,

With the meal finished and the dishes cleared away, the mother showed me some Air Ministry letters confirming the loss of all three. For a moment her own heartache for the boys she herself had come to love, overflowed. Her tears were only momentary; she quickly recovered saying, "Come on, let's go to the village."It was evening and a refreshing time to make the half hour walk to the village. She had friends in the police force there, and they loved a challenging game of snooker. Jim Mudie, Lindsay, Alec and I had previously played evening matches against them. A challenge match had been arranged just for me, and I looked forward to it. However, the evening proved strangely empty, and I walked home in sombre mood.

BOILING THE BILLY

Next day, the family took me driving into the New Forest to boil the billy for afternoon tea. It was something we had shared with them from the Australian bush. A distinctive 614 squadron aircraft flew overhead and prepared to land at the nearby air base of Hurn. Pointing it out to the family, I exclaimed, "Whatever is 614 squadron doing in England?"

The following morning I received a phone call from the Air Force in London, giving me directions about my return to Australia. This day would be my last at Barton on Sea. I walked to the village to purchase a gift for the family and to my amazement I met the pilot and bomb aimer of the 614 squadron plane. Both had flown with me on ops in Italy.

Elated at our meeting, I asked them, "Whatever are you doing in England?" "We've been transporting ex prisoners of war from southern Germany to England." With the war now finished, there remained a big task ahead for the 614 squadron, changed from being a Pathfinder squadron to that of transport. We found a nearby cafe in which we could share news over a cup of coffee; numerous cups of coffee. Delighted by the reunion, I walked back to Rest Harrow with much to think about.

Lunch was on the table when I returned. Bright conversation brought my thoughts back to this marvellous wartime family. How could I ever thank them enough? I had my present for them, a china bowl, but it seemed so inadequate.

Passing the gift over to the lady of the house, my words tumbled out awkwardly. As the representative of voices now stilled in the graves of Europe, I expressed my appreciation of their kindness and care to my friends and me. Quietness followed, then Mrs Newman thanked me, brushed away the moisture that flowed from her eyes, then busied herself with the china bowl. Conversation with the father and two sons turned to what I would be doing when I arrived back in Australia.

Early next morning, my train for London slowly drew out from Bournemouth station. I leaned out the open window to wave my farewell. These people had so excitedly opened their hearts and their home to us who had come from distant places in wartime. Now, with the coming of peace, the Newman family were having to close off a story that had run to its conclusion.

WHERE WERE YOU?

Arriving in London, I moved to my next train taking me to Liverpool. A familiar figure came along, almost hidden by his gear. "Shorty!" I called. He looked, grinned, and joined me excitedly. As he sat, I noticed an air about him that made him seem different. Our train pulled away from the platform, and he asked, "Tommy, where were you, I tried to contact you but I couldn't find out where you were?" "What did you want me for?" I asked blithely. "I wanted you at my wedding! Else and I were married last week and I wanted you as my best man!" My mouth sagged open; my feelings whirled between excitement for Shorty and chagrin for having missed out on such an important event.

Else lived at Bexley on the south side of London. Shorty had continued to correspond with her during all the time we were in Italy. His unscheduled return to England had enabled their romance to blossom into marriage, and I had missed it!

"I can tell you I feel bloody awful about leaving her in England Tommy," the newlywed emphasised. He explained that Else would now have to await a ship becoming available to transport her and other brides to Australia. "And how is she coping with the thought of coming out to Australia on her own Shorty?" "Oh, she's got all her plans worked out. She enjoys mixing with people, she'll be alright." His set facial lines softened, revealing his fondness for this girl of his dreams.

I pictured the tremendous adjustments that Else would face on an Australian farm. "She is a courageous girl," I murmured.

STIRLING CASTLE

On 18th June 1945 Shorty and I boarded the Stirling Castle at Liverpool. She carried a sprinkling of Air Force amongst a thousand or more Australian and New Zealand soldiers, ex prisoners of war from campaigns in North Africa, Greece and Crete. Some of the men had worked in German salt mines in Poland, and were emaciated, with distressing lines of deep suffering on them. Others had escaped to neutral Switzerland, and had worked in hospitable comfort.

Our lone ship headed southwards through the Atlantic to the Panama Canal. How greatly it contrasted with my memories of the Rimutaka sailing in convoy across the Atlantic amidst hazards of submarines and storms on our way to England. The leisurely journey refreshed us, and helped us to adjust to the thought of being in Australia again. Returning across the Pacific, we came to New Zealand, and drew alongside the wharf of Wellington Harbour. We two, warmed by a winter sun, looked down from the top deck upon the New Zealanders crowded on to the wharf to welcome home their boys.

"That's a great welcome those guys are getting Shorty!" He grunted as his eyes focused on to a line of soldiers flowing off the gangway and melting into the waiting crowd. Some of the men had been prisoners for five years, while others had been captured in the more recent bloody warfare of Italy. Lovers, mothers, children, husbands, fathers, wives, friends, arms met and encircled in fond recognition. Intervening years of separation faded within loving embrace. Long felt tears flowed from eyes as they met, and hearts spoke words that lips could not frame.

AUSTRALIA

The Stirling Castle sailed from New Zealand and our excitement mounted as we headed for Sydney. Several days later I was awakened at four o'clock in the morning. Such an awakening did not appeal to me one little bit, and I could not fathom the reason for Shorty's enthusiasm at such an early hour. "Wake up Tommy, I can see the coastline of Australia, come and see!"

Awakening with a jolt, I struggled out of the bunk, donned warm clothes over my pyjamas and followed him out to the deck. "That's Australia!" Shorty breathed. Through the dimness of a wintery morning, I saw cliffs in the distance, coloured orange by a strange effect of the early light. "Do you like it Tommy? It's not like coming in to the Gargarno back there in Italy. This is our country, our home!"

The ship sailed northwards, turned and sailed southwards. The cliffs remained tantalizingly distant. Our ship zigzagged, perhaps awaiting the clearer light of day before sailing into Sydney harbour. Hours passed. We walked, we talked. Here we were, so near to Australia, yet tortured by anticipation, denied the actuality of sailing into harbour.

The breakfast gong sounded, and we went below. Perhaps we would eat, but our eyes kept gazing towards the portholes to see if we were moving nearer to land. Soon back at the railings, we reminisced about our years of flying together, and chose these moments to say goodbye, knowing that on arrival in Sydney, we would part. "Will you have someone meeting you Shorty?" "No, my parents won't be able to leave the farm in Queensland!"

I pictured Shorty arriving home to a farm where a lot of hard work awaited him. "And what do your folks think about you getting married in England?" I asked "They don't know yet Tommy. Else will be writing to them and giving them all the details." As Shorty spoke, I could envisage the many months before Else could get shipping to Australia. It would give time for Shorty and his parents to adjust to each other.

At last the Stirling Castle sailed towards the coast. Nearer and nearer came the coastline until we actually sailed between headlands and into Sydney harbour. Seeing the shoreline with buildings and houses made me want to sing and dance. An overwhelming feeling of exhilaration bubbled within, and I had to walk the decks, round and round, in order to express my excitement. On and on we glided; it was so slow, but at last we sailed under the towering harbour bridge. The ship slowed even more, then tied at a wharf.

Our arrival coincided with that of the Duke Of Gloucester, Governor General of Australia. Out came a red carpet and speeches to welcome homecoming prisoners of war. The protocol proceeded in almost slow motion timing. Would it never end? Eventually all was done, and I stood on the soil of Sydney, Australia. The sun blazed down, and I sweated.

After so much eager anticipation on the boat, I now stood wearily in a busy metropolis I knew little about, and I longed to get moving. Home was still many days journey westward. Buses transported us away from the wharf to an Air Force records section. Shorty went to the Queensland section, I to the West Australian.

Confronted by much paperwork I saw a face I knew, recognition dawned; my interviewing officer was Caldwell Wearne. I had last seen him going down in a flaming Halifax that exploded over Bucharest. He had survived when others of his crew had perished. Our voices rang in joyful recognition. How animated our talk became as we spoke of changes to our lives since last we were together. Then came a call for me to board a bus to my train for Perth. My time with Caldwell Wearne had taken me back into a world I had left behind.

ONWARDS TOWARDS HOME

Melbourne station, July 1945; I was one of a few Air Force officers on the train crowded with returning prisoners of war. What a kaleidoscope of pictures the past three years had given me since last I was here. Hundreds of thousands of miles travelled, friendships made, and many farewells said and unsaid.

Leaning out the window of our slowly moving carriage, I gazed at the eager people waiting on the platform. Surprisingly, I espied two familiar faces. Surely it could not be so. Two young ladies looked very much like two of my sisters. I had not expected to see anyone I knew. Surely my family would not have been aware of my coming here anyway. Melbourne was to be merely my stopover in order to change trains in readiness for a four day journey to Perth.

The train continued slowly along the platform and then stopped. I stared at the two young ladies waiting amongst the crowd further along the platform. Yes, the unbelievable had happened; they were my sisters, Pauline and Elsa; but what were they doing here? My mind reeled as I bounded out of the train and headed for the girls, my shoulder bag flailing behind me. Squeezing along the platform amongst people straining for the sight of long awaited loved ones amongst soldiers returning home, I saw them. Moments later I reached out to them.

Sweeping the girls to me, their arms came about me. Back amongst my family! Was it actual or was I dreaming? It felt so warm to be together. I broke free and began dancing and shouting, then we spoke all at the same time. At last, feeling breathless, we stood back to survey one another, delight in our eyes.

WHERE IS IT?

Both spoke together, "Where is it?" they asked, "Where is what?" I questioned feeling very puzzled. "Where is your decoration?" they chorused.

The only emblems I carried on my uniform were the pilot's brevet and the award of the gilded flying eagle of the Pathfinder Force of the RAF. I thought the girls referred to the PFF eagle, for it was a high honour to wear one, but they had other things in mind. "Where is your decoration?" they again asked together. "I don't know anything about it," I replied feeling mystified.

"Look at this!" Pauline said as she opened her purse and pulled out a folded newspaper cutting. She opened back the folds and I saw a picture of myself. "Is this you?" Pauline asked and began to read aloud; *"Flying Officer Scotland has attacked many well defended targets in Rumania, Southern Germany, Hungary, Bulgaria, Austria, France, Italy and Yugoslavia.*

He has proved to be a most reliable captain of aircraft who has always pressed home his attacks despite enemy ground and air defences."

Pauline continued reading, *"When detailed to attack and identify targets at low level ...... etc. By his outstanding ability and fine airmanship, this officer has made a valuable contribution to the successes achieved by his squadron ... etc etc. You have been awarded the Distinguished Flying Cross kiddo,"* she said smacking me on the back.

"I didn't know about this," I gasped. There were wild shouts and hoots from the girls as they danced around in our circle bounded by the excited crowds of people.

Eventually I turned to gaze at these precious sisters and felt overwhelmed by their expressions of glee. "You've changed" they said in concerned tones, "and the way you talk has changed, you don't speak like an Australian." "Well it will just take time for me to realise that I'm back in Aussie," I admitted, "I guess I've been a long time amongst the Poms."

MUCH TO TALK ABOUT

There seemed so many in the family I wanted news about. Mother came first. "Oh, she's become very lame," they said, "she walks on two sticks now. Pat has left the Land Army to be in Perth with her. We think mother worried about you a lot." My sisters were concerned that all the apprehension had taken its toll of her health. I wondered what I might find when I reached home."

"What's happening to Melita? She wrote to me when I was in Italy to say that she hoped to beat me home. Do you think she will?" I asked. "No, Melita is still nursing with the army in Bougainville. Casualties from tropical diseases are as high as from Japanese bullets. Mother is very concerned about her too." "So Melita is still overseas," I breathed pensively, "Well it looks like I will beat her home after all."

My being on Melbourne Station also brought back rich memories of my eldest sister Norah who had been working in Melbourne with the Air Force. "What's Norah doing now?" I asked. "Oh she's received her discharge papers so as she can be with John. He's been back from Europe for some time and preparing to return to his engineering work in Singapore. You knew that Singapore had been liberated by the British and Australians?" "Yes" I replied, "I heard the news on our ship. There was a big celebration."

TWO EGYPTIAN BROOCHES

My time with the girls passed quickly, and then they had to farewell me on my journey westward. Having duties to perform as service women, it would be some months before they returned to Perth.

As I was about to board the train, I reached into my shoulder bag and grasped the filigree brooches I had carefully selected in Egypt. "Look at these!" I said handing the brooches to the girls. They looked at them in astonishment. "You mean these for us?" they queried. "I sure do. I hope you like them." "Like them? Why they're beautiful!" "Put them on then!" The train began to move. I leaned out of my compartment window and waved as the girls stood together on the crowded platform, excitedly pointing to their two brooches. They looked so fresh and beautiful. What an unexpected and exhilarating reunion it had all been.

Of some surprise to me, the two brooches I gave to Pauline and Elsa, would be questioned after I arrived home in Perth. Blissfully ignorant,

I travelled the hot, dusty, fly ridden miles as our train with open carriages made its way across the Nullarbor and drew closer and closer to Perth.

The time came when my mother, fiercely loyal to all her six daughters, had the news filtered through to her that Pauline and Elsa in Melbourne had received special gifts and I had only lesser gifts for my remaining sisters. She confronted me with the question, "Why only two brooches Tom, what about brooches for all the girls?" Why indeed?

16

YOU MUST BE LAUREL

On August 14th, 1945, mother and I stood talking together on the front lawn of our home in Nedlands. Just two weeks previously, I had arrived from Europe. A good colour now flushed mother's cheeks that had earlier appeared pale and drawn. She had regained more walking ability, balancing her weight comfortably on two sticks, and had so much she wanted to discuss.

The throb of big aircraft motors drew our eyes skyward in time to see a Catalina flying boat letting down for a landing on Crawley Bay less than half a mile away. The patrol aircraft reminded us that war against Japan still proceeded in full fury. "I do hope the war ends soon," mother said sadly. "The signs are that Japan is still fighting on but I can't understand why they are so determined to destroy themselves." I replied.

Next day, in Perth City, whom should I meet but Don Watson, my pilot cobber of 1941/42. We whooped and grabbed each others arms. I discovered he had piloted the Catalina flying boat I had seen landing on Crawley Bay. Don still flew with his squadron and expected to return to the Pacific area shortly. We had much to celebrate, and agreed to meet at a ball that night at the Embassy Ballroom.

THE EMBASSY

A tall striking looking girl called Val became my partner for the ball. I greatly enjoyed her friendship and her dancing. We joined Don and his lass in launching out on to the large ballroom floor to relish the freedom of dance, male and female in bodily movement. They were never far from us nor we from them.

Several hours skipped by and then came the delightful music of the Missouri Waltz. Part way through the swaying and romantic strains of the waltz, the orchestra stopped. There was a loud fanfare, then silence.

Dancing ceased. The orchestra leader, a sheet of paper in hand, spoke into the microphone, "Ladies and gentlemen, I have an announcement!"

I saw the announcer pause, and survey the motionless dancers. Silence shrouded the ballroom; breathing hushed. My body tensed, and my mind grappled with possible contents of the coming statement. Rumours had been filtering through all day that Japan sued for peace. However, all the latest rumours about Japanese defeat had been false. Were we to hear just another one?

The announcer put his hand on the microphone stand, "Ladies and gentlemen, it has been confirmed that Japan has surrendered. Her land forces, naval forces and air forces are laying down their arms. Ladies and gentlemen, the war is over!"

CACOPHONY

The ballroom exploded. A cacophony of sound burst from more than four hundred voices. Don and I dived towards each other, shouting as we hugged, "It's over, it's over, we've come through, unbelievable, ..."

On and on we went shouting to each other above the noise, and all across the huge floored area, people expressed long pent up emotions in screams, cries, shouts, hugs and many streaming tears. Our two partners stood back observing Don and me for a moment. Other girls joined them in excited screaming, shouting and hugging, and then swamping us with their kisses. In all the expressions of inner feeling, none was more important to me than the relief Don and I vented forth to each other. We had survived. We had received back our lives. We could go on with living. The war was over.

The noise subsided. The orchestra broke into God Save the King, and full throated singing filled the ballroom. Two minutes silence followed. Truth bore in upon us; victory had been complete, Germany and Italy had already fallen, and now came Japan's turn. Allied forces had been victorious across the world. Breaking our reverie, there came sounds of weeping. Orchestral strains of "Auld Lang Syne" wove themselves through tender moments, softly at first, then more loudly, as the throng joined hands in moving and eloquent celebration.

Well after midnight, Val and I wended our way to her home in Nedlands. Having expressed my fond goodnight, I walked along the street to mother's home. At this late hour its windows were ablaze with light.

I walked into the front hallway. There they were, mother, my sister Helen and Mr Frank Olifent, a family friend who had stood by us ever since we had arrived to settle in the city.

"Tom, the war's over, have you heard?" mother said in an elated voice, searching for my reaction. "I sure have," I said, putting my arms around her. Then, turning to the others, I continued, "What's more, I've just been celebrating the fact with Don Watson at the Embassy."

"You must have had a good time, look at your face?" Helen laughed. I began rubbing, "I suppose it's lipstick; the girls mobbed us and I've never been so kissed and hugged in all my life." "How did you like that?" Helen looked at me intently. "It was great, I loved it," I assured her as I relived the moments in the Embassy.

Excitement welled up within me. I could hold back my feelings no longer. My exuberance overflowed, "The war's over folks, the war's over, the war's finished." Excited feelings had reached down my body and touched my feet. I began to dance. I would have had them all dancing except that mother had two walking sticks and Frank a wooden leg.

Our expressions of love and relief gradually died down. "Have you thought out what you'll be doing now that the war is over Tom?" Frank Olifent asked. "Well'" I replied, " I must get used to the thought of there being no more war. That's exciting news. But then I have some more flying to do. After that I want to do engineering at the University." I looked at mother and saw her smile. I had talked over these plans with her and she felt at last some of her dreams were being fulfilled.

"Good on you Tommy, that's the stuff," said Frank. Helen piped in, "But I thought you loved flying. It won't be easy for you to give that up will it?" "No," I responded, "it won't be easy but I'll just have to do it if I'm to study."

WINGS ACROSS THE WATER

Next morning Don Watson taxied his Catalina out across Crawley Bay ready for takeoff. The long take off run sent spray billowing out from under his wings. Finally, the great machine lifted off the water adjacent to Mounts Bay Road along which I had often cycled to work.

Water dripped from the hull as the craft rose and climbed for height over the foreshore of Perth City. Don headed to Darwin and to islands of the Pacific. There, Japanese prison camps would be disgorging their British, American and Australian captives. Don's flying boat would become part of a fleet of aircraft ferrying prisoners of war back to Australia.

CATTLE STATIONS

I took up my posting to the RAAF at Guildford airport, on the edge of the city. My flying took me into the northern areas of Western Australia, out from Broome and Derby, ferrying VIPs to bases in the north. Of great interest to me were flights out to the Corunna Downs and Noonkanbah cattle stations where the Air Force had laid down huge runways for big aircraft attacking Japan.

Corunna Downs was east of Marble Bar, one of the hottest places on earth, and covered a vast area. Wherever I went, the sameness of the country stretched from horizon to horizon, and made navigation difficult. On returning, I came to the North West Cape, with the dramatically unfriendly Rough Range stretching southwards from it. Having landed at the Learmonth air base beside the ranges, I saw the Governor General's Avro York come in. What transpired as the aircraft stopped and its door opened, was so unexpected.

Out from the interior of the plane came a stream of men, with their khaki shirts flopping about them. They all engaged in one common activity, covering themselves in red dust that lay abundantly on the surface of the ground. It seemed an unbelieveably exciting corroboree.

These men had been prisoners of the Japanese. Their years of incarceration amidst starvation, filth and stench now lay behind them. They were celebrating their first feel of home, and were ecstatic. How well I knew such ecstasy. As the sun shone through their clouds of red dust, and tipped the edges with a circle of gold, the words from a poem by Walt Whitman came to my mind, and I adapted it to what I now saw:-

For Asian prisons must sometimes yawn
and yield their dead into life again,
but the day that comes with a cloudy dawn,
in golden glory at last may wane.

HOME AGAIN

Early next morning I left Learmonth and flew southward to Perth. Mother met me, and spoke excitedly of seeing my plane coming in and flying quite low overhead.

We walked slowly into the house, and she picked up some letters that lay neatly stacked on a small table in the hallway. "I think some of your boys have written to you." I took them up. They were from fellows who had been in my crew, and were now well scattered. The letters came from Malta, Palestine, England, Scotland, and one was from Shorty in Queensland.

HOPPY ON MALTA

Sitting comfortably in the sunshine, I opened first the letter from Hoppy. He wrote of events after leaving our crew and becoming an air traffic controller on the island of Malta. Malta had much history concentrated into one tiny place, and Hoppy had added his own spot of history to it. He had received news of his father's death, and had grieved alone. His mother and teenage sister, needed him now at home, and his beautiful Olive awaited his homecoming so that they could share their lives together.

Malta sat like a jewel surrounded by high rocky cliffs. On top of those cliffs and overlooking Malta's Grand Harbour of Valetta, a monument would be erected. Fifty feet high and made of marble taken from the hills of Rome, it would list the names of the flyers who had no known grave. The list would include the names of those friends who had flown so near to us in the night, and then they had gone.

As I thought of Hoppy I thought also of my walks and talks with his father, now dead, concerning Hoppy's survival in the war. He had survived, but he with myself, carried many inner scars from air battles we had flown. Such scars would take time to heal.

ED IN ENGLAND

Ed's letter described his flight to Britain after Shorty and I had farewelled him at Naples. His plane had stayed overnight in Paris where he and another RAF fellow had gone to a French Cafe.

Ed wrote, *"At first no one spoke to us, then trouble broke out at one of the tables, and some Americans were sent out of the Cafe. After this* *the French people at our table looked at us and started to shout, `Viva le RAF ... Viva le RAF ....` treating us as heroes. They showered us with drinks, ushered us out onto the dance floor and sang British and French national anthems. I felt wonderfully appreciated. But next morning, oh dear, we paid a big price for our over use of French wines. On flying from Paris to London, the other passengers had great hilarity when they saw that we two experienced flying men became quite airsick."*

Back in Britain, Ed took up duties at the Pathfinder Air Base of Gransden Lodge near Cambridge. There in 1942, the Halifax Bombers had first been fitted with their Pathfinder radar sets. Ed had settled in, but the Medical Officer recognised that he needed medical help. Hospitalisation followed, and then Ed received the heartbreaking news that he would be invalided out of the RAF.

I read Ed's letter and felt sick at the thought of this brilliant young man facing ill health and the termination of his service in the RAF. It was grievous reading.

BOB LEWIS IN SCOTLAND

Bob had taken up the trade of shorthand writing for the courts in Glasgow. He worked with the firm of Hodge and Pollock, and had met Betteen, the girl that one day he hoped to marry.

I thought of Bob and heard again his Glasgow tongue, amidst the clatter of battle, saying "Skipper, that engine needs to be shut down, it's red hot!" I recalled his neat figure literally dancing with the soccer ball as other players came at him on the field. I enjoyed again those wild Glasgow dances he had introduced to me, and I recalled with fondness the voice of his parents saying to me, "We want a photy o' yue un Borbie fur tha hoose."

BILL SCOTT IN PALESTINE

Bill's news indicated he had become navigator on an Air Force plane carrying passengers between Britain, Egypt and Palestine. He had met Wing Commander Lockwood, our flight commander who flew with us on ops. Bill wrote that the Wingco had been awarded the Distinguished Service Order for his leadership on 614 Squadron.

Looking forward to returning to Newcastle on Tyne to marry Lillian, the lady of his dreams, Bill also planned to move back into his studies in power station engineering. I felt stirred as his letter ended, "Skipper this is your navigator signing off!" "Thanks Billy," I murmured.

SHORTY IN QUEENSLAND

Shorty's letter shared exciting news. Else had been allocated a passage on a ship carrying war brides to Australia. He assured me that she knew about the hot dry climate, the infrequent rains, the rough conditions of his Australian farming area, and the courage needed to adjust.

He still chuckled at the thought of a Yorkshire farmer with his pitchfork coming at him and saying, "We'd a kilt yu if yu was a Jerman!"

Shorty had been surprised that people in his farming area hardly knew what had gone on in the war in Europe. He longed for someone who would understand the readjustments he needed to make after returning from wartime activity.

Just then my mother came inviting me to lunch. As we went inside, she became a ready listener to news about the fellows. I told her about their letters, and how good it made me feel in hearing from them.

Mother said casually, "Tom, I'm having a visitor this afternoon." "OK mother," I replied, "that will suit me fine. I just want to relax for a while, then I'll do that job fixing the tap, so I'll leave you to your visitor." I paused, "What's your visitor's name?" "It's Laurel." I seemed to have heard that name before.

SURPRISE ENCOUNTER

During mid afternoon I heard a knock at the front door and went to answer it. A young woman stood smiling at me. "Ah, this would be mother's visitor," I thought. "You must be Laurel," I said, and prepared to usher her inside. "And you must be Tom," she said gaily. "Yes I am," I replied feeling mystified as to how she knew my name. Then I added, "You've come to see mother. Do come in!" I noted her attractive freshness and the warmth in her voice.

I conducted the visitor along the wide passageway towards the beautiful room where mother sat. "Here I am Laurel," mother called. "Laurel!" the name rang another bell in my memory. Probably mother had written about her.

"Hullo Mrs Scotland," the visitor said as she walked into the room and moved towards my mother. "Oh Laurel it is so nice to see you." The women obviously knew each other well. Mother received a kiss and proceeded to direct the guest to a seat near her. I began moving towards the door when mother spoke again, "Tom, you will join us won't you. Those other things can wait can't they?" I thought for a moment, "OK Mother, I'll stay just for a while."

Sitting down, I had opportunity to observe our visitor; her tanned skin highlighted by the white collar at her throat, blue eyes and dark hair, carefully groomed and pulled back into a neat ball. I settled comfortably and she turned to look at me, not speaking. I asked her, "How did you know my name?" Her low pitched voice responded, "Your sister wrote to me from Manjimup and told me you were home from England. I nursed with your sister Helen."

My mind started to put this piece of information in place. I said, "So you come here fairly often?" The girl gazed at me steadily as she answered, "Well I come when I can. I've enjoyed coming to see your mother. Coming here has been like a second home to me, hasn't it Mrs Scotland?"

By now the visitor had turned towards my mother, who responded readily, "Oh Laurel it is so nice to hear you say that." Mother enjoyed the warmth of the words and became effusive about past visits.

I could see that with mother's limited walking ability, such visits had become quite important. The visitor conversed about her life as a nurse at Fremantle hospital, and her friendship with Helen.

On the subject of my being in England, she said, "That's a place I'd love to visit." I explained a little about England and mother said, "While you and Laurel chat, I'll prepare the afternoon tea. Tom would you carry it in for me when I give you a call?" "Surely Mother, " I responded as she moved slowly out of the room.

"When Mother told me that she was having a visitor, I thought you would be older," I began. "Why, how old do you think I am?" she asked seriously. I felt the blood rush to my face at the directness of the question. The girl looked young and yet had an air of maturity about her. "Well you are young enough to be a friend of my sister Helen," I parried. With that, I returned to her questions about England.

We were well engrossed in conversation when mother called, "Tom,

I'm ready!" I excused myself as I went to the kitchen to get the tray.

AFTERNOON TEA

Heirloom crockery, spoons, silver tea pot, and plate of berlina torta, our favourite home made German cake, were all neatly arrayed over a large needle worked linen doily. The weight of the tray surprised me. I carried it to the lounge room, and placed it next to mother's octagonal table brought by her family from Europe. With beautifully inlaid patterns, it engendered much discussion about its age and craftsmanship. I covered the ornate top with a white damask table cloth, as a sense of homeliness and peaceful order came over me, so different from the rough and ready lifestyle I had been living.

Mother came slowly into the room, settled into her comfortable chair, and began serving afternoon tea. She could not have imagined how this ritual had so often come to me during the years I had been away.

"How do you get home to Cottesloe?" I asked our guest as the afternoon came to a close. "I catch a bus from the end of Broadway," she responded. "Then I'll walk with you to your bus." Her face clouded, "But it's a long walk." "It'll do me good, I'd like to walk with you," I replied. For a moment, an embarrassed look came over her face, then she said, "Oh well, if you insist." "I do," I said emphatically, then added, "Laurel."

My use of her name made her smile. She arose to gather her things, saying to mother, "If I am to catch my bus I had better go now, especially as your son has offered to walk with me."

The girl and mother embraced and said their farewells. By the time she and I had reached the front gate, mother had come to the verandah. Lifting her right walking stick with an upraised hand she called, "Do come again Laurel." "I will," Laurel called back. Then we were off.

It took us twenty memorable minutes to walk along Broadway to the bus stop, and by the end I knew that I wanted to know Laurel better.

CORUNNA DOWNS STATION

On my return from the bus, I assisted mother in preparing the evening meal. She spoke glowingly about Laurel's visit for a while, and then asked me about my journey to the north. By the time she and I were ready to sit at the meal table, we were fully immersed in discussions about my flying trips out from Broome. "That's where your father first began life in Australia," mother said. I told her about the waterless miles out there, the dangers of long treks, getting lost easily. "Well, when I first met him, that is where he worked, on a cattle station " she said. I reminisced about my absent father, and marvelled at his ability to migrate here and carve out a livelihood in the tough conditions of the north.

FORGOTTEN SPECTACLES

The telephone rang and I answered it. A wail came from the other end of the line; it was Laurel. "I think I left my glasses in the lounge room" I went to look. "Yes they're here. I can bring them to you tomorrow night, how will that be?" I asked her. "I hate to put you to all that trouble," she said haltingly, then added, "What time do you think you would be here?" "I could be there before eight. Will you be home then?" "Yes, I'll be home." she replied. "We've got a date then," I said boldly.

TIGER MOTHS

I felt strange, next day, sitting in the tiny cockpit of the Tiger Moth. I had to fly some of these now surplus aircraft to Maylands airport to be sold. There were so few instruments, a bit like an early Ford car. As well, it had no brakes, just a tail skid that drew the plane to a halt so long as the wind was not too strong. But the strangeness soon wore off. I opened the throttle for takeoff, the plane rose into the air, the wind rushed by my helmeted head and I began to be right at home. On coming into Maylands airport, the Tiger Moth flew like a glider. It floated merrily across the airfield, as if not wanting to put its wheels on the ground.

Eventually I finished my work and an air force transport dropped me off in the city. From there I boarded an electric trolley-bus homewards around Mounts Bay Road to Nedlands, a route that Jim Layton and I had once cycled daily. It was good to be home, enjoying the comforts and peaceful atmosphere. However, I felt strange each time I entered my room. Walking across the timber floor, my heels echoed back so many memories of past occupants, our boarders, who had experienced so much wartime loss.

Mother had prepared a tasty evening meal, and she and I had much to talk over as we sat enjoying the repast. Before seven o'clock I collected Laurel's reading glasses and headed to catch the bus to Cottesloe.

LAUREL

An embarrassed Laurel met me at the front door, and invited me in. She explained that her parents had gone to meet with friends. It dawned on me that she did not feel comfortable being alone with me in the house. "Let's go for a walk somewhere," I said choosing an alternative and more amenable way for us to be together. She sounded relieved, "That would be nice."

We made our way out the front gate and into the darkness, which was broken here and there by a street light whose beams danced as the trees waved in the wind. Along the road, up over the hill and down towards Cottesloe Beach, the movement of her body next to mine as we walked made me glow within. She talked of her love for the beach, and pointed out landmarks, the beach buildings and the open air dance floor lighted up in the distance. She had grown up here; her life on the beach had greatly influenced her growing years. The sound of ocean waves crashing onto rocks rose to meet us. We walked nearer to the rocks and she said simply, "Isn't it beautiful. I love the sound of the waves." Conversation stilled. Wind and crashing waves had a music all their own. I tuned into their wild sounds, my feelings stirred by nearness to this girl by my side.

DANCING

I discovered Laurel's next night off hospital duty and invited her to come dancing. "I'd like that," she said eagerly with a quick smile.

The dance floor became packed. Moving together with the crowded dancers, I enjoyed this further opportunity of getting to know Laurel. We swayed to the lilting music of the orchestra, and I introduced her to Hoodge, a flying friend I had often met in the Boomerang Club, that gathering place for Aussies in wartime London.

Hoodge came to me later, saying quietly, "Thomas old son, you are going to marry that lass." "What makes you say that Hoodge?" I countered with surprise, for no thought of marriage had entered my head. How could I think of marriage for I planned to be an engineering student for the next four or five years, not a married man. Marriage was just not in my thinking.

Hoodge's eyes stared into mine as he replied, "Oh, I've been watching, Thomas, I've been observing you dancing. You'll see I'm right." His big bushy red moustache twitched as he spoke, and his mop of wavy red hair rocked from side to side.

Returning from the dance to Fremantle Hospital, Laurel and I arrived late, too late for her to go in the front gate of the nurses' quarters. It had been locked. She showed me some well worn steps in the high stone wall that surrounded the quarters. I enjoyed the adventure of helping her climb the steps to the top of the wall, then disappear into the darkness with a muffled, "good night."

Hoodge did not live long enough to find out about Laurel and me. One night he flew a plane load of passengers into a stormy sky and the plane crashed not far from the boundary of the Guilford airport. None survived the resulting inferno. All around Perth, the tragedy touched people's lives.

Subsequent to the dance at Nedlands, I knew that I had found a magical harmony in my friendship with Laurel. I went home with her several times and met her parents, drank beer with her stepfather, and felt great about being in the home.

Some nights later she rang me. A sailor friend had contacted her and wanted to take her out. I felt indignant that she accepted his invitation. "He's just someone I befriended in war years. I would like to go with him," she said. I felt robbed because the sailor had stepped in so easily and invited Laurel out. "Cheeky bugger!" I thought. However, before going out with the sailor, she introduced me to him. Her openness astounded me. Laurel said afterwards that her date wasn't anything special, and I felt wonderfully elated.

OVERLOOKING CLAREMONT WATER

As soon as my jealousy settled, I took Laurel on visits to my father. I had rediscovered him after years of not knowing where he was. Even in later life he exhibited a gentility and strength which I admired. White haired, lantern jawed, and inevitably to be seen smoking his pipe, he and his lady operated a boat hire and tearoom business on the Swan River jetty at Claremont. He had warmed to Laurel, and had offered me the use of his car any time we needed it.

One night, on our way to return the car, I parked it overlooking the water at Claremont. We settled to gaze towards reflections in the distant water and I asked, "Would I have heard your name somewhere before I actually met you?" Laurel laughed and said, "I suppose Helen would have told you about me." Trying to recall something about Laurel, I was bothered when it kept evading my memory. I said, "Helen is down at Manjimup and I haven't seen much of her since I came home."

Laurel became pensive, "Perhaps Helen wrote to you about me when you were in Italy. I passed Helen's room one day and I saw her writing a letter. She said, "I'm writing to my brother." I looked at a photo near her bed and queried her, "Is that him?" She nodded and I joked, `Oh, then you must give him my love.' I didn't know you of course, but I liked the way your mouth turned up at the corners." She looked embarrassed for a moment, then continued, "I knew I could be light hearted with Helen."

My mind conjured up the picture of Helen's letters coming to me in Italy and the words added, "Laurel sends her love." So this was the girl behind the messages.

I teased Laurel about the cheeky messages. She became defensive, trying to assure me that she had done it only as a joke. I turned from banter, and gazed at her. I knew that I wanted this girl to be in my life; how could I tell her my feelings? She looked beautiful against the backdrop I could see through the car window behind her. Street lamps shone dimly on wet leaves lying on a path that melted into the darkness; the same light illuminated Laurel. My heart pounded against my ribs, my feelings overwhelmed me with a sense of oneness with this girl and my words just flooded out, "I love you Laurel!" The overcast sky, the dampening rain, nothing could dampen my enthusiasm for sharing my expressions of love with her. "And I love you Tom." There was a glow in Laurel's eyes as she spoke so quietly, yet so assuredly.

Time ticked by, and I ventured, "Laurel, will you marry me?" She looked at me and seemed to be wondering if she had heard correctly. My words continued to tumble out, "I haven't much to offer you. It will be a tough life, there'll not be much money. I plan to study civil engineering at Uni, so I'll have to study a lot, it's not much to offer you, but I want you to be my wife. Will you?" Her eyes were looking into the distance. I waited, but not too long. She turned to me, "Yes Tom, I'd really love to be your wife!" I was not really expecting her to say this. My mind raced trying to find something more substantial that I could offer this girl in her willingness to go with me.

Then I did remember something, the realisation of which became unbelievably thrilling. I gathered her in my arms. "Laurel," I said, "I have a house!" "You have?" she exclaimed as we shared our warmth. Then holding me at arm's length she said, "Oh Tom why didn't you tell me before. Why, I can't believe it. Where is it?" "It's in South Perth. I invested some back pay and I bought a house!" The humour of my forgetfulness became lost in the moments of committed love for each other. We sat there feeling incredulous at how far our friendship had taken us in the six weeks since we had first met. It had all been so unpremeditated. How could it have happened?

"LET'S TELL OUR NEWS"

Time passed. "Let's go and tell my father," I said remembering that I had to return his car. When we arrived, my father and his lady were sitting having cocoa before retiring. We shared our momentous news. "Have you now?" he exclaimed taking us inside to his lady. "Tom and Laurel have become engaged, isn't that wonderful!" The lady showed her enthusiasm and went to get cake and cups of cocoa. A small celebration ensued, in which my father made no little show of his approval of Laurel.

After a while he said, "You'll need the car a bit longer by the sound of things! You had better take it with you." The car, a 1929 Ford in neat condition, had been well cared for. "Oh bring it back when you are ready." It seemed too good to be true that we had the car for a few more days. Cars were scarce, and petrol difficult to obtain, but I had bought cans of petrol in Broome and had flown them home with me. The eight gallons would be very timely.

I drove her towards Fremantle hospital, and on the way we stopped by rocks that surrounded the Fremantle fishing harbour. Revelling in the sound of the ocean, we rehearsed our night's confessions of love for one another. But Laurel urged delay in the announcement of our engagement as her mother would need time to adjust. We came to a decision. Our official engagement would commence in the new year, two and a half months away.

STRAWBERRIES

Some days later I had a free day, and decided to use it in visiting Laurel's parents. I purchased two large punnets of beautiful strawberries and set out. I walked up the steep hill to the house. Laurel's step father, showed surprise to see me alone but warmly welcomed me in. He and his wife Verna had been enjoying a cup of tea in the kitchen. I made myself comfortable on the top of a stool, and gave them the strawberries. I explained to them that Laurel and I had exciting news, we wanted to become engaged, and I asked them for their daughter's hand in marriage. At my words the atmosphere of the kitchen became electric.

Laurel's mother had not seen me as a suitor for her daughter, and her face darkened, her eyes flooded with tears. Then she broke down completely. Her weeping became most distressing. It went on and on. I sat there dumbfounded at the turn of events. Gradually, recognition of the situation came to me; if I were to have the parents' approval I had some hard work to put in. Laurel was greatly treasured here. For me to take this treasure, the mother would not let go easily. An exceedingly close mother and daughter bond had developed over the twelve years since Laurel's dad had died. Her mother had endured seeing his years of illness end in death after gas poisoning in the first world war. I knew that I must give the mother much more time to adjust to the thought of us marrying.

A BIG PART OF ME

My discharge from the air force came on 5th November. I went walking for miles in order to adjust to the feeling that a big part of me had been taken away. In December, I returned to work in the office of the West Australian Government Railways. I had joined the Air Force from there in 1941, and had a heavy heart facing my return. However, the adventure of getting to know Laurel, and thoughts of full time studies in February, kept me buoyant, and helped to dull my sense of loss in giving up flying.

New year 1946 arrived and with it the announcement of our

engagement. By that time, Laurel's mother had adjusted to our plans, and put on a splendid party. Laurel and I relaxed and enjoyed meeting her parents' friends and neighbours. I began to appreciate how highly these people respected Verna, and esteemed their friendship with her. I drew Verna to the front verandah to thank her for such a fine engagement party. I hoped that a new relationship had begun between us, but closeness with her just did not occur.

A second engagement party came from my own family in our home at Nedlands. Relatives and friends gathered around the big Scotland table sharing goodies and banter. Laurel fitted into our home extremely well, and loved being amongst a stream of family members and friends, so many of her own age group.

VOICE OUT OF MALTA

Invited to hear the story of Malta from the lips of its war time Governor, General Sir William Dobbie, Laurel and I were profoundly moved. He spoke about Malta's survival, and the importance of prayer to him amidst the onslaught of the German attacks, when 500 German Bombers per day had destroyed most of the defences.

I knew about the courage of Malta, for it had stirred the flagging spirits of the British people to whom reverse after reverse had come in the course of the war. For her courageous resistance against the German onslaught, His Majesty, King George 6th had awarded the George Cross to Malta, the highest award for bravery possible.

General Dobbie and the suffering of Malta aroused in me an appreciation that here I faced a man who believed God was real. "Is God real?" The question recalled to my mind, "Some power out there," words that had come to me mysteriously in flying over wartime Europe. I wondered if that was the same power that answered the prayers of General Dobbie. The young lady sitting beside me, and soon to become my wife, could hardly comprehend how General Dobbie had added momentum to a battle that seesawed within me.

THE PADRE

Laurel had a Sunday off duty, and invited me to go with her to church. Church parades in the Air Force had left me assured that church was a meaningless mumbo jumbo routine to which I could not relate.

However, the service was a welcome home to a padre whose wife had befriended Laurel during the war years. The padre, a man who had been in the front line of action with his troops, seemed to have an intensely practical faith in God. I surprised myself by enjoying the service.

Sunday came some weeks later, and Laurel was on night duty. I would meet her when she finished. Aimlessness swept over me. For the evening hours, I decided to go again to the padre's church. A welcoming hand greeted me at the front door, but I did not see the padre. A visiting preacher, recently returned from the war in New Guinea, took the service.

This man annoyed me greatly when he spoke about faith in Jesus Christ. "Ridiculous fellow!" I thought, and began writhing in anger. He should have talked about God and helped me understand about that voice from the stars, but he spoke about the person of Jesus Christ as if he was equal with God. To me this name was only a curse word. To him it had great significance. I decided that he was very much off track, and did not help me at all.

By the time the service finished, I fumed. This fellow had drivelled on and I wanted to tell him so. He stood by the pulpit, so I wormed my way through the crowd determined to vent my disgust on him. I neared him but he spoke first. Looking at me seriously, he said, "Do you know the Lord Jesus Christ as your Lord and your Saviour?" For a moment I looked at him and thought, "You bloody fool!" I wanted to hit him, but found no strength. I tried to talk but no sound came; words locked into my throat.

He discerned my speechlessness and quietly said, "Come outside and we can talk." Not waiting for an answer, he led the way, and for some reason I followed. Walking amongst people talking in the aisle and crowded at the door, he led me into semi darkness and quietness. We stopped under the glow of a street lamp.

His name was Claude DeEvellynes. As he introduced himself his voice came to me with an attractive musical ring that sounded gentle, and he asked me to introduce myself. Here in the quietness, my voice restriction released, "I'm just a visitor, my name's Tom."

"Tom, I'd like to introduce you to a Bible." Claude opened a book, explained about his faith in what it said, and left me in no doubt about his utter belief and trust in this person Jesus Christ. Arguments arose within me; I had the desire to fight him, and I told him that I did not believe those things. Quite calmly, he handed over his book for me to read. "Would you read these lines aloud Tom, and tell me what you think they say?" Quietened by his voice, I took the book and read;

He is despised and rejected of men; a man of sorrows acquainted with grief: and we hid as it were our faces from him. Surely he has borne our griefs and carried our sorrows yet we did esteem him smitten by God and afflicted. But he was wounded for our transgressions, he was bruised for our iniquities: the punishment for our peace was upon him and with his stripes we are healed.

Backwards and forwards we discussed about this person called Jesus. Time slipped by, and I felt myself being drawn along to gain a picture of the name I had blithely used as a profanity. *"I am despised and rejected, yet I have borne your griefs and carried your sorrows."* The words gripped me. Page after page of material followed, simple stories and teachings of Jesus that I had no idea existed.

Gradually I became aware of someone there, out beyond Claude, a person with outstretched hands, looking at me and saying, "Come to me."

"Come to me." The words rang clearly in my mind. "Was this the voice that had spoken to me from the stars?" I really wanted this moment to go away. "No," I determined, "It's not for me, I don't belong here. Jesus Christ is just a word. Everybody uses it. Its just a word." My thoughts kept throwing up an inner argument, "Why am I listening to all this? It's ridiculous. What will my friends say if I get involved here?"

But still I saw the person waiting and patient; his hands stretched out towards me, hands that made me feel loved and cared for, hands that carried an entreaty, urging me to consider all that I had heard this night.

Claude broke into my awareness, "Tom why don't you come? Come into the light of the words we have read tonight?" He drew a circle on the ground around himself, and standing under the street light, he said, "I represent here the light of Jesus. If you want to receive his light, come into this circle. Take my hand as an indication that you want to respond to what he is saying."

He looked at me and I looked at the circle. I felt rooted to the ground where I stood. The blood pounded in my head. Objections kept forming in my mind, "No, no, that name is a name I despise, it's not real, it's not for me!" Then my dominant cry returned, "Oh if only this moment would go away." I wanted to run, I wanted to be away from here, anywhere. But I could not move.

My awareness of hands stretched out to me came again, and there was that voice, saying, "Come to me." An experience of longing invaded my being, and I wanted to respond. I found myself stepping into the ring, looking at Claude, "Yes," I murmured, "I do want to come to him." Lit only by the faint light from overhead, I stood there with Claude in silence. A light had shone within me, and I had made a great discovery. That voice from the stars was real; a caring loving voice. The nail pierced hands of Jesus said it all. I felt surrounded by the love those hands expressed. My heartache over the chaos and killing in the war was known to him. He had carried my griefs and sorrows, like those words from the Bible said. Deep sadness swept over me as my mind recalled the arrogance with which I had treated that name, treading it into the gutter. I had disdained someone I had known nothing about. I stood silent, sorrow overwhelmed me. Time passed as I faced the implications of this night's confrontation with Jesus.

THERE'S A COST
Gradually, everything around seemed ordinary again, the footpath, the street pole, even Claude himself. He said, "Tom, you've taken one step. There'll be other steps you will need to take. Don't be halfhearted in following Jesus. It will cost you, but don't live just as you please."

"Don't be half hearted, there's a cost ..." The words had a ringing sound about them, but I did not comprehend their significance. Then I remembered Laurel and looked at my watch; two and a half hours had passed under the street lamp, and I had to go.

We parted. Claude disappeared into the darkness. I moved away from the lamp pole, and headed for a long walk up the hill towards Laurel's hospital. Feeling wonderfully at peace, I toyed with my discovery about the Voice I had heard during those years of war. The Voice had a name: Jesus. I no longer felt in conflict with that name. I had lighted upon a new meaning, not only for that name but also for my own life. That Voice had intervened to give me purpose and meaning out of the chaos and grief of war. So many answers came tumbling into my mind, answers to questions that had troubled me, and I was elated. My feet seemed to float in an excited dance along the footpath up the hill.

GIFT PACKAGE FOR A BIRTHDAY

Coming out of the darkness into the light surrounding Devonleigh Hospital, I saw Laurel. She gave a lovely impression of outlined whiteness from her uniform and her voice said in measured softness, "Hullo mate!" Then she exclaimed, "Whatever has happened to you? Your face is glowing!" Excited by the night's events I bubbled out, "So much has come together for me; I became a christian tonight." "You did?" she replied, appearing mystified. I noted the change in her and knew I had some explaining to do.

We chose a path that led along undulating cliffs, under trees and beside the unruffled waters of the river. Laurel reminded me that it was after midnight, and my birthday had begun. A gift appeared out of her shoulder bag, and there on the path above the cliffs, I opened the packet. It was a New Testament. She had discerned a battle going on within me and thought a New Testament may help. A few hours previously it would not have been much use, but now I recognised that the book contained words that intrigued me; words I wanted to know more about, and words I wanted to share with Laurel.

In the weeks ahead she saw my hunger to read this book, and find out what this new faith within me really meant. Surprisingly, although she had been attending church, Laurel had not personally heard Christ's call to her. She watched with some trepidation as changes came to my life.

MALARIA

All through the year I had bouts of sickness and sweated a lot. Time was close for examinations in the six units I studied for entrance to university, but still the high temperatures and feelings of nausea continued. My sister Melita, invalided home after nursing the troops on Bougainville, diagnosed malaria, and promptly said, "Tom, you must get off to hospital straight away!"

For weeks the hospital staff worked to get my fevers stabilised. I sweated, felt ill, and gave up hope of being ready for examinations. A fellow student saw my dilemma. He persisted in keeping me in touch with lecturers, and cajoled me into doing the assignments. I felt terrible, far from wanting to study, but my heroic fellow student kept it up.

After six weeks in hospital, I was discharged, unable to stand for long, but having to face my biggest test, the examinations. Day by day, I travelled to the university to tackle the papers and day by day I was so exhausted that I gave up hope of being ready to return for the next examination. Yet at the end, the papers for the six units were completed. When the results were announced, I had sufficient marks for entrance into any faculty I would like to choose. I chose Civil Engineering.

When all was done, I still had not tackled my share of planning our wedding, our honeymoon, and arranging for us to occupy the house in South Perth.

WEDDING BELLS

The day Laurel and I were due to be married dawned exceedingly hot. Don Watson, as my best man, helped me to relax and laugh in recalling that it was in just such hot weather five years earlier, he and I had been filling sandbags as defences against possible Japanese invasion.

We drove to the church at Cottesloe. I paused near the pole where the street lamp had cast its glow upon my confrontation with the person of Jesus, the Voice who had spoken to me from the stars over Europe. That pole represented to me the end of my search to find meaning and purpose for my life. I now felt as an excited child in exploring the vastness of an unknown new world of faith opening up to me.

Entering the church, I gasped. It seemed to be a bower of flowers with a bedecked archway through which Laurel and I had to pass. The music started and I watched as Laurel came up on the arm of her stepfather and stood beside me at the altar. My sister Pauline stood behind her to attend to her dress. Laurel's voice came through to me, "Hullo mate." I squeezed her hand in response, and felt proud of her, and proud of the occasion as she took my arm. She looked beautiful.

Standing before our friend, the Padre, I noticed my arm shaking, my legs also. I had begun the routine of another malarial bout. I cursed the malaria and determined, malaria or not, to enjoy this day to its fullest.

THEY TWO SHALL BECOME ONE

The Padre proceeded with the ceremony, and came to the lines,

"For this cause shall a man leave his father and mother and join to his wife and they two shall become one flesh." At first, the weight of responsibility in "two becoming one," overwhelmed me. Then came quiet assurance. My "Voice from the Stars" would have purposes ahead for us that I knew nothing about. In that assurance I had peace.

MY JOURNEY

I was caught within the centre of a milling frenzied mob,
That spat upon and ridiculed the unflinching son of God,
I beheld them as they mocked him and I heard their taunting cry,
As they jeered him in their madness, well as they did, so did I.

On his head with brutal fingers they did thrust the thorny crown,
And the maddened mob roared louder as the blood came trickling
down,
With the lashes then they scourged him while the mob cried
CRUCIFY!
Dragging forth the heavy crosses and as they did, so did I.

Through the crowded streets they led him to a hill outside the wall,
And the crowd that lately cheered him, loudly scoffed now at his fall,
Then I heard the sound of hammers and I watched the crosses rise,
To the cry of hate, full throated, and as they did, so did I.

Nearer to the cross and nearer, did I work my way apace,
Till I reached the feet of Jesus and could look upon his face,
Then my lips forgot their mocking and I felt my hatred die,
When the thief beside sought pardon, as the thief did so did I.

Then he healed my every heartache, with his blood purged out my
sin,
Promised me his life eternal, gave me perfect peace within,
On the path where earnest christians struggle daily to draw nigh,
To the perfect rest of heaven, well as they do, so do I.

(Author unknown)

✧✧✧

EPILOGUE

LETTER FROM DEVILS GLEN
In 1984 the British newspaper, Yorkshire Evening Post featured an article headed, "Miracle of Drub Lane". A journalist had researched amongst witnesses to my crash of the Halifax Bomber at Devil's Glen near Leeds, Yorkshire in 1943. Drub Lane lay immediately beside the Glen where I crashed. My Australian address appeared in the article, and a copy of the newspaper came to me. Letters followed, including one from a Yorkshireman, Bert Haley, who wrote:-

I think often of the pilot of that bomber who with great skill made a beautiful pancake landing on that hillside of Devils Glen. I never pass the spot without thinking about that pilot and hope he survived the war. I wish I knew.

Today out walking I heard some wonderful news. I met a guy who said he had a newspaper cutting about the air crash. I told him I was there, so he called me to the house to see the paper. The reason for this letter is to let you know that it gives me great pleasure to know you are alive and kicking. I would like to tell you what I saw that day.

When I heard the bomber it was so low I said, "Good Lord it's heading for a crash!" There was this massive wingspan coming straight for me. It went between two telephone poles about head height and cutting the telephone lines. I saw a woman with hands up in the air. I told her to go to a house with a phone and get the Fire Brigade. Then I ran towards the plane and you were just climbing out and you said, "Get to hell out of here there's ammo aboard." I helped you get up to Drub Lane and then I said, "I can't stay as my wife is expecting our first baby today. I will have to push off."

Later, I wrote a letter to the authority to ask them to send a letter to the station commander to thank the pilot for his wonderful skill in clearing the town.

By the way, the birth was a success. She is now a mother herself with a boy and a girl and the boy twenty one years old. Good luck cobber. Bert.

Bert's letter recalled to my mind the drama of my plane arriving in his town on the same day as his baby daughter. I thought about the many people who had been at the crash, and the fellows who had been with me in the plane and had parachuted out. Where were they now? What were they doing? Most had settled down in England, but one lived in Queensland.

In 1980 there had been an early retirement for me, due to a health breakdown. "The war is catching up with you," my medical specialist had said. But after five years of his care, my health had improved enough for me to tackle the thought of going to England, and the feature article stirred a desire to visit Leeds.

DEVILS GLEN
In August 1986, Laurel and I stood with a group of people on a high rise above Devils Glen south of Leeds in Yorkshire. Lower down the hill, a short squat man kicked the earth around some bushes at the back of houses on the edge of the glen.

He turned and walked up the hill towards us, holding in his hands two large lumps of earth. "Look at these!" he exclaimed, as he began removing outer layers of earth. Sections of grey aluminium and rust appeared. Others in the group crowded around. I took one lump and turned it over, recognising a distinctive part of an aircraft. It could be a part of the Halifax bomber I crashed here in 1943.

I looked at the piece of history in my hands, memories flooded in. I stood again beneath the huge wings of a four engined Halifax and looked up into the cavernous opening in the wing. In flight, the Halifax housed its landing wheels there. The part I now held in my hands would have come from that opening that housed the wheels. I turned to the group of people around me and saw them waiting for some comment. "This," I stated simply, "looks like a part of the Halifax, a section of the locking mechanism from the undercarriage wheels." Eager hands reached out for this item from the past.

I turned again to the squat man. He cleaned the last lumps of earth off his second find, a piece of aluminium alloy that had somehow escaped the fierce burning of the Halifax. Most likely it was a part of one of the four big engines. We stood there together, handling these tangible reminders of an event so long ago.

BOY OF TEN

Standing in front of the group, the squat man looked up at me and said, "I was ten when I stood here after you crashed and I asked you for the plane's tail." I looked at him with amazement. "So it was you!" I gasped, thinking of how many times over the years, the face of that boy had come to my mind. But I saw him again; the boy standing before me. Beyond, ugly red flames rose out of the Halifax and a pall of smoke rose high in the air. I heard again the loud noises of exploding ammunition. I felt myself shocked and in pain as men gathered around me. When I saw the crowd gathering, I shouted, "Get back!" They had not realised their danger. At any moment I expected the petrol tanks to explode. Then I felt a pull on my parachute harness. Looking up at me a ten year old boy asked, "Hey mister, can I have the tail?"

NOW A MAN

Once again the boy of ten wanted my attention; but now not a boy, a man of fifty three. He wanted to introduce me to others who had been present on that day.

I recognised the ex-Fire Brigade chief the instant I saw him. His face had registered enduringly in my mind from the effective way he had handled the crowds around the burning Halifax. Tears came to his eyes as he saw Laurel and me, and realised I really had survived the war. "Thank God, thank God," he said repeatedly. Such a highly charged moment of emotion caught me unawares and touched by his words, warm tears of gratitude flowed from my eyes also.

Alec Thomas, an insurance inspector, had been a young man of seventeen at the time. He explained:-

"I was walking along the Leeds Bradford road when I heard this terrific noise. Your plane came straight at me. You were obviously in trouble, you hit some telephone cables beside the road, then you hit a tree and landed on ground that was sloping upwards toward the houses.

When I knew you had survived it made my day."

Then I met Elsie Firth into whose back yard the plane had plunged. She said;

"I was taking my small daughter to visit friends when I saw you approach level with the wall and all lit up. It could have been a real disaster, for there were houses all around. When the bomber crashed, there were flares shooting off and I ran off with my daughter Diane who was two at the time. So I never got to thank you then for the wonderful job you did. I have thought about it many a time and I've told my grandchildren but I think they used to believe that I had dreamed it. I am so glad to be able to thank you now for the job you did that day."

GENEROUS HEARTS OVERFLOWED

Few who witnessed my arrival in Devils Glen in 1943 had known if I had survived the war. Now their generous hearts overflowed in warm welcome to Laurel and me. Bert Haley became their spokesman, and in a voice broken with emotion expressed appreciation on behalf of them all for my return to their town.

I looked for one particular person, Herb Umpleby, manager of a nearby factory who had befriended me and cared for me on that day, and later on leave. "Herb died ten years ago," said Mrs Umpleby as I met her. We embraced and allowed ourselves to feel the significance of this moment without Herb.

THE WALL

Laurel and I walked down the hill and across the glen towards the telephone poles between which I had flown the Halifax, ripping away the cables as I came in. A stone wall lined the main road and tall bushes grew against it. There, below the bushes, twisted and broken telephone cables still lay coiled, washed clean by many rains since repairmen came so long ago.

I looked over the wall. "Laurel, look at this," I called, "See the repair." Rows of building stones had been refitted into the wall with distictive mortar. I explained, "When Herb Umpleby brought me here after my crash there were masses of stones swept into the field. It's where the tail of the Halifax hit the wall and broke off."

We returned slowly up the glen towards the back of Elsie Firth's house. For me the walk meant a pilgrimage. I heard again Herb Umpleby's voice as he stood at this place and pointed to the trees and houses "You know Tom, you are lucky to be alive." Herb had looked at me intently as if to drive the fact home into my mind that the burning Halifax had stopped only a little short of death for me. Some miracle had occurred to save my life.

For a long moment I had stood there with Herb, and I had seemed to be in touch with some eternal power. Then the presence faded; but my search to identify that presence had begun. My search had started here. Herb's penetrating statement to me, had sparked off my determined search to discover the meaning and purpose of my life. Herb had died but my search had brought me into thrilling contact with a caring and lifegiving God. My whole life had changed in that encounter.

I stood quietly in the glen with Laurel, and we bowed our heads in thankfulness to our Creator. Much of my thankfulness was that Laurel herself was able to share these moments with me. She had been my companion in faith serving God's world with me in many years of sacrificial living.

I thought of my seven crew mates who had jumped from the Halifax by parachute. I had contacted three of them, members of my ex RAF Pathfinder navigation team, and they had arranged a reunion for Laurel and me in Northumberland. After various engagements with media and reunions arranged by folk around Devil's Glen, we felt free to go.

HOPPY, BILL AND ED
We had a reunion with my three ex crew members and their ladies at Chollerford, an ancient Roman river crossing near Hadrians Wall in Northumberland. We first met out in the market place underneath the ancient cross. The cross marked the place where, in past centuries, labourers had assembled, waiting to be hired. I looked at the cross, which at one time in my ignorance, I would have despised, but on this day I felt humbled by the sacrificial and caring love that it symbolised.

HOPPY
Hoppy came, tall, carefully dressed, and pink cheeked. In his precise bank officer's voice, he said, "Hullo Tommy." But the part I remembered most was his friendly nervous chuckle. Navigation work had echoed

the preciseness of the man whom we had highly valued as a part of our wartime flying team. In post war years, after much hard work in trying to settle down, he had been promoted to bank manager, reward indeed to a man who had so much to offer in the hazards through which we had survived together.

BILL SCOTT

I gazed at the rugged face and heard that voice; it was Bill Scott. What memories I recalled of him, broad of shoulder, husky in voice and square of jaw. Flying through many long nights with him, I could hear again that gravelly voice, "Skipper, we have a change of course coming up."

Now a retired power station engineer, he had amused us all by dumbfounding newer crews on 614 Squadron by his fabricated accounts of us gaining superior speed in flying to the target by finding the right sort of cloud to fly on.

ED RILEY

Ed Riley's bright sparkling eyes shone out of a sensitive face, highlighted by the lines of added years. His lightly built frame stooped, showing the strain of having to live through the pain of wartime injuries. But his strong Tyneside accent still had its lilt and fun. He had remained single.

Ed had been our brilliant H2S radar operator, whom I had last seen on the tarmac of Naples airport in wartime Italy. In post war years he had given himself to manufacturing and production engineering. We spent days with Ed, getting to know him in the freedom of retirement years. How highly we valued the friendship of this precious man. He never said much about his health, yet we observed his pain.

In retirement Ed fitted in time to scribble away at cartoons epitomising our wartime adventures, and now included in this book. He produced one for our reunion, and he entitled it, "The eagles have landed."

BOB LEWIS

"Skipper, we've an engine in urgent need of shut down!" I could hear so clearly our former Scottish flight engineer, Bob Lewis. He came to us in the form of a letter written by his wife Betteen. Bob had died in Canada in 1970 aged forty seven. I felt a personal sense of loss over not seeing him again. I thought of his family and his wife left alone to raise their sons. I longed to write an account about the bravery of this man who had meant so much to us as part of our flying team.

ARE YOU ASLEEP?

Laurel asked for a photograph of us all out near the cross. "Come on Hoppy, are you asleep?" Ed called as Hoppy held back a bit. Quick to respond, Hoppy said, "I'll bet you fellows didn't know I was asleep and fifty miles off course one night when we were flying home from Rumania!" "Come on now, we knew you were asleep," we chorused, thinking of those long seven and a half hour trips. "No you didn't," retorted Hoppy, "and I'll tell you why. It was because you were all asleep too!" It was banter of the highest order and Laurel clicked the camera in the midst of the hilarity.

Hoppy and his wife Olive loved and cared for Laurel and me during ten days in their home at Alnwick in Northumberland. They were precious days. Hoppy and I were able to experience the balm of talking together and bringing to the light of day some of our inner scars from wartime. We had lived with them, and had felt their pain as post wars years had unfolded.

UNDER THE SHADOW OF THE GARGARNO

Travelling through Europe to Italy, Laurel and I arrived at the airbase at Amandola. Overshadowing Amandola and the Foggia plain, was the Gargarno mountain. The Italian Air Force now roared off from the runways at Amandola, but the exciting thing about that day was a rainbow over the Gargarno. What was more, it sat there for the whole day, and I had not seen a rainbow there in wartime. It spoke to me of a promised healing Presence for the world; that Voice from the Stars I had come to know and love. Over the years he had enabled me to face painful memories and lay them to rest. In 1964 He used a man from Munich to confront wartime hostilities and enmities covered up in my life. Seeds of reconciliation had germinated then. Now I was able to experience their fruit of peace and healing — the promise fulfilled.

DON BENNETT

On returning to England after visiting Italy and Germany, we learnt that Air Vice Marshall Don Bennett had died. He had founded the Pathfinder Force in the dark days of 1942, by selecting crews to lead the RAF attacks on German occupied Europe.

Australian Pathfinders contacted us and asked if I would represent them at his RAF Memorial service in London. I felt honoured to be able to say my personal farewell to a great man. Through him, I had gained a great appreciation for the stars. Such stars had become like friends in our navigating the night skies of wartime Europe. From those very stars had come that Voice breaking into my consciousness.

A thousand people packed into the beautiful St Clement Danes Church. Laurel and I were ushered into seats reserved for the Bennett family, where we felt the warmth of Don's wife Ly. Later, she included Laurel and me with the family in sharing a meal at the Royal Air Force Club. Thus she expressed the fondness that she and Don had for his homeland, Australia.

FAREWELL

Flying over alpine snows as we returned to Australia, we said farewell to Europe. This was the second time I had returned from this great continent. In 1945 I was a flyer going home to an uncertain future, to take my part in an Australia still fighting a war in the Pacific. But this time with Laurel by my side, I was going home with a wonderful sense of fulfilment, and a determination to share some of that fulfilment in a book that I would like to call, VOICE FROM THE STARS.

I would write in thankfulness for the guiding care and love I found through that Voice and have continued to find in the excitement, demands and pain of post war years.

God who commanded the light to shine out of darkness has shined into our hearts to give the light of the knowledge of the glory of God in the face of Jesus Christ. But this treasure we have in earthly bodies so that the excellency of the power may be of God and not of us. (Paul the Apostle)

My book would begin:- *The freckle faced boy first became aware that war clouds threatened his world in 1933* ....

THE AIRFIELD

I lie here still, beside the hill, abandoned long to natures will.
My buildings down, my people gone, my only sounds, the wild
birds song
For my mighty birds will rise no more, no more I hear the
Merlins roar
And never now my bosom feels, the rumbling of their giant
wheels.
Laughter, sorrow, hope and pain, I shall never know these things
again
Emotions that I came to know of strange young men so long ago,
And in the future should structures tall, bury me beyond recall,
I shall still remember them, those wide spread wings of my flying
men.

(Author unknown)